Romance of the Road

Romance of the Road:
The Literature of the American Highway

Ronald Primeau

Bowling Green State University Popular Press
Bowling Green, OH 43403

Portions of chapter 3 have appeared in different form in "The Endless Poem: Jack Kerouac's Midwest," *Great Lakes Review* 3 (1976): 73-86. Reprinted by permission.

Copyright © 1996 Bowling Green State University Popular Press

Library of Congress Cataloging-in-Publication Data

Primeau, Ronald.
    Romance of the road : the literature of the American highway / Ronald Primeau.
        p. cm.
    Includes bibliographical references and index.
    ISBN 0-87972-697-0 (clothbound). -- ISBN 0-87972-698-9 (pbk.)
    1. Travelers' writings, American--History and criticism.
    2. American prose literature--20th century--History and criticism.
    3. American fiction--20th century--History and criticism.
    4. Automobile travel--United States--Historiography. 5. Express highways--United States--Historiography. 6. Americans--Travel--Historiography. 7. Automobile travel in literature. 8. Express highways in literature. 9. Travel in literature. 10. Quests in literature.   I. Title.
    PS366.T73P75   1996
    810.9'355--dc20
                                                                    96-6221
                                                                    CIP

Cover design by Laura Darnell-Dumm

For Katherine, at 25

Contents

Preface

Americans are in love with roads and cars, and we celebrate this romance in song, poetry, film, and video. My focus in this book is on prose narratives—not vacation experiences or tourist diaries but a road genre all its own combining elements of pilgrimage, quest romance, *Bildungsroman*, and the picaresque. My aims are to describe the American road narrative, explore its significance and account for its popularity, and prompt further study of the road tradition it is creating.

Because of the enormous range of available materials, I have placed some limits on this study. By literature of the American highway I mean fiction and nonfiction prose narratives by and about Americans traveling the highway. This sets aside for now other modes of transportation and media as well as accounts written by either foreign observers in America or Americans abroad. Several types of road travel also lie outside the scope of this book: family vacations, the work routines of truck drivers, or the dark side of road crime recorded in tales of highway robbers, for example. And, although I will trace the influence of literature before the coming of the auto, I am leaving for another discussion road quests in which trains, planes, boats, cycles, or walking are the primary means of transportation. A few notable exceptions—*Huckleberry Finn* and *Zen and the Art of Motorcycle Maintenance*, for example—are included for reasons which, I trust, will become apparent. My choice of narrative over poetry, song, or film, however, is based on more than space limitations. I privilege prose for its unique perspective and for the special artistic vision created by a dialogue of authors, readers, and texts. People have always told stories in an effort to make sense of experience; road narratives are an American favorite for that process of composing order and meaning into experience.

In the early stages of this project I resisted genre study—in particular, the formalist agenda which reduces discussion to elements of structure or imagery and tends to diminish the involvement of readers. The central problem of genre study remains classification and definition without reduction. Even if we avoid the prescriptive trap and realize that genre rules evolve so they can be used (and broken) creatively, there is still the danger of isolating the genre in tidy categories that seal it off from the community and culture. The road narrative evolves not just as a generic combination of earlier patterns—no matter how innovative the modifications might be—but because the genre thrives in a culture where writers and readers share clearly articulated literary techniques to question, reaffirm, and explore who they are and where they are going.

While artistic merit is crucial in the study of literature, we cannot decide that books are "great" in isolation from the culture they embody. My selection of road narratives proposes no abstract values about literary or humanistic worth, but rather an attempt to follow the development of a community of writers and readers in motion. Most road books would make anybody's list of good literature, though few have been sanctioned by inclusion in academic literary canons. Those by the best known authors are, of course, read more widely and considered better by repute in academia. Nonfiction narratives, however, are often overlooked for lack of categories or critical terminology. In spite of this lack of scholarly approval, however, road literature continues to grow in popularity outside the curriculum. Protagonists and readers alike want to see what's out there on the road, and the prose narrative is a way of participating vicariously in the adventure, challenge, and fun.

This book examines road narratives from a variety of perspectives. The opening chapter offers some preliminary definitions and suggests an approach to genre study. Chapter 2 traces the development of the genre from early touring books to experimental metafictional narratives more than a half century later. Chapters 3 through 6 examine four major subtypes of the genre with emphasis on social protest, the search for a national identity, journeys of self-discovery, and narrative patterns expressing escape, parody, and metafictional forms. In all of these different quests, the literature of the American highway has been dominated for most of its history by the values and attitudes of white males. When women and minority authors take to the road, they bring a different perspective and experience to their travels and writing. The ways in which they reroute the itineraries and reshape many genre conventions is the subject of chapter 7. Finally, the dynamics of reentry underscores much that is crucial about the road quest. The concluding chapter examines the difficulties of coming home and finding or creating a meaningful pattern in the telling of the story. My own reentry in the epilogue is followed by suggestions for further reading in the notes and works cited.

I am indebted to many people over the ten years in which I have been gathering materials and teaching road literature classes. Not unexpectedly, traveling the highways has also been an important part of my research. Thanks to students in two graduate seminars, I enjoyed a pilgrimage to catch the smelt running in Michigan's Upper Peninsula and a series of memorable excursions to sights in and around Detroit. In the first trip, the students planned a Road Experience for sixteen of us in three vans: stops along the way at diners, class discussion as we rolled along, and plenty of opportunities to live the literary conventions of the genre. In the more recent journey, we all traveled together for part of a day and then continued in groups of four on longer adventures. Besides reading others' stories, then, we wrote our own and created a new category: an illustrated group road narrative composed while in motion. It didn't even matter that in the first quest the smelt weren't running and in the second outing we didn't travel very far. Nonetheless, these shared quests showed us how experiencing and writing about the road influence each other.

While I was working on the early stages of this project, my father-in-law died of leukemia. Henry and I had been planning a road trip to Florida to visit his brother, but Henry died a week before we could leave. I have tried many times since then to write a story about what that journey could have been. At first I planned to include the narrative as part of this book in a series of interchapters, but the story is so far still too personal, and the connections between our imaginary trip and the analysis of road books didn't turn out to be as smooth as I had hoped. In the right time and place, that one might yet gel.

Many supportive people deserve my appreciation for their generous help and encouragement. For insightful questions, fresh perspective, and good cheer, I am grateful to all the students with whom I've studied road narratives. I owe much also to the wisdom and support of many colleagues. Barry Alford, Phil Dillman, Peter Obuchowski, and Jack Stillinger read drafts, set me straight, and kept me going. David D. Anderson, Ronnie Apter, Donald A. Bird, Hans Fetting, Gary Fuller, David Ling, Herbert W. Martin, Francis Molson, Susan Miles, William Miles, Mary Obuchowski, John Pfeiffer, Bruce Roscoe, and Stacy Thompson offered valuable advice and leads. I am indebted to Central Michigan University for a sabbatical leave to begin this project. Thanks to Carole Pasch who typed numerous drafts with great patience and expertise. I thank Katherine, Beth, and Sarah Primeau for all their help and love and for being always my favorite road companions.

1

Introduction: Road As Genre

For most of this century, Americans have treated the highway as sacred space. Roads and cars have long gone beyond simple transportation to become places of exhilarating motion, speed, and solitude. Getting away is a chance at a new start, a special time to discover self and country, glide through vast empty spaces and then come home to write or sing about the adventures. In hundreds of books, movies, poems, songs, and videos, the road journey is an epic quest, a pilgrimage, a romance, a ritual that helps explain where Americans have been and where they think they might be going. Accordingly, the art forms and cultural symbols that have developed express a mode of consciousness, a complex of values, a way of seeing the world. Since the 1950s readers have been fascinated by who goes on the road as well as why, when, and where they go and what they discover along the way. Perhaps the most significant questions are why so many of these highway travelers want to tell their stories and why so many people want to read them. Of the art forms celebrating life on the road, the prose narrative best captures the inner feelings of a wide range of travelers.

To explore these and other questions, this introduction begins with some preliminary definitions and then outlines an approach to the study of genre that emphasizes cultural analysis, genre memory, and a reader-response view of audience.

American road narratives are fiction and nonfiction books by Americans who travel by car throughout the country either on a quest or simply to get away. The most common narrative structure follows the sequence of a journey from preparation to departure, routing, decisions about goals and modes of transport, the arrival, return and reentry, and finally, the recording or reconstructing of events in the telling of the story. Protagonists take to the road for a variety of reasons, and when goals are often frustrated, the irresolution makes telling the story more urgent. The narration of events is not just a record of what happened but a way of trying to understand experiences by finding or making a pattern. The road genre is the pattern in which this mode of discovery takes shape, an artistic rendering of life on the highway.

2 Romance of the Road

Any attempt to define or classify that generic rendering of experience is true to the structure of consciousness out of which it arises only when classification is descriptive and flexible rather than prescriptive and rigid. Just as Aristotle's *Poetics* provided language for describing a tragic worldview, we might today talk about a horror-film description of events or a TV sit-com view of solving problems. Following Whitman and Kerouac, several generations of writers and readers have shaped a prose-narrative vision of life on the road. Because readers come to recognize, expect, and enjoy repeated literary formulas or rituals, authors rely on predictable patterns for some assurance about what has worked so far and for clues on how conventions can be further exploited, developed, or modified within a range of what will still be accessible. At the same time, readers are likely to select a book and bring to their reading expectations based on what they understand to be the genre's appeal. Such expectations create the opportunity for shared communication and allow purposeful deviation from routine. Skepticism about genre study derives in part from the formalist errors of forcing analytic definition or New Critical attempts to isolate a genre from the cultural and social times it expresses. The road narrative is not an arbitrary mix of literary techniques or abstract themes but an artistic vision developed within a specific time and place. The history of the genre is best understood, therefore, not in abstract classification but through exposure to the evolving artistic visions.

As an artistic way of thinking and feeling, a genre is what Mikhail Bakhtin calls a "field" for future expression enabling authors and readers to create by absorption and modification of literary conventions. The genre collects and stores these predictable conventions for later use in what Bakhtin calls "genre memory."[1] This storage system allowed Dostoyevsky, for example, to develop his richly polyphonic works without knowing much directly about specific types of satire. Though unaware of sources or influences, Dostoyevsky nonetheless sensed the genre tradition within which he could best express his views. Bakhtin sees this creative potential as the greatest power of a genre: resources stored in genre memory thus freed Dostoyevsky to respond to the tone, inner logic, and nuances of the genre on the basis of perhaps only a few models. Bakhtin feels that it was not so much Dostoyevsky remembering "but the objective memory of the very genre in which he worked, that preserved the peculiar features" of his satire. It is mostly the great writers who are attuned to a genre's fullest potential, and for them, the opportunity to assume familiarity with conventions of a genre makes "short cuts" possible and expands artistic potential.

In his essay "The *Bildungsroman* and Its Significance in the History of Realism," Bakhtin shows how we can go beyond a static list of characteristics or prescriptions about what a genre ought to be (10-59). He asks us to look instead at the evolution of patterns stored in genre memory. Comparing plots, conceptions of the world, and the types of heroes that emerge, Bakhtin distinguishes between novels of "travel," "ordeal," "biography" and "education" or "emergence." In the travel novel, for example, a static hero is a mere moving point in spatial diversity. The temporal is poorly developed, sweeping contrasts are showcased, and almost no attention is given to the sociocultural. Novels of ordeal feature tests of virtue, saintliness, romance, or chivalry. Human beings suffering ordeals are more developed, though still unitary. Bakhtin sees the novel of ordeal as an ancestor to later adventure fiction and psychological novels of sentiment. The biographical novel added the confessional, hero worship, and, later, family biography—though it was not until the 19th century that the genre depicted heroes in the process of becoming as in the *Bildungsroman* or the novel of education. For Bakhtin, the expression of "education" or "emergence" took several forms over time, from the simple chronology or cyclical stages of epic or adventure tales to the more individualistic growth of personality through narratives of life and work.

In the most advanced sense of the *Bildungsroman*, Bakhtin believes, the emergence of any individual occurs not in isolation but is "linked to historical emergences" (23). The world was fixed in much early travel literature, and heroes either submitted to its fixity or defied order and suffered the consequences. Even when heroes individually broke away from rigid norms, however, the world did not. Further, the hero's education was essentially a private affair with little connection to the static world. But the later *Bildungsroman* shaped a new artistic vision where human experience was no longer a private matter; rather, the hero grows along with the world and even represents "the historical emergence of the world itself." The literary hero is thus created not to fit into a category or imitate a model but to embody a process of growth or a transition between epochs that is "accomplished in him and through him." The American road genre expresses this kind of emergence, reflecting in the road hero evolving social and cultural values and beliefs. Road narratives also express what Bakhtin calls "the spatial whole of the world." Space on the road is not a passive background or a completed scene travelers merely pass through, but is itself an evolving interaction of the pastoral landscape and cultural symbols.

As a practical matter, American road narratives capture time, place, and culture in simple and popular stories. Like their counterparts in road songs and movies, prose narratives of the highway draw on a set of repeatable literary conventions through which readers can explore the major questions of the day. Road travel—as well as reading about life on the road—provides opportunities for a community of fellow-travelers, authors, readers, and critics to share their collective experiences. Customs, values, and ideas are explored in the writing, the reading, the comparing, and the interpreting. The road's appeal extends beyond the merely literary to a mode of expression in which a culture explores and defines itself. While literary elements may be a conservative tug toward preserving tradition, the modification of conventional patterns opens up the form to the individual, the divergent, and even the radical. The process is social as well because it is people in the community who take the trips and write and read the books.

In their conventionality, old-fashionedness, and quiet originality, road stories express what Raymond Williams has called the "dominant, residual, and emergent" elements in our cultural values. Dominant in a culture is what we select and abstract as being the most typical or representative way of life or set of beliefs: we might distinguish, for example, between the dominant features of capitalistic, socialist, agrarian, or feudal societies. Like Bakhtin, Williams emphasizes points of transition between different dominant epochs as well as the importance of past residue and future emergence as cultural systems evolve. He uses the term "residual" to refer to elements of a culture formed in the past and still functioning as an active element of the present. Values or beliefs of the dominant culture may be too inconsistent or controversial to be expressed directly, and so residual symbols may be used instead. For example, road narratives might argue for the individual in a mass-dominated society by celebrating the residual values of the pioneers on the frontier. At the same time, the road is a popular and acceptable place to express new meanings and values that lie outside what is either dominant or residual. The emergent is especially difficult to identify because by nature it is a set of themes and symbols that may not be fully formed and, more often than not, will advocate alternative or oppositional attitudes and beliefs. Moreover, Williams notes that the emergent is in constant jeopardy of being either absorbed or ignored by the dominant. On the road, the emergent is most often manifest as escape, political protest, or social reform and may be particularly evident in road works by women or ethnic minorities (see chapter 7). These diverse strands of dominant, residual, and emergent culture are perhaps easiest to see in times of turmoil or transition. Typically, all three stages operate simultaneously in road narratives which are often at once old fashioned, conventional, and revolutionary.

Road books open dialogues between oppositional elements. Old and new, high and low, traditional and innovative, optimistic and cynical make space for each other in an exploratory mode. The coexistence of dominant, residual, and emergent elements invites people into dialogue that legitimizes new insights not possible in overly restrictive forms. The ritual of conventional pattern thereby invites the modifications that make creativity possible.

To express and influence cultural beliefs and attitudes, road narratives draw upon a rich genre memory of literary conventions extending as far back as ancient travel literature, religious pilgrimages, and mythic quests. In America, the earliest chronicles of movement have been native American storytellers, singers of the slave songs, diarists during westward migration, travelers on stage coach and railroad, and finally, authors of automobile journeys. The earliest road adventurers shaped stories which then became available for later use as people who heard the stories took to the road themselves. New and distinctive in the twentieth century were the power, speed, status, and romance of the automobile, which quickly took on what B.A. Botkin has called the "super icon" of the road to "freedom of activity and movement, to opportunity and success" (Fishwick and Browne 48). Over many decades scholars have produced an abundance of research on travel, tourism, and the role of the automobile in American life. Travel has been seen as the social glue that binds society together, a way to discover one's real self in a release from everyday constraints, a way to participate more fully in daily events, and a chance to repair any number of internal mechanisms.[2] From social, political, and psychological perspectives, travel is seen as the discovery or achievement of identity through interaction with others, as well as a way to validate one's vision of the world. The automobile entered this long tradition of travel literature and added its own unique merging of the frontier spirit and the worship of the machine as a complex icon. The American car has always been more than just transportation: it is status, success, dreams, adventure, mystery, and sex; it is what John Keats has called the insolent chariot and what Marshall McLuhan pronounced to be the mechanical bride.[3]

The evolution of American road literature over the last century has drawn upon several long traditions of travel, quest, and adventure narratives. Travel literature in the Western tradition can be traced back at least as far as 13th-century Icelandic and Norwegian epic narratives or sagas where a people in motion is captured in action tales of feuds and battles. About 1300 Marco Polo's *Travels* brought the East to Europe— and this European perception of the East led to the redevelopment of maps and increased exploration. In the late 14th century Chaucer's

Canterbury Tales presented a journey from London to Canterbury, where 30 people tell stories to entertain each other as they argue their views of the world. From Icelandic sagas to Marco Polo and Chaucer, these storytellers set out to explore what's up ahead and, in the process, to define their own culture's values, attitudes, and beliefs. Following the literature of pilgrimage and *rites de passage*, many road books focus on a goal and pass through what Victor Turner call states of separation, liminality or suspension, and reaggregation (*The Ritual Process* 94-97). Goal orientation provides purpose and organizational pattern. Moreover, the pilgrim's sense of direction provides cultural sanction for the separation and indulgence in transience outside structures. Adherence to the goal often lends the story credibility and gives the characters permission to leave home or even to wander awhile. From the rich traditions of religious and secular stories, the road narrative adapts its own departure rituals for detachment from normal events and everyday delegations, a time of reveling in a free-floating state beyond ordinary spatiotemporal bounds, and a reentry stage wherein the renewed—or at least changed—subject returns to and comments on the cultural and social order.

Other traditions add to this central pattern to make the road narrative an amalgam of different kinds of movement. The frontier myth offers hopes for a new start, more space, healing motion. The *Bildungs-roman* suggests youthful road heroes experiencing initiation and growth. Whitmanesque catalogs sprawl across the pages soaking up "other" in the "profound lesson of reception." Adding tension and power is the displaced religious quest where fallen heroes suffer the anguish of separation from the divine and seek restorative motion and a recovery of paradise. Stories of life on the road are often romantic quests for healing grace and apocalyptic vision followed by a return to the ordinary, with a transformed consciousness.

Although the road narrative is neither a tour guide nor an ancient epic quest, the genre does draw from travel literature and the mythic hero journey. In *The Tourist: Travel in Twentieth-Century North America*, John A. Jakle has summarized several distinct stages in the travel process. Drawing on Marion Clawson's five parts of the recreational experience and ethologist Fred Fischer's ten phases of animal movement, Jakle describes eight successive stages of travel: "predisposition to travel, trip preparation, departure, outward movement, turnabout, homeward movement, return, and trip recollection" (10). One begins with a need to be somewhere else, renounces home while feeling anxiety about leaving, enacts a ritual departure, and experiences the euphoria of outward movement, a climactic point where moving away turns into moving back home. The traveler also undergoes the difficulties of reentry and relives the experiences in postcards, photos, souvenirs, and travel diaries.

The literature of the American highway is also a modern version of what Joseph Campbell has called the monomyth. Central to the pattern is the journey of the hero who sets out on a quest, experiences ordeals, and ultimately returns triumphant, bringing restorative powers back home. Key phases of the cycle are successive purification trials leading to self-annihilation and rebirth, the hero's possible refusal of challenges and the need for magical flight or rescue, jealousy of those who remain behind, and the necessary reentry where, in epic terms, "the speech-defying pronouncements of the dead" are rendered back into "lightworld language" (243). One function of the monomyth is to effect "a reconciliation of individual consciousness with unconscious will," to find a "true relationship of the passing phenomena of time to the imperishable life that lives and dies in us all" (242). A recurring hero deed in modern America is the automobile journey with its call to adventure on the open road, its initiation rites of trials, threshold crossings, conflict, return, and resurrection. Although the pronounced optimism and naivete of the highway quest evade some of the struggles and burdens of the ancient mythic stories, the pattern of flight, trials, and reentry repeats the motivating power of the monomyth.

Beyond travel literature and the hero journey, two additional patterns etched into road genre memory contribute to the diversity and popularity of road narratives. From picaresque tales, the road story gives us rascals and rogues who wander aimlessly to undermine the status quo in episodic adventures that mock acceptable routines and values. Like the picaro antihero, protagonists on the road are cut loose from everyday restraints of work and daily experiences. As they revel in their wandering, picaro road characters may have difficulty with, or even refuse, reintegration and choose instead to extend their journeys indefinitely. Finally, like the epic tradition, road literature captures the oral dimensions of shared experience, or what John Fiske and John Hartley have called bardic expression. In the telling of adventures that may be as available as the nearest set of car keys, the highway myth-maker articulates a cultural consensus about what is real and what matters in the society. The bardic road narrative draws readers into the dominant value systems of the culture, celebrates individual achievements within the larger group patterns, and provides assurance against fears of inadequacy. At the same time, because life on the road exposes the inadequacies of people and institutions back home, road narratives develop overt countercultural protest or use the conventional form to subvert present ideologies. In reaching a very wide audience, road stories function like the mass media in their creation of a place for negotiated definitions and redefinitions of values and political choices within an ever-changing institutionalized system. Shared texts reaffirm traditional values even as they challenge the status quo. The lure of the road invites the search for individuality within a community of people in motion. Moreover, the genre often takes on the tone of pilgrimage to search for origins, to define a culture separate from the old world, or to explore vanishing regions of a land becoming homogenized. Various myths—paradisal, frontier, individual, success, growth—reinforce one another in the open spaces and on fast roads in powerful machines.

Although road stories are indebted to a variety of older travel forms including the pilgrimage, the *Bildungsroman*, and the picaresque—the genre came to be recognized in its own right only as readers began to recognize familiar patterns of structure, theme, and style closer to home. Beginning about 1900, cross-country auto trips were popular subjects for essays and short stories, and for several decades mainstream writers from Theodore Dreiser (*Hoosier Holiday*, 1916) to John Steinbeck (*Grapes of Wrath*, 1939) included elements of the highway quest in their works. Jack Kerouac's *On the Road* (1957), however, brought formal recognition of the cultural ritual, and the genre began to accumulate its own distinctive features. Others followed over the next four decades either repeating with some variations the road pattern Kerouac had made popular or trying to get out from under his influence. As readers got used to certain road genre conventions, authors were both restrained to follow those paths and freed to modify the form and manipulate expectations to their own ends. Thus the cultural and social uses of the form became more complex. Road authors grew increasingly aware of genre conventions, and a self-reflexive critical commentary developed within the texts themselves. Moreover, readers aware of the road tradition entered into dialogue with road heroes, narrators, and authors—making the genre a particularly revealing measure of evolving cultural values.

The typical American road story plot grows out of a series of decisions about structure and narrative perspective. In nonfiction, the initial questions are straightforward. Will the author be a participant narrator or choose a distanced narrative frame? Will readers be addressed directly or kept in the background? What kind of structure—sequential, flashback, dream sequence—is likely to capture events as they actually happened? How much of the compositional process will be shared with readers? Similar questions in prose fiction are only slightly more complex as authors presumably invent the stories and relate them in a narrative frame. For example, to what extent will a protagonist step out of the action to draw attention to the fact that a story is make believe? After everyone gets back home, how does the story get told and reach readers? And, of course, there are always the questions of how much fiction and nonfiction overlaps—on or off the road.

Even prior to the construction of a narrative frame, motives for setting out on a road quest establish some criteria about what will be observed and included later. The desire to get back in touch with people, values, and landscapes creates a loose pattern of apparently aimless wandering. In *Travels with Charley*, Steinbeck wants to hear the people again, and Charles Kuralt's video essays set out seeking the real American behind the scenes. Often the pursuit of a specific goal creates the urgency of pilgrimage: returning the Big Bopper's car to Iowa in Jim Dodge's *Not Fade Away*, blowing up a dam in Jim Harrison's *A Good Day to Die*, getting a divorce in Anne Roiphe's *Long Division*. Sometimes the pattern is a retracing of a previous well-known journey. Richard Reeves (*American Journey*) follows Tocqueville and Beaumont, Jonathan Raban (*Old Glory*) goes down the river with Twain, and Dayton Duncan (*Out West*) follows in the paths of Lewis and Clark. Less like pilgrimages or heroic quests are the picaresque wanderings that often seem aimless or even manic-depressive; Kerouac searches for "It," Kesey's pranksters (*The Further Inquiry*) create a sprawling video, and Tom Robbins's cowgirls (*Even Cowgirls Get the Blues*) pursue everything outrageous to mock the *Bildung*, the picaro, and the narrative frame itself. Many narratives follow a pattern of loss and recovery where the road journey attempts to repair or heal. Philbert in David Seals's *The Powwow Highway* hopes the highway will help him recover his identity as a warrior, Robert M. Pirsig tries to repair the ruins of dualistic philosophy, William Least Heat Moon travels the blue highways to heal his failed marriage and career. Still others travel in desperation, as the Joads in *Grapes of Wrath* or to numb the pain as does Maria Wyeth in Joan Didion's *Play It As It Lays*. Road protagonists leave home with many diverse goals in mind, and narrative structures reflect these differences in motivation and perspective.

Often three or more distinct structural patterns overlap in a road narrative. The travel experience itself is distinct from the way events are first remembered and then reconstructed in the discourse pattern used to tell the story. The unfolding of highway adventures and the organizational frames for telling about them generally follow predictable patterns. In turn, both the conventional patterns themselves as well as successive modifications of those patterns make books understandable for readers who know what to expect. Literary conventions also enable authors to introduce variations into the established order. For example, some conventions develop based on relationships between the person going on the journey and the narrator who tells the story. Most nonfiction narrators and many fictional protagonists travel alone. In *This Is My Country Too*, John A. Williams initially discusses the difficulties the road hero experiences finding traveling companions and then concludes that the presence of fellow travelers might often actually inhibit mobility, thought, and—most of all—the writing process. If an author's powers of observation are spent in conversation along the way, John A. Williams notes, much could be "lost to the typewriter forever" (6). Protagonists set out alone also for the purity of the experience, as in Least Heat Moon's search for himself, Steinbeck's search for America, Henry Miller's desire to have another look at the country he left (*The Air-Conditioned Nightmare*), or Mary Morris's memoirs of a woman traveling alone (*Nothing to Declare*). Alone behind the wheel, road heroes experience the creative disengagement of driving, where the monotony frees the mind of clutter and creates a disinterested state. In sharp contrast, other road protagonists travel in groups to capture shared experiences. Beat writers create the carnival atmosphere of "dharma bums" or "desolation angels" or the huge grids of mythologized characters in *On the Road*. At times the groups are small as in the threesomes of Harrison's *A Good Day to Die* or Toby Olson's *Seaview* where a third party creates new tension or changes the dynamics of a relationship.

Road travelers are often paired as driver and a more-or-less "reluctant companion."[4] Perhaps most reluctant of all is Lolita as Humbert Humbert drags her along on a mock epic highway quest or the hesitant children travelers such as Chris with his father in Pirsig's *Zen and the Art of Motorcycle Maintenance* or the mother-daughter car companions in books by Anne Roiphe, Hilma Wolitzer, and Mona Simpson. In each of these twosomes, the reluctance of the companion sharpens the lines of the protagonist's quest and allows for change as their interaction unfolds. To underscore evolving relationships, an author will often maintain limited narrator perspective through at least the early stages of the story or use a separate omniscient and often comic narrator. In David Seals's *The Powwow Highway*, Philbert and Buddy are reluctant companions for each other on two separate quests: Buddy's attempt to rescue his sister and Philbert's ride on his pony warrior into his mythic past.

Another series of decisions modifying genre conventions involves the question of demand for the books. Who reads them and why? How are readers influenced by the stories? To what extent are readers brought along on the journey, invited to participate in the exploration, and challenged to confront the issues raised and the values presented? Road authors use their expectations about audience in the creation and modification of genre conventions. In "The Writer's Audience Is Always a Fiction" Walter J. Ong suggests that authors generally target readers they imagine as they compose and thus provide for themselves a kind of antecedent feedback that guides choices about everything from subject matter to style and tone. Most road narratives set out to be popular books, hoping to attract readers of traditional fiction, autobiography, adventure stories, and travel narratives. The audience includes the academically trained as well as ordinary bookstore clients, "mass readers" who might be anywhere on the political spectrum from the far left to far right. Literary conventions begin and develop as readers get used to certain patterns. Road narrative texts create "implied readers"— Wolfgang Iser's term for an audience the text creates for itself.[5] In other words, readers start into and then warm up to a work, as they get used to the poetry of *On the Road*, the raw edges of Jim Harrison, the philosophical quandries of Robert M. Pirsig, the multiple perspectives of Mona Simpson. Public relations, talk show appearances, and reviews may help identify targeted readers, but mostly discourse patterns themselves tell a potential audience how they are expected to respond as readers.

Whether or not they are formally trained, readers become "competent," in Jonathan Culler's term, when they become familiar with and internalize the conventions of the genre. Recognition of genre conventions is most apparent when authors manipulate standard expectations to modify the way they work or as in Toby Olson's *Seaview*, which inverts the standard quest pattern in order to parody the form of the quest. Perhaps an overdefined species of the competent reader is what Michael Riffaterre calls the superreader who has read all the books and can synthesize all background allusions. The superreader of Dayton Duncan's retracing of Lewis and Clark (*Out West*) would be conversant with the *Journals of Lewis and Clark* and have some expertise about American history. Another version of "competence" is found in the concept of consensus put forth by David Bleich, Stanley Fish, and others wherein a community of readers agrees to agree on definitions and interpretive strategies. Even consensus reading tends to further validate authorities with credentials, though some models would involve more fully collaborative decisions. Robert J. Connors attributes the strong connection between reader-response critics and genre study to the way interpretive communities form reading strategies "based on previous experience of similar works, and that is but another way of talking about genre" (Simons and Aghezarlan 42). Again, elements of expectation and predisposition about genre conventions are crucial in both the composition and interpretation of road narratives.

Adaptation to fictionalized or actual readers shapes the road narrative's manipulation of point of view and directs attention to the storytelling process as it takes shape. Narrators in works by Tom Robbins or David Seals address readers targeted specifically for mock epic or other political effects. This technique of calling attention to readers as readers is at least as old as Laurence Sterne's *Tristram Shandy* and fits in particularly well with swift and daring highway antics. Psychoanalytic approaches have given us reading as defense, where the lure of the road satisfies our needs psychologically as well as culturally, socially, and politically. Subtle defensive strategies suggest we find in Charles Kuralt what we need America to be. Single parents may identify with Wolitzer's *Hearts*, and angry or frustrated audiences may experience catharsis or sublimate aggression in reading Hawkes's *Travesty*.

Reaching a very wide range of readers, the American road narrative remains a popular literary form that has received only hesitant and reserved attention from academic critics. Road novelists like Tom Robbins, Jim Dodge, or even Kerouac have been excluded from or at best tolerated in college courses—though we are now experiencing a renewed interest in Kerouac. Women and minority road authors continue to experience double-jeopardy neglect. Most nonfiction road authors are considered journalists (Kuralt, Moyers, Reeves) or fall through the categories still adhered to in the literary canons (Is Pirsig writing fact or fiction? Is Duncan "doing" literature or history?) The famous authors who went out on the road (Henry Miller, Steinbeck, William Saroyan) get more attention, though their road books are treated less seriously than even less successful nonroad novels. Despite uneven treatment, however, road narratives express both popular and elite views without apologizing for either. In its popular appeal, the road story invites readers to trust their own readings. Road narratives affirm the value of everyday people and celebrate the ordinary and mundane. The books are accessible to large numbers and types of readers who enjoy their dialogue with text, author, and each other.

For the most part, road narratives have survived the war between the popular and the elite by sidestepping the confrontation. Considered old-fashioned, road stories avoid pressures to be in the vanguard or even to be original or fresh. Retracing old paths is acceptable as are conventions associated with travel narratives or classical quests. Innovation is not a primary consideration when "back to Whitman" can be heard from the 1950s up to the 1990s. Rather, road literature finds its originality in a return of the very old when the recent—academic or otherwise—seems at a dead end. On the whole, intellectual tastes and road literature as popular culture have given each other a large dose of *No Respect,* as Andrew Ross titled his book. Most "elite" criticism has treated the road with benign neglect. At the same time, road literature has served up a large portion of what Ross sees as "the popular, resistant appeal of disrespect." Road narratives are often popular precisely because they express "indifferent attitudes toward the life of the mind and the protocols of knowledge," they appeal "to the body in ways which cannot always be trusted," and they celebrate "pleasures which a training in political rationality encourages us to devalue" (231). Ross argues further that the popular appeal may not be indifference to mind or pleasures of body as much as a blatant and deep distrust of the intellectual agenda. In fact, the sexism, racism, and militarism that often pervade popular genres are never expressed directly but "articulated through and alongside social resentments born of subordination and exclusion" (231). This pervasive disrespect may account for why so much road literature is escapist, angry, or confrontational.

Still, the road narrative straddles popularity and official recognition by literary critics. Brash, disrespectful, mundane, and satiric, the pop side of the road mocks the high seriousness of the quest. At the same time, road journeys unfold with high seriousness and religious zeal. This multifaceted appeal creates special uses for popular literary formulas similar to the way commercial television enacts complex artistry through the simple and the topical. In his discussions of TV melodrama, David Thorburn calls the recurring features of formulaic plot and stock characters "the enabling conditions" for an encounter with "forbidden or deeply disturbing materials" (in Newcomb, ed. 628-44). Media formats or literary conventions become popular according to Thorburn, not because they are simplistic or undemanding or "an escape into blindness or easy reassurance," but because formulas are "an instrument of seeing." While reading road adventures, readers confront the complex and terrifying and even the cerebral in ways that are less intimidating or intellectualized. While critics maintain that TV melodrama panders to its audience, Thorburn sees the genre as "a peculiarly significant public forum . . . in which traditional ways of feeling and thinking are brought into continuous, strained relation with powerful institutions of change and contingency." In other words, "serious" reading is occurring during all the road fun and the significance of the genre rests in no small measure on its broad-based appeal. Even the sameness or monotony of the ritualized elements of genre support the popularity and the cultural significance of road narratives. What some call contrivance or predictability in TV drama, Thorburn attributes to "the multiplicity principle" wherein a drama will "draw not once or twice but many times upon the immense store of stories and situations created by the genre's brief but crowded history." With the aid of this genre memory, road narratives follow recognizable formulas that give authors and readers a base on which to build. The multiplicity principle makes the telling of road stories easier and more effective and frees narrators to construct intricacies beyond basic plot. Authors are able to present symbols elliptically with the assurance that much of the work has been done already for readers through the evolving tradition. Thorburn's concept of "enabling conditions" accounts for how familiar road types and predictable situations can be "more suggestive and less imprisoning," more a starting point for exploration than an end in themselves. What can be taken for granted is more than mere convenience. Familiar with shortcuts made possible in the formulaic, readers are free to respond to the way each work treats the formulas. Readers or critics not familiar with the genre's storehouse of conventions are likely to miss not only nuances, but also the reasons for the popularity and significance of the genre. Even external constraints can be liberating, Thorburn notes. Ratings for TV or sales and academic pressures for road narratives, for example, may become "instruments of use." Somewhat paradoxically, then, the road narrative not only survives its own restraints and prohibitions but thrives by incorporating certain confinements into its artistry.

On the road we mourn the loss of the old stretches of highway, the disappearance of distinct regions, the homogeneity and commercialization of the individual. Road narratives invite us at the same time to celebrate heroes and places and values that were never there except in our hopes, our imaginations, and our ability to construct myths. The small town has probably never been idyllic, no individual has ever fully discovered a self, and the national identity is hard to find in part because it is constructed rather than found. The carnivalesque playfulness of road travel draws attention to the way the mind reshapes through imagination. Gentle parody of the quest and the pilgrimage underscore both the wanderlust and arbitrariness of what a dominant culture takes to be the norm. Irreverent protest on the journey further attacks the dominant values as imposed constructs and multicultural questers demythologize interpretations as they critique the old stories.

Over time, variations of conventional road patterns have evolved a set of four subgenres with their own norms and deliberate violations of norms. Road authors have drawn from the genre's history to create formulaic patterns emphasizing protest, the search for a national identity, self-discovery, and experimentation or parody:

1. The decision to go on the road most often arises from some dissatisfaction or desire for change. The ensuing adventures and the writing of the narrative often take the form of social and political protest.

2. American road authors feel strongly that their country's history is short by world standards. This need for defining a national identity sends many writers on the road in search of their country. Many of these questers actually retrace earlier journeys of, for example, Lewis and Clark or Tocqueville and Beaumont in order to study not only geography or social structure, but also the road as a cultural phenomenon. Such modern explorers are often overwhelmed still by the expanse and magnitude of the country on the whole. As a result, they both celebrate and bemoan the slow disappearance of distinctive regional characteristics. The search for a national identity turns, therefore, to the study of regional attitudes and values.

3. Many road travelers take to the road for the freedom to explore or redefine themselves; they then tell their stories as a way of finding out who they are so far and where they are or could be going.

4. Deviating from standard road formats are the experimental narratives that stretch conventions into the radically discontinuous, the futuristic, or the parodic. One of the continued attractions of road literature has been its reliance on older and more traditional narrative structures at a time when readers may tire of what they see as pointless experimentation. Thus, experimental road books are rare and seem to follow parallel developments in American fiction on the whole. In this area the road narrative is more likely to break ground through subtle variation rather than radical departure from norms.

Before looking more closely at these four subtypes or formulaic variations within the genre (chapters 3 through 6), the next chapter will consider chronology as one important way new forms develop from what older forms make available. Over time, the American road narrative has accumulated genre conventions or certain strategies and modes of consciousness from which each new text can draw. Examining the chronology of a genre demonstrates how authors and readers use the multiplicity available in a tradition to advance, recombine, or subvert conventional patterns into new creations.

The lure of the road is simple adventure, escape, and the offer to break the routine. The appeal is in part the road's carnivalesque disruption of the ordinary. The freedom of the pilgrimage is a social alternative, a pure quest for something beyond the mundane. The genre's transforming power is also its ability to get us talking together as we meet other people on the highway, swap travel stories, or discuss what we've read. The genre continues to appeal because it lets us recast our image of ourselves. Getting away, we are free to be different; in the invigorating, free-floating space of the temporary nomad, we can challenge what has been dominant and explore emergent values and dreams. The genre opens up into irresponsible wandering and radical protest even as it closes off the expansiveness by insisting on conventional literary patterns. A multiplicity of possibilities narrows into shared cultural norms as the dialogue between new and old, strange and familiar, individual and society goes on. On reentry, the norms at least momentarily assert dominance, and it remains for the work of art to create a community exploration of the indeterminant. Each road narrative is an individual text, but it becomes a part of the genre that represents a culture in dialogue about national and self identity, social values, and opportunity. The form is particularly American and immensely popular because so many of the questions remain open to debate.

Though the highway quester often drives alone, the trip sooner or later involves a community of fellow travelers with similar goals. Similarly, reading a road narrative is not so much a text-centered interpretation of an individual work as much as a dialogue about what the genre has come to count for in the culture over time. Stored in genre memory is what the culture chooses to remember or repress about itself as it shapes a mythos and sets an agenda to explore. While literary forms are a conserving force in the mnemonic devices of our story telling, the road narrative stretches beyond literary constraints and into a socially constructed dialogue about who we are, where we've been, and where we might yet still go.

2

Backgrounds: A Chronology of Genre Memory

The backgrounds of any literary genre are more than sources or influences. In very real ways, the old is still present in the new as a set of evolving literary conventions available for the use of authors and readers. To reach an audience successfully, any new creation reinforces or modifies what has worked before. Familiarity with a context of established conventions makes both the predictable and the innovative accessible to an audience. A genre stores what we may have forgotten or forsaken, and that genre memory makes possible at the same time shortcuts as well as creative uses of formulaic patterns. Repetition and innovation bring pleasure to the extent that they are recognized as either accepted conventions or modifications of the predictable.

A genre's memory stores not only literary conventions but also the social and cultural factors that bring about their expression. The road narrative has evolved into a socially constructed vision of a community defining itself in motion, a genre identified over time through what Steven Mailloux identifies as "interpretive conventions" or "communal procedures for making intelligible the world, behavior, communication, and literary texts" (149). We tell stories to remember and share experiences and to make sense out of what we couldn't otherwise understand. The evolution of conventional symbols in a community makes intelligibility possible. Americans have found in the road narrative a way to connect or defuse the contested oppositions between "high" and "low" culture, tradition and innovation, the dominance of the status quo and the subversive direction of protest. Each new community of readers places each new road narrative in context not by learning abstract rules but through group strategies for constructing meaning. Each new road story is read and interpreted in context by a community of readers who know the history and potential of the genre. While conventional literary forms tend to constrain, the stretching and manipulating of conventions is a measure of how a community continues to redefine its own culture.

Reconstructing the history of a genre requires attention to elements of past culture that are still powerful as present symbols. Whitman's lesson of reception or the motivating force of the ancient pilgrimage, for example, are still present in our cultural traditions even as we discover new symbols of perspectives (often described from later hindsight as forerunners or precursors). Nothing in a genre memory is ever fixed, therefore, because old and new evolve together. T.S. Eliot described this evolution as the reciprocal influence of "tradition" and the "individual talent" wherein any new work of art takes its place alongside the "pastness of the past" and reshapes its presence. With every new creation, we reshape the whole existing order of what we think of as literary tradition. In looking to the past, what is "rediscovered" is being recreated with each new look. Thus we find and shape the symbols we need in our cultural evolution. Every new entry in a genre's history takes its place within—and itself reshapes—an evolving tradition of audience expectations and authorial prerogatives.

The social implications of the American highway extend considerably beyond its literary dimensions. The American road narrative, for example, reaches back over hundreds of years of storytelling about a culture on the move. Before white settlers began a westward migration, Native American tribes moved across the plains in paths that Black Elk identified with the power of the circle (Neihardt). Throughout history, Americans have wandered on horseback, in stagecoaches and wagon trains, on rivers and bicycle paths, and on the modern highway. As Daniel J. Boorstin has reminded us, American migration before and during the frontier experience was movement not in a direct line but in a "churning, casual, vagrant, circular motion around and around" (95). The special quality of this movement throughout history offers clues to the restlessness of American culture even now. Whereas most travelers of old in pilgrimages or quest romances moved with deliberation toward goals, Americans were nomadic in their trust that the power of movement itself would bring happiness, success, and fulfillment.

This Bedouin-like pattern of European immigrants combined with the circular motion of Native Americans to shape the nomadic and rootless character of later American highway literature. American road heroes revel in what French philosopher Gilles Deleuze and psychoanalyst Felix Guattari call deterritorialization as they wander across vast open spaces in order to replace a linear and hierarchical ordering of roots with "a thousand plateaus" of rhizomatic offshoots linked together by a "circulation of intensities" along an infinity of connecting routes (10). While Western European literature prefers the metaphors of trees and roots reaching for ancestry and goals, the American search is different. "America reversed the directions," Deleuze and Guattari suggest, putting "its Orient in the West, as if it were precisely in America that the earth came full circle; its West is the edge of the East." It is as if the linear quest with its persistent search for origins is but a norm against which the restless wandering, the encircling within, and dialogical protest flourish: "Everything important that has happened or is happening takes the route of the American Rhizome: the beatniks, the underground, bands and gangs, successive lateral offshoots in immediate connection with an outside" (19). The American rhizome is found in the tribal spirit, in Whitman's grass, on the frontier, in apparently aimless rebellion, and in movement seemingly for its own sake in what Deleuze and Guattari see as Kerouac's dream "to saturate everything" and "become everybody/everything" (280). From the circling, churning pattern of motion and rhizomatic multiplicity, the modern highway traveler inherited a tradition of ambivalence wherein movement itself would become at least as important as reaching a goal.

The distinctly nomadic movement typical of American travel literature underscores at the same time a tension between the restlessness of an actual journey and the more orderly ways in which the experiences are relived or reshaped in the telling of a story. In what William C. Spengemann terms a "poetics of adventure," American travel writers of the 19th century began moving away from the view of travel as the recorded observation of an already established world order toward the conviction that order is composed into the travelers' experiences as they are remembered, constructed, and shared in artistic form. Romanticism and travel adventure tales begin to overlap, therefore, when the writing process is seen not just as reporting ideas already formed but as a mode of discovery equal to the experiences of traveling itself. Nineteenth-century American travel writing also blended imagined stories with recollections of actual experiences. As a result, writers presented a world that is defined not prior to experience but rather through the recorded observations of people in motion (Spengemann 3).

The traveler's remaking of the world in writing is one legacy of the American quest motif. The rootless search for personal and national identity, for example, reaches back at least to Emerson's self-reliance, Thoreau's self-suffiency, and Whitman's self-celebration. Students of American literature can readily cite Emersonian aphorisms on the dangers of "foolish consistency," the importance of being misunderstood, and the necessity to unsettle everything in great orbs of circular journeys. Emerson's cry that each person develop an original relation to the universe would further encourage the youth of the next century to take to the road to unsettle the routine. Thoreau prefigured much of the promise of American road narratives. "Every walk," he proclaimed, "is a sort of a crusade preached by some Peter the Hermit in us, to go forth and reconquer this Holy Land from the hands of the Infidels" ("Walking" 598). Perhaps the greatest kinship between Thoreau and the heroes of American road narratives is their insistence that one must draw nourishment and vitality from wildness and daring.

From 19th-century travel writing, the road narrative also acquired a check on itself as the highway traveler became skeptical of progress, machines, speed and human intrusions into the landscape. Thoreau objected that new roads are made for horses and business: "I do not travel in them much, comparatively, because I am not in a hurry to get to any tavern or grocery or livery-stable or depot to which they lead." Like many contemporary road heroes, he preferred old back roads and warned of the day "when fences shall be multiplied and man-traps and other engines invented to confine men to the *public* road" ("Walking" 606). He thus contributed to a long tradition of movement that looks for its strengths in wildness, adventure, and self discovery even as it warns about the dangers of speed, progress, and alienation from the self.

The American road tradition includes as well a heritage of river journeys, foremost of which is Huck Finn's escape from civilization, his sometimes free-spirited float down the river on a raft, and his encounters with a variety of characters who advance the rebellious American quest motif. The many layers of satire in Huck's insights resemble the social criticism expressed by later road nomads. Hypocrisy, high culture, religion, racism, and the Puritan ethic are examined from the perspective gained in motion on the raft. Getting away from it all not only creates adventure for Huck but enables him to clear his head, sort through some problems, and decide what he believes. Though his adventures when he steps off the raft are anything but peaceful, while he floats down river the atmosphere is solemn, quiet, and lonesome. What Huck calls the "monstrous big river" provides the stimulation and peace found by so many who later roll down the highway.

Prominent also in the history of road travel are the stagecoach journey conventions illustrated by Twain's trip from Missouri to Nevada in *Roughing It,* described in the preface as an account of "several years of variegated vagabondizing" (v). Twain relates adventures on the overland stage via a route not yet taken over by the railroad. *Roughing It* begins with what Kenneth S. Lynn identifies as a "pastoral vision of the West" in which the stagecoach trip serves as "an escape from all the cares and obligations of the contemporary world." Lynn notes that "to a people publicly committed to the frantic hustle of the American way of life, the idea of quitting work, of simply walking out, suddenly and without an explanation, on all responsibilities, has been a haunting one" (Lynn 41). Whether in the stagecoach or on Huck Finn's raft or in the many cars used by later highway heroes, the motive is to move away from the clutter of daily life and out on to a road to regroup and build the world anew. Perhaps the closest affinity between Twain's stagecoach questers and later road heroes is their restlessness. In *Roughing It* the narrator declares that he gets tired of staying in one place very long. In his pursuit of action and constant motion, the stagecoach adventurer seeks in the process of change, according to Lynn, what he cannot find in permanence. Unwilling to settle down and unable to rest, Twain's narrator prefigures the frenetic road heroes of the next century.

Of 19th-century influences, Walt Whitman contributed most to the modern road narrative in his synthesis of quest conventions and his expansion of the genre's protest against the status quo. In "Song of the Open Road," the speaker casts off burdens and takes to the highway to find what is latent in "unseen existence." Listening to "the cheerful voice of the public road," he learns the wisdom that is "not finally tested in schools" but through the "efflux of the soul." People, places, and events merge into one another during the journeying or movement along the road where, "all other progress is the needed emblem and sustenance." "Song of the Open Road" is an epitome of the themes and concerns of later American road narratives which invite readers to move against the grain and to challenge dominant values.

In *Democratic Vistas* Whitman called for American literature steeped in "the average, the bodily, the concrete, the democratic, the popular." For nearly a century and a half readers have speculated and argued about how Whitman or anyone else could manage that. Recently David Marc says he has found in TV sitcoms the ironic fulfillment of what Whitman was looking for. The situation comedy, he notes, represents rational types, styles, customs, issues, and language in didactic allegories that temporarily disturb but then restore order and happiness. Marc argues in his *Demographic Vistas* that Whitman's democracy has given way to media demography; and while his case is in part convincing, an even more likely candidate for Whitman's homegrown genre is the literature of the American highway. Whitman's contemporaneity is in large measure his ability to involve an audience in dialogue about their own lives, the values they hold, and what they encounter along the highway.

The commentator who heard Whitman's radical challenge most clearly was D.H. Lawrence in his *Studies in Classic American Literature*. For Lawrence, Whitman was the first "white aboriginal" and the first to "smash the old moral conception that the soul of man is something 'superior' and 'above' the flesh" (257). On the road, the soul is at home in its fully passionate and unqualified acceptance of and exposure to all. Paradise is neither above the world nor within the self but in the accumulated highway experiences. Whitman's "lesson of reception," says Lawrence, was that the soul and body bring into being and celebrate the inseparable unity of the self on the journey:

> It is the American heroic message. The soul is not to pile up defenses around herself. She is not to withdraw and seek her heavens inwardly, in mystical ecstasies. She is not to cry to some God beyond for salvation. She is to go down the open road, as the road opens, into the unknown, keeping company with those whose soul draws them to her, accomplishing nothing save the journey, and the works incident to the journey, in the long life-travel into the unknown, the soul in her subtle sympathies accomplishing herself by the way. (257)

Lawrence sees this unqualified receptivity as the essential message of the American open road, a message that even Whitman would stray from as he "failed to get out of the old rut of Salvation" (258). The trap is the lingering of the old morality with its notion of saving oneself—as if reception and openness to the road are never enough. Whitman's road espoused, for Lawrence, a passionate rather than a didactic morality:

> It is not I who guide my soul to heaven. It is I who am guided by my own soul along the open road, where all men tread. Therefore, I must accept her deep motions of love, or hate, or compassion, or dislike, or indifference. And I must go where she takes me. For my feet and my lips and my body are my soul. It is I who must submit to her. (Lawrence 263)

This sense of letting go and opening up without qualification to the road's healing powers is part of the emerging values of the genre. In conflict with that passionate receptivity, however, are the restraints of dominant values such as the need to feel in control, to reach personal rather than collective insight, or to seek solutions that can be expressed in monologues with closure rather than in unsettled dialogues. That lingering interplay between the homiletic and the dialogue accounts for the diversity and wide popularity of the road narrative even today.

Another informing link between Whitman and automobile travel is the enduring attraction of the "frontier myth."[1] When Frederick Jackson Turner in 1893 announced the closing of the American frontier, the modern road hero's quest was just about to begin. The frontier may have been closed and the virgin land beginning to vanish, but Americans' roaming spirit was anxiously awaiting the new form of quest brought about by the motorways. Even the earliest motorized travel would speed up the movement and transform America's external and internal landscapes. In 1904 A.B. Filson observed that "the miles, once tyrants of the road, the oppressors of travellers, are now humbly subject to the motor car's triumphant empire" (qtd. in Pettifer and Turner 59). At first, the transformation was slow and required considerable promotion by car manufacturers who competed with each other to demonstrate that cars were superior to horses. Early publicity included races and trials, stunt shows, and highly publicized cross-country journeys undertaken by wealthy car owners. Beginning in 1901 Phineas Fogg became the first man to tour the world in a car. The journey took him eight years— traveling with his wife for 46,528 miles at 17 miles per hour. Though not read widely today, many of the earliest road narratives were adventurous accounts of challenge and hardship. Others were the products of promotional campaigns for companies—such as the Maxwell Briscoe Motor Company in the case of Alice Ramsey's two-month journey in 1909 from New York to San Francisco.

Marketing dominated early road adventures, with marathon drivers and wide-ranging sales promotions targeted to sell cars. Inevitably, there followed the Sunday drive, the motoring holiday, motels, roadside diners, and a system of expressways that led Booth Tarkington to make these dire predictions: "Within only two or three years, every one of you will have yielded to the horseless craze and be a boastful owner of a metal demon. . . . Restfulness will have entirely disappeared from your lives; the quiet life of the world is ending for ever" (qtd. in Pettifer and Turner 83). From the first sponsored road races in 1895 and the first motor show in 1898 to the song "In My Merry Oldsmobile" in 1901, the love affair was on. Car travel soon became a new form of entertainment spawning autocamps, billboards, cabins, drive-in theaters, motels, and superhighways, as documented in Chester Liebs's *Roadside Architecture* (4). In *Open Road: A Celebration of the American Highway*, Phil Patton has examined the effects of these roadside phenomena on "the metaphorical landscape of the American mind" (8). Taking his title from Whitman, he traces how in music, photography, and literature the road became etched in the national psychology and culture. From Tocqueville to Emerson, William James, and Kerouac, Patton finds a national obsession with mobility and change on the new frontier. Because automobiles and highways "froze the values of the frontier by making movement a permanent state of mind" (13), what had been migration turned into circulation. While once a means of getting from one place to another, roads themselves slowly became *the* place to be: the place for searching, escape, and self-discovery.

More even than improved roads, the power of the automobile gave the continuing restless quest increased energy and a new direction. Cars introduced in American culture what Rudolph E. Anderson describes in his *The Story of the American Automobile* as a "Jovian power to create a new love of stirring might and of hurricane speed, a new sense of spatial proportion which in turn was reflected in the evolving national psychology" (72). Turning up the speed and reducing distances between destinations soon altered travelers' feelings for the journey as well as their own identity. To a greater degree than ever before, people had access to personalized, fast, and powerful transportation of their own. Artists and writers in every medium watched closely the automobile's impact on American culture. Stunt-shows, jingles, slogans, and popular songs sang the praises of "the merry Oldsmobile," the Sunday joy ride, and "love in an automobile." Soon cars were celebrated as symbols of prosperity in not only advertising but musical plays, poems, and movies. In 1934 James Agee, writing in *Fortune* magazine, identified the American roadside as a major growth industry and called for someone to write a trilogy in honor of the restlessness that moves the "American autoist." Increasingly, popular and highbrow writers alike included the automobile journey motif in autobiographies, short stories, essays, and novels. Road travel soon figured prominently in the fiction of the 1920s and 1930s from Fitzgerald's *The Great Gatsby* and William Faulkner's *The Sound and the Fury* to Erskine Caldwell's *Tobacco Road* and John Steinbeck's *The Grapes of Wrath*, and Theodore Dreiser's *A Hoosier Holiday*. Common themes included a fascination with the novelty of the automobile, an emphasis on the expanded horizon, and the effects on the landscape of the speed, power, and convenience of highway travel.[2]

In these earliest automobile trips the quest motif is expressed externally in travel through an expansive landscape and internally in the discovery of personal identity. Even in its earliest manifestations in fiction before World War II, however, the modern road narrative differs from prior literature of exploration in several important respects. While pioneers made and used maps to guide their search, modern highway maps are seen as monotonous and restrictive of the experiences sought. Danger lurked everywhere for the early settlers, whereas safe and dull roads soon lulled modern travelers away from adventures. Even nomadic pioneers lived essentially in one place at a time, and travel was often an undertaking of epic proportions. Modern drivers, on the other hand, take for granted a highly mobile, throwaway society. The pace of the stage coach was slow and deliberate, but more recent highway travel has often followed in the Neal Cassady school of frenetic trip planning. While the explorer's first concerns had to be external, modern comforts give modern road questers the luxury as well as the burden of turning their search inward.

The legacy of automobile travel includes also the expansion and clutter of modern life. In *The Beer Can by the Highway*, John A. Kouwenhoven traces this American waste and abundance to the increased mobility made possible by democracy. With the closing off of the frontier, modern life has provided fewer opportunities for the traditional heroic quest with its clearing of empty space and the achievement of new goals. In a "disfrontiered civilization," Kouwenhoven suggests, security becomes more important than mobility. With plenty of new space to be explored and new resources to exploit, romance thrives on each new journey (242). Once there are no more worlds to conquer, however, modern explorers seek status and other assurances to relieve the insecurity about who they are, where they might go, and what awaits them next. Looking back to Emerson, Kouwenhoven argues that the quest for self-reliance and equal opportunities goes beyond the frontier thesis proposed by Frederick Jackson Turner and Walter Webb. Over and above any attempt to displace status and wealth, the mobility that democracy makes possible symbolizes a healthy irreverence for security and authority. The discarded beer can is a challenge to ownership and a hint of the rootless and rhizomatic quality of later road narratives. If the characters along the road are often disruptive, manic, idealistic, and beat, they just might share Emerson's, Thoreau's, and Whitman's conceptions of humanity's potential to seek fulfillment.

Though the freedom of the open road can be traced back into 19th-century America, the quest on wheels developed much faster following the unique combination of post-Depression, post–World War II prosperity combined with the social protest of the Beats and the introspection of the existentialists. In a line of American outlaws that stretches back at least as far as Huck Finn, the protagonists of Beat literature in the 1950s broke sharply with the norms and values of those around them. Sal Paradise in Kerouac's *On the Road* and Clancy Sigal writing in *Going Away*, for example, were searching for a way of life at once radically different from the pretentions they saw in their midst and in tune at the same time with old traditions that had been blurred by modern life. Again the American road narrative offered these protestors what their culture had forgotten or chosen to ignore about its own past. The Beat movement in literature was primarily a protest against what the writers felt to be self-defeating and hypocritical in the American dream. In their view, success beat down the best of human energies and values in the pursuit of power and material gain. The dreams of the early settlers had degenerated into the building of expressways and shopping centers. The Beat quest romance looked for new father figures, as epitomized by Dean Moriarity's search for his own lost father. When the immediate past is bankrupt, however, the search for origins jumps leapfrog back generations or even centuries to overlooked or misunderstood cultures. One of the paradoxes of Beat writers is their desire to combine rebellious and unorthodox living with the simple and even conservative views they find in Whitman or Zen Buddhism.

Such was the climate of thought that Jack Kerouac entered and helped to develop. While considerable protest was expressed in poetry and novels throughout the 1950s, the road narrative seemed to be waiting for that special kind of driver who brings the road highway quest in line with his own frenetic pace. The opening sentence of Kerouac's *On the Road*—"I first met Dean not long after my wife and I split up"— proclaimed the arrival of that new American road hero. *On the Road* is indebted to both the nomadic elements of road genre memory and the forces of protest gathering in the '50s. Kerouac's nomads are runaways like Huck Finn, adventurers like Ahab, and radicals like Emerson, Whitman, and Thoreau. It wasn't that Kerouac and his Beat cohorts introduced so much that was new in the road tradition, but they did synthesize a wide range of themes and techniques in ways that no one else had yet managed. Although Kerouac's heroes were dropouts and runaways, they created a community of protestors who, in their irreverence, opened up the quest romance, the picaresque, and the pilgrimage to ever-wider audiences. In Kerouac's hands the potential of the road quest was social as the form broke new ground for new readers.

Kerouac also reshaped a variety of literary conventions. He compressed—as Tim Hunt has shown—the diffuseness of travel narratives, the sprawling detail of Whitman, and the sonorous cadences of Thomas Wolfe.[3] In the development of road literary conventions, Kerouac was that great writer who understood clearly what Bakhtin calls generic potential. He created, that is, the prototype of the genre that others developed and modified over the next three decades. Kerouac triggered, for example, a frantic quest that continued in the exploits of Ken Kesey and the Merry Pranksters. In his introduction to Kerouac's *Visions of Cody*, Allen Ginsberg recalls Kerouac's "panegyric to heroism of mind" in his farewell to Neal Cassady. "Jack thought Cody'd gone back to California, Marriage, would settle down, be silent and die of old age," Ginsberg recalls:

> Little he knew the Psychedelic Bus, as if *On the Road* were transported to Heaven, would ride on the road again through

America, the great vehicle painted rainbow colored as Mahayana
illusion with its frantic Kool-Aid and celestial passengers playing
their Merry Pranks further thru the land. (*Visions* xi-xii)

A decade after the publication of *On the Road*, Tom Wolfe reported on
the later activities of the Beat writers. *The Electric Kool-Aid Acid Test*
follows the travels of the Merry Pranksters who drive in an elaborately
painted bus wired for every form of sound transmission on an epic quest
for *the* ultimate experience. Wolfe's tone is half-serious, half-whimsical
as he documents the Pranksters' attempts to make a 40-hour movie
capturing their peak experiences (415).

The 1960s was also a time when many older, established novelists
took to the highways and tried their hand at the developing road
narrative tradition. Faulkner showed his fascination for cars in *The
Reivers*, as he had done in 1929 with in *The Sound and the Fury*. John
Updike's *Rabbit Run* used the road motif to question the American
dream, and John Steinbeck's *Travels with Charley* resulted from his
now-famous trip across the country to get back in touch with people. In
1966 William Saroyan toured the country picking up riders in his
renovated old limo, a chronicle that became *Short Drive, Sweet Chariot*.
Not surprisingly, many road narratives of the '60s and early '70s also
reflected the social turbulence of the times. For nearly a decade political
uncertainty was the norm, and the country's romance with the road could
get stormy. Beaten down, worn out, or disillusioned with the quest itself,
some road heroes saw the highway not as renewal but the sheer frenzy of
escapism. Even when depressed or disillusioned, however, narrators
would turn to the conventions of the road genre as a way to think
problems through and to express the ambivalence of their feelings. The
road in the 1970s was a place of satire where authors felt free to
reexamine and to experiment with metafictional forms. Futuristic
landscapes and absurdist parodies emerged in a genre old enough to
comment on itself. Though some absurdism and self-corrective mockery
continued into the 1970s, road narrative patterns of the '80s returned to
standard genre conventions that could be modified for a variety of
effects and uses.

Progress would exact its price along the road, as increased speed,
power, and more sophisticated interstate systems led in the 1980s to
what Phil Patton calls in *Open Road* "the road culture's loss of
innocence" (267). In the early '60s, President John F. Kennedy had
spoken of "the new frontier," but the energy crises of the '70s slowed
the wheels, and at least for a while, the power and glamour were
tarnished. Over the two decades after Kerouac, gas prices quadrupled

and road heroes shifted from large sedans to fuel-efficient smaller cars. Energy conservation and a new belief that "small is beautiful" also created renewed interest in back roads, a slower pace, and exploration along the "blue" highways where drivers could once again find the lost America that the superhighways had bypassed. Patton sees in the period of long gas lines and high prices a resurgence of "the camaraderie of the early auto days" wherein there was a "sense of wartime . . . shared national deprivations and efforts," a sense in which "the highways seemed like wilderness again" (267). Once dulled by interstates, national franchises, and increased crowds, the road journey retrenched became once again restless and celebrated a community in motion where dialogue about cultural norms and values could be explored and redefined.

Far from surrendering the road quest to car pooling or space travel, the '70s and '80s brought a great outpouring of highway literature that increased the visibility, popularity, and influence of the genre. Kerouac's presence had been felt for 25 years, and for many readers, Steinbeck's *Travels with Charley* had provided sanction and respectability to the otherwise suspect notion of aimless wandering. Films like *Easy Rider* (1969) and numerous popular road songs brought the highway as cultural symbol into the forefront of mass consciousness. Television journalists continued to include the road on their beat. Charles Kuralt's "On the Road" features were prominent on the *CBS Evening News*, and Bill Moyers chronicled his travels in *Listening to America* (1971). In *Beyond Our Control: America in the Mid Seventies*, Tom Engelhardt attacked the "vampirization" of the American road quest by corporate America. Figures from the past like Jan Kerouac reappeared to shed new light on old stories (*Baby Driver*, 1981, and *Trainsong*, 1988). Protagonists from different backgrounds broadened the perspective on why people went on the road and what they might be looking for. Michelle Cole, Stuart Black, and a group of New York's inner city students took a cross-country trek, described in their *Checking It Out*, 1971. Women climbed out of the passenger seat, got behind the wheel, and in a wide variety of narratives, changed a great deal about the male-dominated road quest. (See chapter 7.) Over the 30 years after Kerouac and the Beats, the road narrative invited readers to explore greater diversity and contrast in a form particularly well suited to motion, change, and dialogue.

In the evolution of a genre, there is a stage in which conventional patterns display a self-consciousness about their own conventionality. Narrators thus become self reflexive as they draw an audience into closer participation in the way the work is shaped. Songs about singing, poems defining poetry, and movies dramatizing filmmaking, for example, provide opportunities for artists to comment on their goals in the art form itself. In the late '70s and early '80s, road narratives began to discuss not only traveling but the process of writing about travel. Self-reflexivity also meant that new road literature would allude to earlier narratives in the tradition. Sissy Hankshaw in Tom Robbins's *Even Cowgirls Get the Blues*, for example, attacks Jack Kerouac's excessive goal orientation, and Dayton Duncan, in *Out West*, writes with an awareness that not only Lewis and Clark but also Steinbeck, Least Heat Moon, and others had traveled the path ahead of him. Duncan provided a list of "road rules" that codified precepts known to frequent road travelers or regular readers of road narratives. A more recent self-reflexive road narrative is Douglas Brinkley's *The Majic Bus: An American Odyssey,* which records the experiences of a six-week course at Hofstra University in 1992. Seventeen students read 12 books while visiting 30 states in search of their country, their heritage, their selves, and a good time. In this classroom on wheels, students read Twain in Missouri, Hunter Thompson in Las Vegas, Steinbeck in California and Whitman and Kerouac everywhere. The *Majic Bus* is a road narrative about road narratives—shaping an itinerary that "wouldn't simply study America" but "grabs it by the scruff of its neck" (4). Just as cinema becomes a richer experience for frequent filmgoers, readers who understand allusions to earlier road books reap the benefits of their inside knowledge.

In the '70s and '80s the heroes of American road narratives were still breaking away, seeking their own space, and discovering new identities. They began to show at the same time, however, an increased historical sense about earlier authors who had been there ahead of them. In 1992, Richard Reeves in *American Journey* followed in the path not only of Tocqueville and Beaumont but also countless narrators who reshaped road conventions each time a new work entered the increasingly complex tradition. Each new work reshaped what readers would emphasize in road symbols. For some, Whitman remains the standard by which Least Heat Moon's meditations on the open road would be judged. Similarly, Pirsig's warnings about the confinement of car travel would alter the views from many literary windshields. Sissy Hankshaw's mockery of Kerouac redirected in some sense where Beat quests seemed to be heading. A self-conscious tradition of road narratives can also be felt in the growing number of humorous journeys like William C. Anderson's *The Two-Ton Albatross*, Alex Atkinson and Ronald Searle's *By Rocking Chair Across America*, and Fred Bauer's *How Many Miles to Hillsboro?*

At times drawing from an ongoing tradition can be discouraging or even intimidating. In *The Burden of the Past and the English Poet* Walter Jackson Bate has focused on the modern writer's "accumulated anxiety" in the face of past accomplishment. Confronted by earlier writers who have already been where they want to go and done what they hoped to do, authors are tempted to increase the pressure on themselves to do something new and original. Ideally, each new creative effort will overcome this burden by relating to past accomplishment in a way that is liberating without undue intimidation. "The greatest single cultural problem" we face is, according to Bate, "learning how to use a heritage, when we know and admire so much about it, how to be ourselves" (134). Harold Bloom has also described, in *A Map of Misreading,* the anxiety later writers can experience when they confront a flood of creative precursors. For Bloom, "strong poets" make and remake literary tradition "by misreading one another, so as to clear imaginative space for themselves" (5).

Though Bate and Bloom had other genres in mind in developing their theories, road authors have experienced some of that anxiety as they hope to use and, at the same time, swerve away from being absorbed by past achievement. Nearly every author who took to the road after Kerouac, for example, has had to contend with *On the Road.* The road genre tradition, however, isn't as much the combative place Bate and Bloom describe. Rather, on the road, there is more often than not a dialogue involving not only authors and readers but all those who have taken trips themselves and read or written road stories of their own. As later road narratives appear in the merging lane, the effect is not combat but a collaboration in which genre conventions recombine and emerge into new visions.

Typical of a popular genre, road narrative innovation often consists of variations on a theme and multiplicity of formulaic patterns. Widespread nomadic restlessness thrives, therefore, in a comfort zone linked to the very old. Road heroes of the '50s and '60s for example, break out of confinement by returning to what they see as solid and true in the tradition. Many road quests of the 1970s chart a new kind of optimism rebuilt on the buried ruins of traditions that had been long neglected or forgotten. Pirsig resurrects the chautauqua, for example, and Least Heat Moon traces his ancestral roots in the Hopi maze. Road narratives aren't afraid to leap over the distractions of the immediate past and join fellow road travelers and readers in a dialogue about what might be dormant in a tradition of wandering.

Each new road narrative participates, therefore, in revisionist history, entering an ongoing dialogue governed by genre conventions and interpretive strategies. All road texts follow predictable patterns which they both imitate and modify to advantage. For example, road experiences are expressed according to shared assumptions about what road symbols, heroism, and motion have come to mean and what possibilities they offer for writing, reading, and interpreting road stories. At any time in the chronology, there will be residue from outmoded conventions as well as emerging beliefs and values that seem inconsistent or contradictory. Just as the emergent is difficult to understand as it takes shape, so also dominant values are hard to define until their dominance has either subsided or been challenged by contrast. As Roland Barthes has shown, dominant views maintain control in part by refusing to be named or defined as anything other than the norm. What Barthes terms "exnomination" or "naturalness" allows dominant views to call themselves "natural," "real," or "common sensical" rather than a label that would suggest a particular perspective (*Mythologies* 11). The study of a genre's evolution redirects attention to how dominant cultural values are formed, maintained, or challenged.

The study of a chronology is always less than precise. Trying to capture artistic thinking in analytical terms can reduce the genre to less than its full expression. The evolution of a genre is not a linear cause-and-effect pattern but a complex discontinuous flow of the culture expressing itself in artistic form. At any given time, in other words, the road narrative is an evolving genre in which writers and readers explore together who they are, where they are headed, how things are going, and what might still be possible.

3

Disharmony and Protest

Going back at least to Whitman's "Song of the Open Road," the literature of the American highway has expressed the apparent opposites of protest and patriotism. Although Whitman in the mid-19th century and the Beats a hundred years later attacked establishment views, they also shared allegiance to older, traditional values which could be renewed. In some ways, all road trips are protests. People leave home to change the scene, to overcome being defined by custom, tradition, and circumstances back home, and—at least for a while—to construct an alternative way of living. Time on the road creates opportunities to question the existing social order and explore values that run counter to what is dominant in the culture.

The earliest automobile travel books were slow to discover the genre's potential for protest. Showcasing the amazing new automobile was at first the major concern, though many authors worried about where industrialization and commercialization were heading. It would take a combination of economic factors for the road journey to evolve more fully as a mode of artistic expression especially suited to social protest. In mid-century, Henry Miller and Jack Kerouac saw that potential. Expatriate Miller came back to write just one road book, *The Air-Conditioned Nightmare,* and then left for good. Kerouac, on the other hand, wrote one continuous road story that he continued to reshape for 15 years in a variety of settings and forms.

Before baby boomers and the flight to the suburbs in the Eisenhower years, Henry Miller's 1945 *The Air-Conditioned Nightmare* provided a glimpse of the protest road narrative to come. Though the spirit of the European quest romance influenced Miller significantly, his story is a prophetic outcry about what was turning sour in the country. Miller had lived in France for a decade when he decided to return home for a last look at his country so he could leave with a "good taste" rather than feel he was running away. Surprisingly, he decided to travel the country by car, even though he needed both the car and driving lessons to get started. The trip produced a shrill appraisal of the national scene. Mired in comforts and luxuries, the nation's thoughts, he judges, are not "brave, chivalrous, heroic or magnanimous" but "smug, timid, queasy and quaky" (17). He doesn't hold back in expressing his impressions: "We are a vulgar, pushing mob whose passions are easily mobilized by demagogues, newspaper men, religious quacks, agitators and such like. To call this a society of free people is blasphemous" (20).

Miller analyzes endlessly as he tells his story. He compares America to European culture, to the rich and neglected history of the North American continent, and to ideals about what the country should have become. Though angry about his "lugubrious trip about America" (68), he is nonetheless caught up in the flow of motion and wants to "get out in the open" (12). Echoing Emerson's cry that America "begin afresh" (Miller 17) and pursue its own dreams and possibilities, Miller places his hopes in the artist who is unfortunately suppressed by the pressures of conformity, utilitarianism, and profit. His form in the book is a series of personal essays, presented as a collage and connected by the loose chronology of his travels. By assaulting readers with fire-and-brimstone homiletics and drawing them into his discontinuous patterns, Miller opens up a dialogue on the American culture he had left. The cultural negotiation he initiates is both condemnation of the vacuous majority and celebration of the isolated artistic visionary heroes he finds along the way. In structure and theme, Miller prefigures the Beats and prepares the way for Kerouac's fuller development of the genre.

From the outset, Miller takes readers behind the scenes for a view of how he structures his narrative. Before the trip began, he lived it imaginatively just as Thoreau had planned long journeys he would never take. "It seems a pity," he recalls, "that I didn't write an account of that imaginary journey which began in Paris." To his cinematic descriptions of events along the way and extended analytical essays, he adds dream vignettes on the old South or on what each explorer must have felt in the West. He recalls hearing stories of peoples' dreams of America, where romantic sounding names would roll off their tongues and dreamy scenarios would unfold in ways that no actual trip could match. The most elaborate sketch is his "dream of Mobile"—an extended surrealistic description of an imaginary place he kept to himself. Needless to say, the reality doesn't match the dream, which begins to die either from lack of nourishment or because it is replaced by another dream. This contrast between reality and the dream provides the narrative frame within which Miller explores the achievements and values of the nation.

Predictably, the daily life he sees through his windshield offers little encouragement to leave the dream or come back home. His list of places, institutions, and attitudes to condemn is long. For over 10,000 miles he meets sad people living on a treadmill of false success. In montage style, he records impressions of Detroit ("capital of the planet that will kill itself off" 41), Cleveland (prosperous but dead), sewer rats in Chicago, man-made sterile parks everywhere, rust and bile in St. Louis, and a landscape dominated by architecture that expresses the "morbidity of the American soul" (68). The conclusions are pointed and grim: "Nowhere else in the world is the divorce between man and nature so complete. Nowhere have I encountered such dull, monotonous fabric of life as here in America. Here boredom reaches its peak" (20). Instead of the American dream, he comes up against an "avalanche of false progress" (36). The great American individualist is, in fact, "mild, blank, pseudo-serious and definitely fatuous" (45). From the start, Miller observes, America developed a complex about itself, and the cause wasn't being cut off from the world by oceans. Instead, he blames a mania for practicality wherein nothing is given attention or resources except utilitarian projects in a place where "you can ride for thousands of miles and be utterly unaware of the existence of the world of art" (157).

Not everything is so negative in Miller's tract. On the positive side, he also discovers heroes and visionary artists who operate against the grain of utility and profit. There is hope yet, too, in the old southern cities—particularly Charleston—and in southwestern ties to ancient North American cultures. At the rectangle of Utah, Colorado, New Mexico, and Arizona he feels enchantment, sorcery, and phantasmagoria. In the Southwest, he rhapsodizes: "Perhaps the secret of the American continent is contained in this wild, forbidding and partially unexplored territory. It is the land of the Indian par excellence. Everything is hypnagogic, chthonian, and super-celestial. Here nature has gone gaga and dada—Man is just an irruption, like a wart or a pimple" (239). Somewhere in the mountains, Miller comes upon a scene validating that California is actually the paradise it claims to be. Climbing a thermometic landscape where trees and farms and houses "climb with you," he revels in "rugged, towering mountain ranges" that fade in "dancing heat waves of midafternoon" to leave "only the pink snow shimmering in the heavens—like an ice cream cone without the cone" (244-45). He enjoys too "a burst of green, the wildest, greenest green imaginable" with everything but the ocean "jammed into this mile-high circus at sixty miles an hour." But soon he feels again the clash between the dream and what the place had become as the man inside of him tries to imagine the thrill of the pioneers who first encountered the place on foot and on horseback. "Seated in an automobile, hemmed in by a horde of Sunday afternoon maniacs," he quips, "it is no longer possible to experience the emotion which such a scene should produce in the human breast" (245).

Exploring further the contrasts between dreams and reality on the road, Miller is intrigued by the way writers shape the myths by which a culture lives. Ringing in his ears is a key sentence from John Masefield's introduction to *The Travels of Marco Polo*: "When Marco Polo went to the East, the whole of Central Asia, so full of splendour and magnificence, so noisy with nations and kings, was like a dream in men's minds" (qtd. in Miller 180). The mystery, inspiration, and unharnessed energy of magical Asia come forth from Polo's dream—a process Miller likens to his own dream of Mobile and the dreams of travelers everywhere. "It is only the wonderful traveller who sees a wonder," Miller asserts—to which he adds a telling commentary on the disappointments of actual experience alongside reading fiction. There is romance in wandering, he conjectures," though the romance has been over-estimated by those whose sedentary lives have created in them a false taste for action" (180). Miller's surrealistic dream scenes challenge readers to reexamine dominant American values in light of their own experiences. Just as Marco Polo "created Asia for the European mind" (181), so also America's myths of progress, success and utility replaced the artistic vision with easy solutions. In America, the fruit became "rotten before it had a chance to ripen" (118), and only the artist's dream can once again stir the wonder. Miller appeals to the world jury to speak out on what went wrong with the American dream. Coming in 1945, *The Air-Conditioned Nightmare* anticipated by only a few years Kerouac's hope that the dream as well as the realities might live again on the road.

In 1952, John Clellon Holmes published *Go,* a novel that Dennis McNally has called one of the first public reflections on the "emotional, aesthetic, and spiritual deficiencies of the nation" (168). Holmes's protagonist, Paul Hobbes, his wife, Kathryn, and their friends Pasternak (Kerouac), Kennedy (Cassady), and Stofsky (Ginsberg) reflect the early stages of Beat life in New York. Hobbes tells his story of trying to reassimilate and find direction following the war. He goes back to school, reads, and writes frantically in "fragments of wild rhetoric" (33). Ambivalent about finding his place in society, he becomes depressed and the road offers the hope of fleeing to Mexico. Neal Cassady is behind the wheel in the person of Hart, who drives the new Cadillac "with a reckless precision, manipulating it in the sluggish midtown traffic as though the axle was somehow attached to his body." Hart would "doodle on the dashboard with both hands beating out little rhythms, his eyes continually sizing everything up" (117). They cruised New York's tightly packed grid of streets and avenues, providing a microcosm of the wild chases across Route 66. Their panoramic sweep is stated in epic tones:

"As though they were the creations of that night, it drove them, drunk and sober, towards the dawn, through a jumble of dreary streets to still drearier precincts, conglomerate with derelict houses where no light showed." Through streets of crusted and squalid tenements, their car swerves around corners as they mutter "Go! Go!" (137). The frenzy, the dreams, the holy dedication are embodied in their shrine the Go-Hole, where wartime America had created a vision of America "as a monstrous danceland, extending from coast to coast, roofed by a starless night, with hot bands propelling thousands of lonely couples with an accelerating Saturday-night intensity." In jazz they "heard something rebel and nameless that spoke for them, and their lives knew a gospel for the first time" (161). Holmes thus predicts in 1952 much of what was to transpire in road narratives and in the culture on the whole for the next two decades.

In Jack Kerouac's *On the Road*, the road novel gained notoriety, respect, and a sense of direction. The most famous account of Beat travels gave the genre its name and brought the counterculture into classrooms and the pages of literary reviews. Kerouac is, of course, synonymous with Beat protest literature, but his legacy for the literature and film of the American highway goes beyond labels.[1] He was not the first to live on the road or to celebrate that life in literary form, but he did have an exceptional understanding of the genre's potential to at once protest the current scene and return to the values of Whitman and the Buddha. Kerouac's energy, vision of what can take shape along the literary road, and dedication to traditional quest conventions pointed the way for the development of the road genre over the next three decades.

More has been written on Kerouac than on any other American road author.[2] Numerous biographies trace the evolution of his thought from the 1950 *Town and the Country* through works published posthumously in the 1970s. Whatever else might be conjectured about his place in contemporary fiction, *On the Road* became the prototypical road narrative from which others have drawn and with which they have had to contend. As Regina Weinreich has demonstrated, Kerouac revised by repetition as he worked out stylistic variations in a series of novels over many years. In his now famous *New York Times* review of *On the Road*, Gilbert Millstein proclaimed that Kerouac captured a generation as well as anything since Hemingway's *The Sun Also Rises*. In *The Majic Bus* Douglas Brinkley describes *On the Road* as "the seminal book of my coming of age" (21). Brinkley questions those who dismiss Kerouac's importance as a writer for the young: "Kerouac is best understood when you are older, for after all the hitchhiking and madcap driving, and zany adventures, his despair lingers. . . . His final message is that you've got to get out and look for America—both within yourself and on the road—and no matter what you find, you are better off than sitting in a cage" (22).

At once an underground cult favorite and a bestseller, *On the Road* is rightly given credit for bringing America's Beat culture into the mainstream of American letters. The version of *On the Road* that Viking Press published in 1957 is a distilled version of at least three narratives that Kerouac had been writing for almost a decade. It is a fast-paced picaresque tale of numerous cross-country trips with narrator Sal Paradise recording his observations mostly about the genre's most famous driver, Dean Moriarity. Dean is looking for his father, though frequently the purpose of his trip seems to be pure adventure, chasing women, or the fulfillment of driving itself. One trip after another—from east to west, west to east, and then down south—stretch out along an endless line of fast pavement where "the road is life" (175). All along that road Sal is in pursuit of the ultimate in experience, a Beat quest for what philosophers in the Western tradition have called the Good or the Real. Commentators have described the book's mad adventures as elegiac quest, spontaneous bop prosody, a pilgrimage forward beatific enlightenment, a theological displacement of Kerouac's French-Canadian Catholic upbringing, a Whitmanesque and Wolfian hymn to America, and a discontinuous angelic romp in search of "it." Organizing and energizing this quest is a rhythm of loss and recovery—a Miltonic pattern of fall, the search for redemption, the pain of lost bliss and the search for ways to repair the ruins. The lure of the road is enormously diverse and complicated for Kerouac's heroes, but always the underlying motive is the "displaced theodicy" that M.H. Abrams has traced to 19th-century quest literature (95-96). For Sal and Dean, the search for God—what they call "it"—becomes secularized even as it gets more intense.

This Edenic quest is not new to American literature. R.W.B. Lewis long ago described the American Adam in the wilderness, and Leo Marx called our attention to the machine in the garden. Like so many modern paradisical myths from the wagon trains to *Star Trek*, the highway offers relief from the pain of lost bliss for Kerouac. Whitman's open road had become a holy place in the modern quest to restore a lost harmony. Whatever else Sal's and Dean's adventures might be as they crisscross America, Kerouac depicts the overwhelming sadness of Sal's loss and the mythic redemptive force of Dean Moriarity and life on the road. Trying to identify the "something, someone, some spirit" that had been "pursuing all of us across the desert of life," Sal decides that we yearn all our living days for the remembrance of "bliss that was probably experienced in the womb and can only be reproduced (though we hate to

admit it) in death" (103). Like Satan's anguish in *Paradise Lost,* this
relentless feeling of loss prompts Sal to follow Dean along the road
where he hopes to find some healing relief. Though this pattern of loss
and recovery can be found throughout most of Western romance quests,
Kerouac epitomizes his era's sadness as well as the healing grace and
redemptive power Sal seeks racing down the highway in his '47 Hudson.

Sal Paradise is lost and sad in all his adventures. The Ferris wheel
in Nebraska is sad, babies cry sadly in Iowa, and California is "end of
the land sadness" (141). In Denver when Florestan sings gloom in
Fidelio, Sal cries over "the mournful sounds of Beethoven and the rich
Rembrandt tones of his story." For a while Sal can numb the pain with
alcohol or a speeding car, but soon again gloom stalks him everywhere:
in the lights at a baseball game (149), Billie Holliday's songs (83), the
stories he writes that are "too sad" for Hollywood (53), the hum of neon
lights (72), and the "raggedy lives" of old photo albums with their
"senseless emptiness" (208). Alone, Sal feels he can make only "ripples
in the upside-down lake of the void" (208), but with every new arrival of
Dean it is time to get moving in search of the healing power of the road.

Like the prototypical religious redeemer or quest hero, Dean
Moriarity will first make the journey for his people and then show them
how to do it for themselves. For Sal, Dean is beatific (161), the holy
goof (160), the angel whose "jalopy chariot with thousands of flames
shooting out from it" burns a path over the road and makes its own road
through cornfields, cities, bridges, and rivers (212). At once following
old ways and making new paths for his followers, Dean is demonic and
seraphic (215), transcending time and space in his pursuit of It (172). Sal
likens Dean to the Prince of Dharma who has lost his ancestral home and
"journeys across the spaces between points in the handle of the Big
Dipper, trying to find it again" (184). He is both symbol of perpetual
motion and a model for Sal's own redemptive road experiences.
Alternately joyous and brooding, a hustler and a seer, a drunken
Odysseus and a solemn mystic, Dean is the world's greatest driver, a
master of control and then later—as a hitchhiker—the model of
resignation to the All. As the focal point, the energizer and the barometer
of vision on the road, Dean helps keep Sal moving—even though he
doesn't seem to be heading anywhere and recharges Sal's confidence
whenever it lags. "I was never scared when Dean drove," Sal admits, "he
could handle a car under any circumstances" (102). In a snow storm at
night Dean drives "with his scarf-wrapped head stuck out the window,
with snowglasses that make him look like a monk peering into the
manuscripts of snow" (93). All Dean's and Sal's efforts are dedicated to
the purity of the road. Hugging the winding white lines, they are

delighted in the realization that they are "leaving confusion and nonsense behind and performing . . . the one and noble function of the time, *move*" (111). Their goal is not just escape but the achievement of wisdom enacted in the road's holy rituals: "I knew, I knew like mad that everything I had ever known and would ever know was One" (123). Again it's Dean who helps Sal along the Tao road: "What's your road, man?—holyboy road, madman road, rainbow road, guppy road, any road. It's an anywhere road for anybody anyhow" (206). Dean's antidote to Sal's sadness is his "wild yea-saying overburst of American joy" (11).

In their wild searches for lost bliss, Dean and Sal hope to achieve an infinitely elongated liminality in which they can challenge the status quo in American life. Sal repeatedly attacks post-war greed, commercialism, and hypocrisy as ordinary people in the tradition of American pioneers are victimized by the big grab of business and world politics. Juxtaposed with his rhapsodies on dreams and saviors, Sal attacks the repressiveness of the "law and order mentality" (56). He rails against New York's millions "hustling forever for a buck among themselves, the mad dream-grabbing, taking, giving, sighing, dying just so they could be buried in those awful cemetery cities" (89-90). Old Bull accounts for the origin of inferior goods and services: "They prefer making cheap goods so's everybody'll have to go on working and punching timeclocks and organizing themselves into sullen unions and floundering around while the big grab goes on in Washington and Moscow" (124). These and other comments suggest the kind of protest that Kerouac would develop more fully in his later works.

For Kerouac, social protest is a collective experience as the road brings people together in sacred space uniting everybody in the country (78). Like Whitman, he sees America as a massive poem in progress, a collage of Sal's "riotous angelic particulars" (172). Sal makes himself "ten sandwiches to cross the country on" and dreams of all the babies in the country crying together, all the bus stop floors everywhere with the same stains, and Main Street in every city the same. He is more worried about fragmentation than uniformity and monotony. "Everywhere I went," he recalls, "everybody was in it together"—racing through the same crazy streets, sharing the same loneliness and sad separation from the lost vision. Dean thus proclaims "Yes! you and I, Sal, we'd dig the whole world with a car like this because, man, the road must eventually lead to the whole world" (189).

Sal's critique of the American scene and his search for lost bliss draw him in a special way to the innocence and meditative aura of the prairies and open plains.[3] Setting the pace for road books of the next 30 years, *On the Road* expresses adulation for the landscape and values of the Midwestern plains and prairies. In one of his several brooding philosophical passages, Sal sits in a gloomy old hotel on the plains reflecting on his position "halfway across America, at the dividing line between the East of my youth and the West of my future" (16). Images of what Sal considers to be typically Midwestern recur throughout his narrative. Alluding to farmers, cowboys, and the mystique of the land which he describes as lyrical and Beat, Sal creates patterns of images in crucial positions in the novel. Often the midpoint of his quests, the Midwest is alternately expansive and optimistic or confined and brooding. The pace of life is slower, yet the roads are faster. He finds diversity in the amalgam of East and West concentrated in people and customs—capturing what Ann Charters has called the rhythm of the Midwest (*Kerouac: A Biography* 86). In Sal's first four chapters especially, Dean Moriarity sings an ode from the Plains. In Chicago, Iowa, and Nebraska, Sal realizes for the first time that he is on a quest; in the Midwest he also experiences a rite of passage between his youth and his future, and he takes the greatest ride of his life. Valuing the land as a purifier of experience, Sal recognizes that the opening-up of the Western plains "was really the way that my whole road experience began" (10). Dean revels on one of those Nebraskan straight and fast roads in Iowa, as Sal clings to the car floor: "As a seaman I used to think of the waves rushing beneath me, unfurling and flying and hissing at incredible speeds across the groaning continent" (193). Soon after, Sal remarks on the rivers flowing softly through the peaceful Illinois prairies. Traveling through the region by bus, he elaborates:

> The dark and mysterious Ohio, and Cincinnati at dawn. Then Indiana fields again, and St. Louis as ever in the great valley clouds of afternoon. The muddy cobbles and the Montana logs, the broken steamboats, the ancient signs, the grass and the ropes by the river. The endless poem. By night Missouri, Kansas fields, Kansas night-cows in the secret wides, crackerbox towns with a sea for the end of every street; dawn in Abilene. East Kansas grasses become West Kansas rangelands that climb up the hill of the Western night. (209)

The Midwest performs a rite of passage for Sal in at least one further episode. As in a passage through the Underworld, Dean and Sal spend the night in a moviehouse in Detroit's skid row and at daybreak he feels an osmotic experience in the convergence of the strange "gray myth" of the West and the "weird dark myth" of the East.

In addition to being a recurring mid-point in his quests, the Midwest for Sal has its own mystique. After a bus trip with crying babies and hot sun through Ohio and Indiana, he takes long walks through the midnight jungles of Chicago, a city interchangeable with no other in the novel, a place where Sal finds "strange semi-Eastern, semi-Western types going to work and spitting" (196). It is a city that represents at once the whole nation in microcosm as well as a jumping-off point toward Sal's mythic West:

> The fellows at the Loop blew, but with a tired air, because bop was somewhere between its Charlie Parker Ornithology period and another period that began with Miles Davis. And as I sat there listening to that sound of the night bop has come to represent for all of us, I thought of all my friends from one end of the country to the other and how they were really all in the same vast backyard doing something so frantic and rushing about. And for the first time in my life, the following afternoon, I went into the West. (14)

In Omaha Sal celebrates the residual values of the Western frontier. He meets his first cowboy in a ten-gallon hat and Texas boots, and finds that he looks "like any beat character of the brickwall towns of the East except for the getup" (18). While in the rest of Nebraska, Sal is primarily conscious of being on the way somewhere else. As a West-bound train passes, the faces of pullman passengers whiz by in a blur, and he responds that "the train howled off across the plains in the direction of our desire" (20). A carnival owner asks Sal, "You boys going to get somewhere, or just going?" and he recalls later: "We didn't understand his question, and it was damned good question" (20). Sal the carnival-worker briefly turns narrator-philosopher: "And the ferris wheel revolving in the flat-lands darkness, and Godalmighty, the sad music of the merry-go-round and me wanting to get on to my goal" (21). In a somewhat different mood, Sal takes the greatest ride of his life and caps it off with a big swig of rotgut "in the wild, lyrical, drizzling air of Nebraska" (22).

In "The Origins of the Beat Generation," Kerouac insists that he stands for an America "invested with wild self-believing individuality." "There's nothing to get excited about," he prophesies. "Beat comes out, actually, of old American whoopee and it will only change a few dresses and pants and make chairs useless in the living room and pretty soon we'll have Beat Secretaries of State (*Playboy* interview, June 1959: 79). As they drift through the sacred and lyrical Midwestern plains, Dean is Sal's savior, his "western kinsman of the sun" (11), and his dime-novel hero who crosses Mid-America's wide expanse on a quest for the limitless. On a ride through Ohio that nearly undoes Sal, Dean seems to gain momentum: "Dean was so exhausted and out of his mind that everything he saw delighted him. He was reaching another pious frenzy" (202). All throughout Sal Paradise's Midwest, the reader finds the straightest and fastest stretches of road. Like Kerouac, many road authors of the next 30 years would stop a while in the heartland to take stock of their trip and/or redefine the direction of their quest.

As much as any single book, *On the Road* established a wide range of genre conventions that later authors have taken for granted. Working with recognizable elements of the picaresque, the pilgrimage, and *the Bildung*, Kerouac shaped a distinctively American Beat version of the pain of lost bliss and the attempt to recover paradise through the power and speed of the road. As redeemer, Dean freed Sal to be himself, taught him the requisite madness, and helped him formulate his paradoxical combination of optimism and social protest. Though not "intertextual" or "dialogic" in the way recent critics use these terms (Sal's forté is always the monologue), Kerouac's renegotiation of cultural values places his work firmly in a tradition of social protest. *On the Road* rejected many of the dominant values of its time while embracing the pioneers or Ahab on the high seas. Perhaps most important, the book made significant contributions to the political protests and social upheaval of the '60s and '70s.

If Kerouac created in *On the Road* a prototypical road pattern of frantic movement, in *Visions of Cody* he anticipated the structural experimentation that followed in the '70s and '80s. *Visions of Cody* repeats details of the famous trips in *On the Road*, but as Tim Hunt's discussion of manuscript revisions reveals, Sal Paradise is telling a story while Jack Dulouz meditates on experiences (Hunt 37-38). Hunt sees *Visions of Cody* as "a dance in language," recording not so much an analysis of experience as the process of discovery taking place. The book's narrative technique is epitomized, for example, in the one-paragraph, six-page letter from Dulouz to Cody in which he recalls how much he digs "1,000 things in America, even the rubbish in the weeds of an empty lot" and how he makes notes about it and penetrates its secrets (40). Just as Dean Moriarity is always front and center in *On the Road*, Cody Pomeroy is here the star and the symbol of a vanishing America. "Have you ever seen anyone like Cody Pomeroy?"—Dulouz asks in a refrain that sets up the rhapsodic catalogs that follow. Cody has, quite simply, "the face of a great hero—a face to remind you that the impact springs from the great Assyrian bush of a man, not from an eye, ear or a forehead—the face of a Simon Bolivar, Robert E. Lee, young Whitman, young Melville, a statue in the park, rough and free" (*Visions* 49). In Cody, Dulouz conceptualized all to America; he was "a mad genius," "a

Nietzschean hero of the pure snowy wild West, a champion" (*Visions* 338).

The feel of driving a car is a major topic in *Visions of Cody*. Dulouz revels in the wonder and magnificence of moving from ocean to ocean in hours, in cross-country journeys that unroll like "a mighty thread of accomplished moments" (348). One trek begins in San Francisco "in the heat of wildest excitement, great jazz, fast driving, women, accidents, arrests, all night movies," and ends "all petered out in the dark of Long Island, where we walked a few blocks around my house just because we were so used to moving, having moved three thousand miles so fast and talking all the time" (350). Cody is manic with endless talk, speed, excitement, and rhapsodic praise of "all those tremendously frightening two-lane bumpy roads with those ditches on both sides." Despite larger-than-life characters experiencing nonstop adventures, a pervasive sadness hovers over all. Much of *Visions of Cody* turns off the highway for interviews, descriptions of living on either coast, letters, flashbacks to Cody Pomeroy's early life, and meditations on every conceivable subject. Dulouz spends a good deal of time playing Boswell to Pomeroy's Dr. Johnson and, in monologues that stretch ten pages, analyzes the process of getting his own and Cody's experiences down in a form so that the reader can "dig it" too. The quest motif, however, never leaves Dulouz's sight, and he links his own work with Melville, Thoreau, Whitman, the Bible, Montesquieu, Abner Doubleday, and the Koran as a kind of "Third Coming" (349-50). More intense and wilder than *On the Road*, and more the phenomenologist's experiment waiting for the reader's uptake, *Visions of Cody* is a significant breakthrough in the literature of the American highway.

In *The Dharma Bums* (1958), Kerouac's continuous road quest has moved from Dean's frenzy and Cody's visions to Japhy Rider's search for the Zen way to Dharma. The bums are once again actual beat characters with narrator Ray Smith, who stands in for Kerouac himself, describing himself as "an old time bhikku in modern clothes wandering the world (mostly New York to Mexico City to San Francisco) to turn the wheel of Dharma. A religious wanderer on an immortal trail, Smith concentrates on the Zen lunacy of old desert paths. Japhy's search for ultimates is clear—perhaps even heavy-handed—as he reminds Ray that "it's only through form that we can realize emptiness." Alvah's determination to grasp after life as much as possible because of its sweet sadness and Rosie's "God is *you*, you fool" (88) reinforce the paradox of Ray's "Pretty girls make graves" (257) and his "zest for life, for Thy ever-recurring forms in Thy Womb of Exuberant Fertility" (100). Ray's message is, in short, that apparent opposites are resolved only when one understands the compassion of Buddhism. Alongside Ray's and Japhy's optimism, the narrative attacks society's forced conformity, the perversion caused by "American whoopee" (72), and the intrusion of mass media in "the millions and millions of the One Eye" (83). Finally, the picture of the man who had everything provides Kerouac's summary of the price of postwar progress: "he had a nice home in Ohio with wife, daughter, Christmas tree, two cars, garage, lawn, lawnmower, but he couldn't enjoy any of it because he wasn't really free" (102). For Japhy and Ray, the journey to the mountain is free of all this clutter and offers the Buddhist insight that suffering brings growth. This realization requires, however, that they reject mystical transcendence and find salvation in the simplicity and clarity of their daily lives back home. Coming down from the mountain top, Ray kneels on the road and says "Blah" to what he must leave behind: "I knew that shack and that mountain would understand what that meant, and I turned and went on down the trail back to this world" (192). Like prophets and pilgrims of old, Kerouac's heroes confront the difficulties and accept the inevitability of returning home.

Over the next three decades, a succession of protest road narratives followed Kerouac's lead. Published five years after *On the Road*, Clancy Sigal's *Going Away: A Report, a Memoir* (1962) is a sprawling work of over 500 pages blending autobiography and fiction, fast-paced trips around the country, and considerable philosophizing about American life and culture. Sigal's story focuses on 1956 but stretches back two decades in flashbacks to recall the narrator's growing up in Chicago, his life as a reporter, and the repeated trips in which he visits old friends and relives past experiences. Along the way, we are given an extensive analysis also of how the book came to be written. The narrator of *Going Away* is described in an italicized prefatory remark as "an American with a crew cut and a 1940 Pontiac sedan automobile, whose childhood had been spent in many cities." Traveling all his life, he became a cab driver, a journalist, and a factory worker. Most of all, however, he drove from one end of the country to the other in a red-and-white DeSoto convertible. Paradoxically, he admits to never really enjoying his time on the road; it was more something he felt compelled to do: "If I lived in one city," he remarks, "when that city got used up, in order to step up in the world, to achieve vantage, I had to go to another city, sometimes near, sometimes across to the far coast, and to do that, I had to use the highway. And it was the highway, the road that was the education" (137). For Sigal, roads are memories of earlier times, a chance to think, and an opportunity for renewal. He develops, for example, a brooding sense of history on the California emigrant trail and along Highway 30 following the route of Lewis and Clark (92). For a person who is always going away, he learns, movement and speed soon become obsessive. At 95 mph with the top down "on a dusty, moonless, wind-filled night," the speed is frenetic, hypnotic. "We of the road," he proclaims, "are the residual legatees of struggle, of cultural involvement, of personal meaning, of the search for justice and honesty" (273).

There is no shortage of social commentary in Sigal's critique of the American scene. He regularly confronts head-on the problems he sees in the "nausea of experience," and he is perhaps most disturbed by a "national conformity" breeding a terrible sameness from state to state. In his travels he finds heavy consumer debt, huge mortgages, more appliances than anyone knows what to do with, and a ferocious national self-absorption (143). From coast to coast, he visits old friends and tries to recapture the fervor they shared in leftist political activities earlier. Mostly, it's gone, he finds. People have forgotten, become too tired, or experienced comfortable prosperity. He finds the American dream a lie, a sham. "We never had, never had lived, an alternative in America . . . we never touched that *source* of life which provides alternatives, meaningful, stark, and immense" (188). When the liberals' vision is dashed to ruin, Sigal decries that the Left in America, "failed to prepare us for defeat, to train us in the art of custodianship" (298). Ultimately, then, he writes his narrative to quell his own great unrest. "I am writing this novel," he concludes, "to find a point of stillness in the rush to my own extinction, which at the moment seems close" (471). Typical of the optimistic dissent of the road protest tradition on the whole, Sigal's periods of despair never diminish the exuberance that sprawls over the adventures related.

Road dissent was often prophetic in its warnings about the backlash the country would experience in the seventies. Nonetheless, road protest outlived Kerouac and the politics of the late sixties. Over the next two decades narratives by Tom Wolfe, Jan Kerouac, and Jim Dodge continued the legacy of quests that opposed the dominant culture and turned on to the road for alternatives.

In a series of books in the 1970s Tom Wolfe documented the further activities of the descendants of the Beats. In *The Electric Kool-Aid Acid Test*, the Merry Pranksters set out in their infamous psychedelic bus to stir up what they hoped would be "consternation and vague befuddling resentment" and to alter "the usual order of things" wherever they went. Following the motto "haul ass, and what we are, out across the Southwest, and all of it on film and on tape" (74), these intrepid travelers see their trip as "an allegory of life" (73) where everybody gets manic and euphoric like "a vast contact high, like they have all suddenly taken acid themselves" (76). Their holy mission is to move through the face of America "muddling people's minds. It's a short-lived high, however, after which the bus is gone and "all the Fab foam in their heads" settles "back down into their brain pans" (72).

Neal Cassady drives once again with the same vengeance he displayed parking cars and speeding through Nebraska in Kerouac's accounts. Cassady's "Gestalt Driving" is built on speed; even when he doesn't hold the steering wheel or look at the road, he still listens to nonstop radio and produces "an incredible oral fibrillation of words" (159). While commandeering the bus, he spins off non-stop monologues of memories punctuated by "you understand" (17). Linking these LSD trips to the pursuit of religious experience, Wolfe suggests that the Pranksters hoped to find in drugs "a mindblown state such as the world has never seen" (232). Further, Kesey hoped the culmination of the journey at the trips festival would lead to a vision "Beyond Acid" (397). Through mind expanding drugs, they hoped to reach the Emersonian experience of the All, Zen's Oneness of all things, and the Beats' attraction to the instantaneous and everlasting Now. In addition to the pages of Wolfe's books, the Pranksters wanted to save all the fun in huge media archives of tapes, diaries, photographs, and a 40-hour movie of the bus trip.[4]

Another direct descendent of the Beat road books, Jan Kerouac's *Baby Driver* (1981) is an important road protest for two reasons. An insider's account of events by Jack Kerouac's daughter as well as one of the few nonfiction road narratives written by a woman, the book presents her journeys from New York to California and down to the end of South America, interspersed with flashbacks of childhood in New York and then later life on the West coast in a vagabond tale that captures the intensity and frenzy of a beat-style epic quest. "Playing hide and seek with truck drivers," Jan feels like "Marco Polo bringing wondrous bounty to amaze the folks back home" (89). She is playful with classical allusions: a girl named Carol driving a green bread truck is "arched over the wheel like a slinky water nymph" (91), and "on the Albuquerque highway, 7,000 feet up," her '55 Caddy is "grimacing in her black chrome armor" (112). A blue correctional bus that transports Jan from a detention home in the Bronx to Manhattan for juvenile court is a "nightmarish vehicle of cold cruel Hell," a "chariot of heavenly prospects, delivering us from gray limo into the colorful world of real life for another chance" (154). From high-school drug trips to "hitching free rides on the fuming back of the Tenth Street Crosstown bus" (84), *Baby Driver* keeps moving with a "giddy sense of independence" (189).

For Jan Kerouac—as it had been for her father—this freedom comes only on the road.[5]

Even as the country settled deeper into the conservative 1980s, countercultural protest road narratives continued to revel in fast motion seemingly for its own sake. In *Not Fade Away,* of 1987, Jim Dodge introduces tow-truck driver George Gastin, who confesses to "a bad case of the romance, sitting way up there above the road balling it down the pike, eaten up with white line fever" (20). Floorboard George takes Benzedrine and other drugs on a mission to transport the Big Bopper's Cadillac from California to Iowa where the Bopper, Ritchie Valens, and Buddy Holly had died in a plane crash in 1959. George's tone is philosophical in the way of Kerouac and has the irreverence and exuberance of Kesey. As a kid riding with his dad, he had loved the power of diesels and "all the people asleep in their houses and dreaming all those dreams as the moon burned across the sky" (19). Later he learns to drive like John Coltrane's music, feeling a "surge of purpose" behind the wheel, yet generally content to let his itinerary sort itself out along the way. George drives with his "right foot nailed to the juice" (203) as he stands on the gas. The amphetamines bring "a rage for order, a craving for the voluptuous convolutions of routes, schedules and plans" and wire him to the road so tight he doesn't even want to stop for fuel. For fun in route, he pretends to be Kerouac, picks up a host of outcast hitchhikers, dances with cactuses, and laughs with the stars—"the laughter of honest commiseration, of true celebration for the splendid and foolish tenacity that keeps us hanging on despite the blows" (99). He admires the Beats for their "passionate willingness to be moved" over and against the "rational Sunday School for the soul" which was the smugness and meanness of the '50s. George didn't really know much about "the Day the Music Stopped" in 1959, although he does know that Dylan and the Stones brought back the music after a time of "pretty-boy idols and teenybop dance fads" (56). From the beginning George is aware of being on what he calls with mock-epic solemnity "a pilgrimage" (19). Aiming to "Doo-Wop to the Bopper's Grave," he takes off not "contemplating the exquisitely bottomless metaphysical definition of freedom" but "*feeling* the wild, crazy joy of actually cutting loose and *doing* it" (85). He starts out wanting to "make the trip clean and clear, with elegance, dispatch and grace" (88), but half-way there, he begins to question what his search is all about: "I wondered what I actually wanted out of all of this. I wanted to get there, wherever *there* was. I wanted to deliver the gift . . . then I wondered why I was delivering Harriet's gift to the Big Bopper when both were dead, gone, and done with. Was it that I couldn't deliver my own gift to the living?" (101).

With the help of the motion, drugs, the Big Bopper's records, and two ghosts—his own and "the Holy Ghost"—George finds that he's really traveling to honor "the lost gift of love" (146), as well as the "invincible joy" and the "cleansing energy" of the music (115). With the help of hitchhiker the Reverend Double-Gone Johnson, George changes his destination from the Bopper's grave to the crash sight, and from the sheer fun of the music to its spirit of love. Going back to 1965 and the Rolling Stones, George had held onto the music for salvation and healing. Twenty years later, however, he was beginning really to hear it for the first time, and he noticed, "the consolation of its promise, its spark of life, its wild, powerful synaptic arc across spirit, mind, and meat" (201). During the quest, his fellow-pilgrim ghost (along with Goethe) tells him that "the self-seeker finds nothing" (201). Wandering from his resolve and lacking at first the courage to perform the pure act of love by burning the Cadillac at the death sight, George listens to his own ghost-spirit and redirects his quest. "If you need some miraculous conversion to bolster yourself, preach your madness at me" his ghost admonishes (261), suggesting that he may be stuck in a motion-trap. Finally, George torches the Cadillac, but only after his ghost tells him "If you want to live you must throw yourself to death like a handful of pennies in a wishing well" (283). Once again George is a dropout, a social critic and a pilgrim, but finally he lets go and shares the love of the journey. George's pilgrimage honors "the ghost in all of us who would dance at the wedding of the sun and moon" (291).

Like many later road protestors, George admired the Beats' "passionate willingness to be moved" which was "a whole helluva lot better than . . . what the 50s were generally like—a rational Sunday School for the soul, smug with dull virtues, mean with smothered desires" (23). Displaying the courage of their appetites and visions, the Beats added to the growing protests found in Henry Miller's nightmare and Biff Loman's warnings, in *Death of a Salesman*, about the sour dream his father had bought into. The most prolific commentator on a country adrift into disharmony was Jack Kerouac who combined scathing satire and patriotic longings. For nearly a half century—from Holmes and Sigal through Kesey, and the Merry Pranksters, and Floorboard George, the road became a place where people who were beat down could regroup and express their vision of how the American dream had gone wrong.

Many have found it fashionable in recent years to ridicule the oppositional political views of the '50s and '60s. Beats, hippies, and other "radicals" are portrayed as an amorphous blob of naive youths with nothing shaping their views beyond a generation gap. As Theodore

Roszak has argued, however, the underlying target of dissent was "the social form" that "an industrial society reaches at the peak of its organizational integrations." With no satisfactory answers forthcoming from the postwar engineers of the American economy and its suburban life style, young people turned in increasing numbers to jazz, Eastern philosophy, and religion, and what had been overlooked in mystical and occult thought in the Western tradition. In attempting to recall the shamanistic magic of forgotten ancestors, the counterculture turned to heroes like William Blake, Walt Whitman, Native American singers, and Zen Buddhists.

More often than not, the route from social protest back to the old masters passed through what Andrew Ross termed a "hipster pseudo-scholar sensibility" with its "codes of aristocratic self-extinction" and its aesthetic of transcendence projected on to the lower class (86). At the same time, the oppositional thrust of the protest road narrative has managed to avoid what Ross sees as the bombast and trivialization typical of hip "creative nihilism" by aligning itself with cultural forms that "draw their popular appeal from expressions of disregard for the lessons of educated taste" (231). Disharmony and protest on the road have avoided the trappings of hipsterism by appealing successfully to both popular and academic tastes without compromising its vision or pandering to either audience. Legitimized in the academy by links to the very diverse authorities of Whitman and the ancient hero journey, established writers made no apologies for trying their hand at the genre. Voices of opposition are less restrained on the actual highway as well as in an old storytelling format that evolved before the split between popular and elite forms widened over the past 20 years. Highway protestors have taken little stock in the radical leftist position that mass appeal is merely mind control in behalf of hegemonic ideology. Road authors continue to feel that protest can do some good, agreeing with Douglas Kellner that popular culture can be "emancipatory" as it challenges and subverts and takes revenge on dominant cultural values (qtd. in Newcomb 471-503). Commercial forms are not inferior watered-down versions of the real thing but legitimate vehicles for protest. Road narratives give themselves permission to be popular. Their link between popular and elite is not the fakery of what the music industry has called a "cover" recording but rather the legitimate, though rarer, "crossover."

4
Search for a National Identity

A nation only two hundred years old will understandably spend much time and energy trying to find its identity. By world standards, America is very young, restless, and less secure than older nations about its history and traditions. Highway travel has a special lure for this kind of restlessness as reflected in such titles and subtitles as *In Search of America* and *A Journey into America*. From Whitman's invitation to join him on the open road to Charles Kuralt's most recent video celebration of small towns and American traditions, the road genre has expressed the mood of the country, the character of the people, and the sense of mission Americans feel so central to their national experience. Road stories in search of a nation often are told around a motif of loss—lost towns, highways, regions, and values—where narrators want to recover the old ways or to clean the lenses of perception to see again what is still there. Frequently an itinerary retraces an earlier famous journey (Lewis and Clark, Tocqueville and Beaumont, Twain's Mississippi travelers, Fraser's exploration of the Northwest.) Because the nation is immense, exploration readily focuses on particular regions, and authors lament the slow absorption of, for example, Midwestern or Southern values and beliefs into the larger whole. In an effort to define a national identity, therefore, road genre conventions develop in three basic patterns: a quest for the soul of the nation, retracings of earlier classic journeys, and studies of specific regions.

Since 1966, Charles Kuralt has been creating road stories for *The CBS Evening News*, his own feature show *On the Road*, and the news program *Sunday Morning*. His 1985 book *On the Road with Charles Kuralt* provided an overview of his video stories. Commenting on how in TV journalism "one's best work vanishes at the speed of light," Kuralt captures one motive for getting road experiences on paper: "To call some of it back from the ether and place it in the pages of a book is immensely satisfying." His pages are a compendium of Americana with sections appropriately entitled "Unlikely Heroes," "Different Drummers," "Small Towns," "Hallowed Ground." Kuralt is aware of the road genre conventions, for he has read "Tocqueville, Mark Twain, John

51

Steinbeck, and all the rest" who "caught a little bit of the truth about America and wrote it down." He pays tribute to Alice Huyler Ramsey, the first woman who drove a car across the country. He knows, however, that "even the best of them never got it all in one book because the country is too rich and full of contradictions" (41). That richness is the core of his interviews with "the bicycle man," "the bird lady," "the singing mailman"—with bridge builders and canoe makers, auctioneers, prospectors, blacksmiths, toy makers and fixers. Kuralt's 92 chapters are Whitman's catalogs expanded, updated, and photographed. Rejecting the notion of the melting pot and its assimilation, he looks for the alloy that will not be melted in ordinary people in out-of-the-way places.

The America Kuralt finds is one of quiet optimism, "a multitude of gentle people doing good for others with no expectation of gain or recognition" (3). He acknowledges classes in the country, but not much of a class system: "The rich are always willing to move over, make room for one more" (66). Like Emerson and Whitman, he hears a poet at every crossroad—not "a writer of verse" but "somebody who had inside of him such a love of something—farming, flying, furniture-making—and talks about it so lyrically and intensely, that in telling you about it, he makes you love it too." During the 1976 Bicentennial year, Kuralt and his crew went looking for these poets. From coast to coast they talked to cow punchers and con men, teachers, soldiers, sod busters and politicians. His book may not be able to define the national identity, but it does soak it up in tall tales, roadside sculpture, the ingenuity of a man who built his own road, the music of American place names, and even the multitude of American burgers. He finds something particularly American in the small town's agelessness and continuity. Above all, he is sure that all this is still there for the looking—a recurring theme in most road narratives: "American history is gaudier than a dime novel and a lot better reading, and the places where it happened are mostly still there to be seen. If you go to some of these places early in the morning, say, when there's nobody else around and think what happened there, they'll give you the shivers" (301). In his celebration of a national ethos, Kuralt promotes what Hal Himmelstein has called "the myth of the middle landscape" or a tribute to pure country values and hard work.[1] Kuralt's books and videos profile strong-willed and commonsensical folks in order to distract from the chaos of the rest of the news. The aura he finds remains a part of the road's residual culture as well as a mythic ingredient in the dominant culture's view of itself as yet unspoiled for those who take the time and make the effort to look underneath what appears otherwise.

The tradition of American journalists on the road extends back to Whitman and to naturalist writers like Theodore Dreiser and Stephen Crane. The genre owes a good deal not only to Kuralt but also to Hunter Thompson's gonzo reporting and Tom Wolfe's new journalism. The tradition includes the 1989 *Lost Continent* by Bill Bryson, an American writer now living in London, and well-known figures like Bill Moyers and Richard Reeves. In the political turmoil of the late 1960s, Moyers described, in *Listening to America: A Traveler Rediscovers His Country, 1971*, his 13,000-mile quest to hear people speak for themselves. The America he finds, however, is a place where "man is born to trouble, and experience teaches that he endures those troubles by talking about them." The talk mirrors the paradoxes revealed in so many road narratives. The president of Antioch College tells him that the tumultuousness of the '60s is valuable because "human beings can tolerate a much higher level of conflict than they think they can," and "this conflict can be healthy" (46). Moyers also listens to a debate about small towns, concluding "it is hard not to lament their decline, although life in these rural towns was never as idyllic as our poets remember it" (48).

Traveling from Hartford, Connecticut, to California and then back east, Moyers sees deterioration everywhere. In Denver he notes the gradual disappearance of the West as more people arrive bringing "patches of suburbs with fancy names" (128). Highways are overloaded and billboards scream Americanese slogans from coast to coast (194). Pockets of crime in Washington thrive short blocks from national treasures. The danger in it all, he feels, is that the impatience people express can become "an intemperance, an isolation which invites opportunists who promise too much and castigate too many" (342). People don't know what to make of it all, he notes, as war, protest, congestion, wandering, intransigence, loneliness, boredom—all threaten to overwhelm the country in turmoil. Nonetheless, Moyers finds people indomitable and their contradictions a source of strength for democracy. The destructive tendency to define the good Americans as people who resemble each other is countered by increased emphasis on ethnic differences that give America its true character. In Whitmanesque style, he calls Lawrence, Kansas, a microcosm, "the epitome of a troubled, spirited, inspired, brightened, complacent, industrious, selfish, magnanimous, confused, spiteful, bewitching country" (83). Indeed, *Listening to America* hears hope as Moyers rediscovers in people a "hunger to talk." "They are not often heard," he concludes, "but they have something to say." Moyers is steeped in Emersonian optimism, schooled in Tocqueville's contradictions, and just a bit more apprehensive in his conclusions than many of America's road questers.

In another variation of the quest for a national identity, J.R. Humphreys tells, in *The Lost Towns and Roads of America* (1961), the story of places and people cut off from the progress of modern civilization by new highways. Humphreys is looking for a Rip Van Winkle experience, hoping to recapture "the whole nation still . . . pretty much as it should look" before the intrusion of strip cities already spreading from the Atlantic Ocean to the Mississippi River. Quoting Melville's Redburn who reminds us that we rely on guide books which eventually are "used for waste paper" (31), Humphreys searches the old maps for directions to the lost towns and roads. "If I followed one of those old lost or abandoned roads," he hopes, "I could go back into an earlier time, not only in the life of the land, but in my own as well" (37). His trip is deliberately slow—7,484 miles in 45 days, pausing to study Amish settlements and black towns that "sprang up along the Underground Railroad (52) and studies the "old faces in tintypes that so many Americans have in their family albums" (127). Looking for every little town cut off by the highways, he feels "like a tourist from outer space who had managed by the single trick of birth to reach this planet for a visit" (154). Humphreys's answer to the alleged disappearance of the frontier is to suggest that the quester asks the wrong questions and seeks the wrong goals. Go back in time, he urges, to rediscover what has always been in our midst: "I thought of these places, empty, beautiful, unwitnessed before I'd been born—and remaining unchanged, living on, long after I'd be gone" (154). With his old maps, Humphreys turns off the main highways and makes many discoveries. His preconceptions about the West, for example, don't hold up. He had thought that America's roots were in the East, only to discover the ancient West he had neglected. He learns also that his quest is impossible to complete. When he reaches the Pacific Ocean, Humphreys doesn't experience "the grand finale" he thought it was going to be. Instead, "it was more like old Whitman facing West from California's shore: inquiring, tireless and seeking what was yet unfound. So this is not an ending. There isn't any, for trips through time" (189).

The most famous American author taking to the road to define the country is John Steinbeck. In *The Grapes of Wrath* (1939) the Okies' world was defined for them as they searched for work along old Highway 66. Almost a quarter of a century later, Steinbeck felt "out of touch" and went out again "in search of America." His reputation as a major author of world status provided his rationale or excuse for taking off across this very pragmatic country. Writing a book was an acceptable reason, that is, for what might otherwise be considered a frivolous trek. For the 60-year old author, the trip was a 12,000-mile test of endurance as well as an "antidote for the poison of the professional sick man" (20). When he wants to eavesdrop on the locals, he tries breakfast at a roadside restaurant and listens to morning radio shows that take the place of the local newspaper. What he hears suggests that he had neglected his country for too long. He finds that American society has become oversanitized, obsessed with the Russian threat and embroiled in racial tensions. But in spite of all its problems and contradictions, the American he finds is a new breed amalgamated from diverse nationalities, races, cultures, and regions.

Steinbeck's actual journey was perhaps less restless than most, for his plans, paraphernalia, and other road trappings were elaborate. He and his wife, Elaine, meet along the way, with an extended stay together in Chicago. He also telephones home three times a week and equips his vehicle with many of the comforts of home. Nicknamed Rocinante after Don Quixote's horse, Steinbeck's truck is a minihouse on wheels in which he could host people and take refuge from the elements, the dullness of long road stretches, and the pervasive loneliness. As a famous writer whose face would be recognized, he takes pains to preserve anonymity, though he finds most people recognize notoriety "only in context." He avoids maps, takes back roads, and focuses on distinctive regional traits in people and events, and compiles catalogs of his experiences and observations. In a straightforward style and uncomplicated structure, *Travels with Charley* became the non-specialist's participation in the continuation of the Beat quest. Steinbeck likens his adventures to the picaresque, perhaps a toned-down version of the Beat search, akin to what he calls the Spanish *vacilando*—setting out for somewhere, but not quite caring whether you get there. The *vacilando* is apparent aimlessness, but with direction.

The direction Steinbeck finds in his own travels and in the American identity itself is a rootless desire to be "any place away from any here." In one of his many conversations with Charley, his French poodle, he proposes that "we have overrated roots as a psychic need. Maybe the greater the urge, the deeper and more ancient is the need, the will, the hunger to be somewhere else" (104). As a road person himself, he finds his place in the long tradition of American wanderers: "I was born lost and take no pleasure in being found" (70). This rootlessness pervades the book. Friends told him maturity would cure the itch he had always had to be someplace else, but the disease becomes incurable. He learns that people don't take trips, trips take people. Wanderers value roots far less than being set in motion so that when the trip ends on one level, the journey is likely to continue a lifetime.

Speculation on the role of memory in the writing of stories leads Steinbeck to consider the relationship between his day-to-day life on the road and his reconstruction of these experiences. Early in the book he searches for a pattern and finds instead a poetic wandering. He concludes that his observations are highly personal and that he is presenting "not an America that you'll find but mine" (77). Ultimately we have no choice but to make over the object of our attention as we become intermeshed with how we feel at the moment. In writing the road journey Steinbeck discovers the macrocosm of his microcosmic self. He rejects the phoney American motive for traveling where "one goes, not so much to see but to tell afterward" (161). At the same time, what is more telling afterward than the writing of the story? Embracing that challenge, he rests at times to get "a little time to think" (112), and leaves out the Chicago part of the trip because it would bring "disunity in writing." The job of writing, he finds, is just too difficult if experiences aren't allowed to gel. He can't do justice to his home town of Salinas, California, because he can't distance himself as he had in other places along the road. The writer can't go home again because memory reshapes. In the end, the patterns he wanted to create are shaped by experience and the struggle to interpret: "Every safe generality I gathered in my travels," he concludes, "was concealed by another" (157).

Within conventional road patterns, Steinbeck challenges readers to reconsider a wide range of American institutions and traditions. The personal tone and conviction of voice suggest that the form of the book may have started out as a series of letters to his wife. Letters from September 1960 to January 1961 show that he tried out some of the ideas while writing to her. Most notably, he tells Elaine on October 10: "If I am ever looking for a theme—this restless mobility is a good one" (Elaine Steinbeck, *A Life in Letters,* 684). In one of her return letters, Elaine noted how much she was enjoying his diary letters: "They remind me of *Travels with a Donkey.*" He replied: "You've just given me my title" (686). What started out as diary entries with the tone of a travelogue grew through the quest for definition and the *vacilando* conventions Steinbeck found in genre memory. Readers who knew those earlier quests would find something distinctive in this accomplished author's return to the highways. The protests of the 1960s were about to begin, yet it was also "Camelot" time where a journey could go on forever even after the physical trip had ended. Steinbeck invites his readers to come along with him to overhear his conversations with Charley. Like Whitman, he suggests that the wandering should be celebrated, and he challenges readers to break away and let a trip take them somewhere.

Whether in tones of adulation or harsh satire, the American road narrative's search for identity is abiding. Recently many authors have looked for the national identity in the paths of early voyagers. In May 1831 Alexis de Tocqueville and Gustave de Beaumont began their nine-month journey from Rhode Island through New York and Michigan to Green Bay and then back east to Philadelphia, down to New Orleans and eventually through the South to Washington. They came with a practical goal—to observe selected prison systems—but Tocqueville hoped also to study the American system of government and record his observations in "some publication." In 1835 *De la Democratie en Amerique* appeared in two volumes in Paris, and its influence on the study of American culture has been incalculable. *Democracy in America* is acknowledged by historians and political scientists to be an enduring classic. The most direct attempt to recreate Tocqueville's journey is Richard Reeves' *American Journey: Traveling with Tocqueville in Search of Democracy in America* (1982). Awe-struck reading "the notes for what was probably the best book ever written about my country," Reeves decided to "travel the same roads, see the same things or what had replaced them, and talk to the modern counterparts of the men and women" Tocqueville had questioned. He soon discovers that they are asking the same questions about American democracy: "What had it become? Did it work? Could it peacefully translate the will of the people into life, liberty and the pursuit of happiness for each of those people?" (15).

Reeves looked for verification of Tocqueville's hypothesis that Americans are a nomadic tribe which, "having reached the Pacific Ocean, will reverse its steps to trouble and destroy the societies it will have formed behind it." He finds that the prophecy has come true and the destruction has been advanced on "those societies called Louisville, Memphis, Saginaw, Detroit, New York. All for the American reasons, old and new: money and an easier way of life" (325). Increased mobility is, of course, a well-known phenomenon of American life in this century, and Reeves notes the contrasts in the landscape and the speed of travel introduced over the nearly fifteen decades between his and Tocqueville's journeys. So much territory is covered and with so much speed, that the West soon gets won and there's nowhere else to settle. The wheels of the quest keep spinning, however, and the displacement of the traditional quest pattern is not without significant consequences. "Our ancestors left the old country or they moved West from New England—they left relationships for opportunity," Reeves hears from Ellen Goodman, the Boston columnist: "Now people do the same thing personally, psychologically. They leave each other for real or imagined opportunity.

Americans are living alone—it's the centrifugal force at the end of individualism" (71). Supreme Court Justice Potter Stewart suggests some new roads open for modern travel: "When this country was new, a nonconformist or someone who just wasn't making it could always go west. There was always space. Now there is no more space and the courts have been called on to protect the rights of these individuals. . . . Now they are needed to provide the economic opportunity that the frontier was" (99).

The American road quest continues as well for commuters as better and faster highways expand freedom of movement and allow people to live farther from their jobs than anyone else in the world. As a result, the cities empty out as people take taxes, industry, and shops with them. In Saginaw, Michigan, Reeves bemoans the American way: "Use it and move on—like nomads" (187). Quoting David Riesman's observation that "this is the only country whose living patterns were determined by real estate speculation" (182), Reeves worries that democracy's most freedom for the most people had bred a new self-absorption beyond the wildest imaginings of Emerson and Whitman. While Tocqueville was sure that democracy turns man from externals to concentration on the self, Reeves sees democracy and the psychoanalyst as synergistic. The dean of the Harvard Divinity School proposes, for example, that "the social gospel and the introduction of psychological jargon into religion led to the whole attitude that you're not responsible for your own action" (203). In some ways Tocqueville's America had been "turned upside down—from aggression to defense, from books on public solutions to books on private problems, from republicanism to psychiatry" (268). In all the contradictions and paradoxes of modern life, consensus about democracy is difficult to attain, so long as "each of us has the right and the power to disagree about what it should do." Reeves concludes his journey with remarks that explain why the American road narrative will remain a vital part of our modern quest as a nation: "The glory and the frustration of American democracy is that greatness is defined by each American—and that's the way we meant it to be" (357). Tocqueville would not be surprised by the directions we have taken and the variety of roads followed to get there. Just as Reeves followed the path of Tocqueville and Beaumont, Dayton Duncan continued the most famous American journey along the Lewis and Clark trail.

Out West is a road narrative *about* road narratives. Most directly, it is Duncan retracing Lewis and Clark's American epic quest and rereading *The Journals of Lewis and Clark* at the same time. In the process, he also analyzes both the rules of the road travel and the literary conventions used to tell the road story. From the opening sentence, he sets a relaxed tone: "My idea of a good time has always been getting in a car and driving nowhere in particular" (ix). In this story of adventure, wonder, and exploration, the keynote is the freedom "associated with a steering wheel in my hands and a new section of America somewhere out past the windshield where the yellow center line dips over the horizon" (ix). The story intertwines three separate journeys: Lewis' and Clark's in 1804-06, Duncan's in 1983 and 1985, and the American West's during the years in between. Reaching into every part of the American road's genre memory, *Out West* is a pilgrimage to Lewis and Clark shrines, an epiphany on the eternity of nature, a corrective history lesson on the facts of our past and the mythology we substitute for reality; Duncan sees motion as both a way to stir up the settled past for reinterpretation and a regenerative act of healing. The experiences he seeks and the way he tells his story are deliberately and self-consciously in a tradition he both embraces and critiques.

Duncan sets out to crack the code of highway literature in his 26 Rules of the Road—complete with numerous corollaries inserted at appropriate places along the trip. His rules become a commentary on the road literature that has gone before and a guide to the way he shapes the discourse patterns of his own presentation. One type of rule involving day-to-day moving around includes advice on why one shouldn't ask for directions, drive the interstates, follow maps, or frequent certain types of businesses. Where to eat, how to plan an itinerary, and how to meet people are addressed with the ironic wisdom of one who has both traveled and read a good deal about others' adventures. Another set of rules speaks to the conventions of experienced road travelers who plan to write about their quest. "Never retrace your route" considers the effects of the itinerary on the telling of the story later. The rules also speculate on what kinds of roads to choose or avoid. Straighter roads and higher speeds cause thoughts to meander and release the power of memory to reshape. Chronology, Duncan finds, is more than a sequence of events: "Each place you stop exists in layers of time as well as space." These rules consider "the many strains of road fever" and the "folk remedies" that can be applied. Finally, there are the rules of "road theology," of the mythology that has grown up through decades of travel and literary conventions. Ultimately, road questors create their own religion: "Its Deity is the road spent; its principal practice is the pilgrimage." Failure to adhere to road rules brings down retribution, Duncan warns, whereas "great are the rewards for those who have strayed but return to the rules." In this theology, the only certainty is change, the access to which is the mystery of the open road. With Whitman, Kerouac, and the road novelists of the '60s and '70s, he admonishes in Road Rule 12: "You can learn a lot from books, maps, and statistics, but the road is a better—and sterner—teacher."

Duncan's Road Rules reveal how the national identity is constructed rather than discovered. Along the Lewis and Clark Trail, readers are asked to reconsider how myths and symbols are created to meet national interests. Duncan notes, for example, that the frontier spirit of optimism and restlessness soon "became self-promotions for the country." It wasn't long before aspirations hardened into expansionism and eventually Manifest Destiny and anything that buttressed the divine plan was "vaulted automatically into the pantheon of folk religion." From behind his windshield, Duncan opens up a wide gamut of myths for reexamination. From the St. Louis Arch to the Pacific, he reconsiders America's propensity for easy superlatives, progress at all costs, and the shaping of romantic heroes like the mountain men. He contrasts the myth of the small farmer with the reality of agribusiness. Duncan calls the modern shopping mall a symbol of our frontier quest to replace rather than fix. He quips about media intrusion into nature ("I'm driving through a beer commercial" 29), and mulls over the many examples of how we worship mythical heroes to avoid facing atrocities, false ends, or empty promises. Everywhere the white settlers' pursuit of conquest is in sharp contrast to the basic Native American view that human beings are but a part of the landscape. Even Lewis and Clark fell prey, he notes, to Eastern cartographers who never saw the Rockies but drew a range that "conformed to the myth of easy Passage" (276).

Above all, *Out West* exposes the myths we create to "sanitize our history" or to make it bearable (53). "Free to choose what we believe," Duncan notes, "Americans choose myth over reality every time." The highway quest for an American identity is thus steeped in controversy: "Our national dreams have always edited out any nightmarish realities and rewritten popular history whenever our actions fall short of our ideals" (55). Buffalo Bill Cody, to name only one legend, emerges as a synthesis of fact, myth, and self-promotion. (62). Demythologizing about the national identity can be disillusioning and terrifying. Duncan points out that there is no greater disparity between reality and our popular myths than in the nation's treatment of native Americans. Though they were cheated, subjugated and killed, the romanticized symbol of the American Indian was enshrined nonetheless. Seen alternately as caricatures of either a barbarous or noble savage, the Native American was smashed by a machine of progress that rolled across the prairies and everything in its path" (67). In the quiet but firm tones of *Out West*, these and other myths are exploded by seeking out the facts of history behind the glossy tales.

The most recent highway search for the soul of America is Douglas Brinkley's *The Majic Bus: An American Odyssey* (1993), an attempt "to discover America by sleeper bus" in a classroom in perpetual motion. Teaching a Hofstra University course on "Art and Culture Across America" for 17 students, Brinkley wants to "ignite (or reignite) an intense passion for the United States in high school and college students, their parents, and educators" (xiii). Over six weeks in 30 states he hoped that living together and visiting the places they studied would "help bored and jaded students develop a sense of democracy's potential and of community responsibility" (xiii-xiv). Being fully on the road, Brinkley notes, means there has to be a record of the experience in a journal, photo, video—or book. The *Majic Bus* would be that road book which captured "the tensions between obligation and freedom, creativity and convention, between America as-it-is and America as-we-want-it-to-be" (10). The book captures what it means to be lost in America, how it feels to be restless and rambling and to find healing in motion, in the journey which is "a brief, sweet moment" of mystical nourishment (70-71). Their American odyssey sweeps through Thomas Jefferson's Virginia and Thomas Wolfe country through Mississippi to Lincoln's Springfield and Chicago; they visit with William S. Burroughs in Kansas and Ken Kesey in Oregon; they travel on Route 66 and experience D.H. Lawrence's enchantment of New Mexico; they linger in California with the works of John Steinbeck and Jack London; they fall in love with the redwoods and relive legendary tales; they listen to the music of the highway everywhere and return again and again to Jack Kerouac's "religious poem for America" (26). Just as Whitman saw the entire country as a giant poem in progress, Brinkley's classroom is the nation itself on the move pursuing truths which emerge only while in transit.

Whenever movement along the American highways doesn't lead to the discovery of anything as sweeping as a national identity, that lofty and exhausting search often pulls up short and settles for a smaller patch of earth. Instead of sweeping along on cross-country treks, the road winds in and out of particular places and distinctive regions of the country which embody local customs. These regional characteristics often define elements of a people more accurately than what can be found in any search for a national character. The wide expanse and diversity of the American landscape—together with the sheer size of the country— encourage road narrators to focus more precisely on geographical and cultural regions. The attraction of more manageable regions is two-fold. First, travelers hope to experience the distinct ways of life found in clearly defined places. Regretting that regional speech was in the process of disappearing, Steinbeck hoped to get a feel for localness before it was destroyed by media standardization (*Travels with Charley* 106). Moreover, this detailed attention to local places, events, and customs also provided a way of organizing experiences into narrative patterns. John Jakle, for example, has noted the early traveler's desire to verify stereotypes about regions derived from reading (101). So also writers of road narratives collected their own samples of regional differences— especially as the burgeoning superhighway system threatened to blur distinctions. Their observations repeat stereotypical ways of describing regions, of course. While the East coast is notable for its urban sprawl and monuments of an Anglo-American heritage, the South embodies political controversy, racial innuendo, and clash of old and new. Travel itself is almost synonymous with movement West, the region that still offers the most spaciousness and for many is still the promised land of Montana or Idaho. In the West also, road travelers discover many of our monuments to Native American traditions. The Midwest, on the other hand, is an amalgam of other regions combining the more conservative ways of New England traditions, with the questing spirit of the frontier.

American road narratives visit, analyze, and celebrate all regions of the country on a search for the soul of the nation. From Lewis and Clark and the Joads of *Grapes of Wrath* to the present, the West has been a symbol both of new hope and of the terrors of the unknown. Western motifs vary widely from William Least Heat Moon's exploration of his Native American heritage on the Western plains to Jim Harrison's tribute to Chief Joseph and the Nez Percé. Anne Roiphe's *Long Division* and Henry Miller's *The Air-Conditioned Nightmare* rediscover the monuments of ancient North American culture in the neglected history of the Southwest. The South is both setting and object of political and cultural analysis in Faulkner's *The Reivers*, Caldwell's *Tobacco Road*, and more recently Leon Driskell's *Passing Through*, set in Owen County, Kentucky. Jonathan Raban's *Old Glory: An American Voyage* follows the Mississippi River down south. In works as politically diverse as *Easy Rider* and *Travels with Charley*, Southern responses to race and political dissent are explored. Due perhaps to weather, driving conditions, and more densely populated areas, the North and the East are not the locales for as many road narratives or the sources of regional definition. Travelers do head to Alaska, of course, and the landscape shares that Western sense of expanse. Jim Harrison remarks on the effect of the cold on Northern sensibility, making folks less friendly and more taciturn. The crowded Eastern roadways belong to Willy Loman who is "a New England Man," Rabbit Angstrum driving the freeways, and John

Clellon Holmes and Jack Kerouac whose Beat characters circle in and around Greenwich Village.

The power of the Northwest unfolds across the landscape of John Keeble's *Yellowfish* where a "catechism of history" is etched in rivers, rocks, mountains, and inexplicable glaciers. On his drive from Vancouver to San Francisco transporting four Chinese aliens (the "trash fish of Chinese waters eaten by the poor" of the title) Wesley Erks meditates on the 1808 travel journals of Simon Fraser. Erks is attracted to Fraser's "violence of dream, of visions exceeding his ideas." His aggressive language is "akin to the excessive, often brutal, and yet exact language of other Westerners to come: Joaquin Miller, Norris, London, Jeffers, Ginsberg, Kerouac, Spicer, and Bukowski" (106). *Yellowfish* is a history lesson on the founding of towns and the customs of the region's people including the Paiute Indians who "took on the color of all things alive" and "thus took the desert inside their skin" (227). With 90 miles between each town, the terrain opens into "the space of the gatherers, the American *agrapha*, the unwritten—a land whose settlement showed as it had for centuries the thin power of the land to uphold dwelling, the great power, instead, residing in space" (208). American road narratives want to read and write the agrapha still speaking in the distinctive power of every region of the country.

Most road narratives focus on several different regions and emphasize how distinctions are being disregarded by the media and travelers in a hurry. Humphreys, Moyers, and Kuralt, for example, worry about missing subtleties of regional identity. In *American Journey* Reeves is alarmed that our interest in what makes places unique is being replaced by the ubiquitous "sameness of tract homes, shopping centers, and hamburger stands." He conjectures that uniformity is actually defended as an antidote to traumatic mobility. Noting that he can move for days without experiencing change, he feels a sense of dislocation made worse by nationwide TV superstations and national daily satellite newspapers. A century and a half after Tocqueville, American road narratives continue to regret the apparent fading of regional differences. One theme repeated frequently is the loss brought about by improved superhighways. Trying to correct an overemphasis on speed and efficiency, the road narrative hopes to restore contact with the landscape, people, and customs of distinctive regions throughout the country. With Whitman, road authors want to examine the riches of the whole by exploring and holding on to the local. In keeping with the highway quester's desire to preserve or rediscover the very old, special attention has been given to the land and people found in the nation's heartland.

Indeed, the Midwest is a crucial region in American road narratives—most of which follow coast-to-coast itineraries with the plains and prairies serving as places for taking stock along a dull and flat landscape that frees the mind from excessive goal orientation. Highway questers enter the region in the way pilgrims move into sacred space. For Kerouac, the area is wild and lyrical, while Pirsig discovers a Zen contentment with "hereness and nowness." For Least Heat Moon, the region is the beginning and end around which he comes full circle, and Tom Robbins's cowgirl Sissy Hankshaw sees the Midwestern prairie as the ultimate feminine embodiment of life's energies. The common links found in these four writers are the magical expansiveness of the landscape and the unifying power of the region's simplicity.

Steinbeck found in the Midwest the most intense sights and sounds of the America he wanted to recapture. He worries about the postwar spawning of superhighways and seeks to rediscover the uniquely regional elements before it becomes "possible to drive from New York to California without seeing a single thing." Even truckers, he speculates, who would appear to have their ears tuned to local sounds actually rivet themselves to the radio and therefore "cruise over the surface of the action without being a part of it" (92). Steinbeck and Charley approach the Midwest from the East into Ohio and Michigan and with considerable commentary on the "noble land" of Wisconsin's fields. He finds Midwestern people more open and more outgoing than people elsewhere as they exhibit an electrifying flow of energy (105). The countryside is rich and beautiful, generous and outgoing, and the people "take a cue from it" (106). Steinbeck hopes to catch the tempo of the region, "to listen, to hear speech, accent, speech rhythms, overtones and emphasis"—all of which, he feels is disappearing because of mass communications. He predicts many events of the next twenty years in his lament that a national standardized speech will replace local speech and tempo. Against this dystopic flavor, Steinbeck's Midwest is a major force in his attempt to discover the essence of America.

Robert M. Pirsig at first encounters a nondescript and dull Midwestern landscape as he rides across the plains in *Zen and the Art of Motorcycle Maintenance*. "Flatness and great emptiness as far as you can see," he recalls, with "extreme monotony and boredom as you drive hour after hour, getting nowhere, wondering how long this is going to last without a turn in the road, without a change in the land going on and on to the horizon" (19). He soon finds, however, that this Zen-like monotony captures an inner harmony which contrasts sharply with the clutter and distractions of his friend's city life:

I hope later she will see and feel a thing about these prairies I have given up talking to others about; a thing that exists here because everything else does not and can be noticed because other things are absent. She seems so depressed sometimes by the monotony and boredom of her city life, I thought maybe in this endless grass and wind she would see a thing that sometimes comes when monotony and boredom are accepted. It's here, but I have no names for it.

Pirsig underscores the differences between the remoteness of modern electronic media and the immediacy of the Chautauquas or the traveling tent shows that used to cross the country. Because standardized mass communication increasingly displaces local media with their regional differences, he concludes that "the stream of national consciousness moves faster now, and is broader, but it seems to run less deep" (8). In the Midwest, Pirsig finds people content with being simple as well as secure enough to accept being ordinary, and he compares those regional qualities with the calm energy of Zen Buddhism.

The primary motivating force of the American road quest is a longing to return to the time when the stream was deeper, when local customs and regional culture were preserved—a time before the landscape was pasted over with billboards and interstates circumvented the old highways. This desire to rediscover America's hidden essence along the secondary roads dominates William Least Heat Moon's *Blue Highways*—a work which takes its title from the color used on old maps for back roads. The author insists on a "circular trip over the back roads of the United States" because a straight line does not enable one to "come round again" (185). His journey is an Emersonian encircling, a process akin to the Hopi emergence symbol of cosmic human movement. Beginning in Missouri, Moon heads east, south, northwest, then back east and once again west to where he began. Appropriately, his last two pages celebrate the mystical Rappites of New Harmony, Indiana, whose 1820 circular privet-hedge labyrinth was symbolic of "the Harmonist idea of how the circuitous and difficult way leads to true harmony (411).

The circle is a central metaphor also in Tom Robbins's *Even Cowgirls Get the Blues* as Sissy Hankshaw hitchhikes her way from Richmond, Virginia, to the Dakotas and on to the Rubber Rose Ranch. As she rides through the grasslands, the Midwestern prairie gives off the scent and feel of "American loneliness, which is like no other loneliness in the world" (137-38). Robbins's Midwest includes the huge prairie pancake and the badlands ruins with their poisonously bland landscapes. Though these hymns to the flatlands have their satiric edges, ultimately the prairie is portrayed as a female meadow preferred to its male counterpart because it is "more coarse, more oceanic and enduring, supporting a greater variety of life" (254). Sissy marvels at the wonder of "the hard, flat-belly-of-America prairie" which becomes in September a "garden of gentle blooms." On her solitary sweep across the fullness of the Midwestern landscape, she merges with the peaceful rapture of the swaying asters "forcing their way to the light" (158).

Typical also in the Midwestern leg of the road pilgrimage is the way infinite space is punctuated by roadside sculpture, a phenomenon which Karol Ann Marling in *The Colossus of Roads* has compared to the function of the pilgrims' shrine as "a stopping place in time, where the everyday rules of reality are suspended and an idyllic dream commences" (101). In its grand scale, sweeping scope, and positioning along the route westward, the roadside attraction is a monument to the frontier myth. What was always larger than life in American dreams, stories, and daily life is personified in the iconography of roadside sculpture that extends the aesthetic of the frontier. Marling points to F. Scott Fitzgerald's jazz-baby narrator in *The Great Gatsby* who portrays the "temporal, the geographic, the spiritual, and the aesthetic dimensions of the American roadside colossus, the popular monument through which the Midwest has, for almost half a century, articulated a sense of regional identity" (5). Just as Fitzgerald mourns the tragedy of the closing of the Western frontier, he also played out again in spiritual terms the motion of the quest. Because the East was too small for Paul Bunyan, the Midwestern expanse becomes the ground on which to work out what Marling calls the American riddle of "how the finite individual can find his bearings in the infinite immensity of space; of how to symbolize and come to grips with a wholly new world, sized for Titans or for gods" (6). It's the aesthetic of the prairie that Whitman had celebrated in 1882 in *Specimen Days* and which turn-of-the-century sculptors worked into their colossal works.

The art and architecture of the American highway provide symbols to reinforce the urgency of the road quest. For generations of Americans who had seen travel as an escape from routine, the roadside became a "privileged zone, strewn with marvels for the delectation of the wayfarer," a nearby frontier, a place of hopes and dreams where all things are possible (42). The spin-off has given us miniature golf, increasingly adorned motel complexes, and roadside colossi post cards. In the enthusiasm and glitter, roadside dreamers became hoaxsters who want to fool themselves with the highway's magic and wonder. Like the road itself, the collossus reproduces the paradoxes of the American quest: perpetual motion that attempts to freeze time, monuments to antiquity made of the ever-new and the grotesque, the search for the infinite in the finite, expanse symbolized by enclosed space, the lonely individual in tourist-trap crowds, and the self-exploration of a single identity in a mass society.

Whatever the realities or fantasies of the Midwestern prairies and small towns at any given time, the region has served in four decades of road narratives as a symbol of wholesomeness, friendliness, and contemplative movement going nowhere. Highway literature speeds across vast, flat stretches of land even while it lingers in peaceful cornfields and open prairies. An amalgam of cultures and beliefs transplanted from other regions, the Midwestern soil blends the possibilities Whitman hoped for in *Democratic Vistas* (1871). The Midwest was admired by Dean Moriarity for its fast roads, by Least Heat Moon because of its blue highways, by Duncan because it was the way West. In *The Better Country* (1928), Dallas L. Sharp sums up the attraction of the area for those seeking freedom and greater self-awareness: "Nowhere in the world have I felt a more perfect harmony between earth and man than among the farms of Iowa, nor more comfortable space and spiritual freedom between man and man" (57). This is the harmony that Pirsig felt in the nowhere of the Midwestern plains, that Least Heat Moon saw in New Harmony, Indiana, that Sal Paradise found in the Pooh Bear in the Iowa sunset. It is also the region where Lewis and Clark, Dayton Duncan, Richard Reeves, Bill Moyers— and countless others—stopped to regroup, recharge, and sort out. Whitman too foresaw the attraction as he made celebration of regions a main theme of his "Song of the Open Road": "I inhale the great draughts of space, / The east and west are mine, and the north and the south are mine. / I am larger, better than I thought, / I did not know I held so much goodness" (151).

The literature of the highway wants to find or create—and ultimately to celebrate—an American identity. Kuralt's interviews, Steinbeck's and Moyers's attempts to listen to the country, Humphreys's travels on the lost highways, and the demythologizing of Duncan and others—all are the kind of travel Emerson encouraged as part of his plan to push away from the courtly muses of Europe. For Emerson, the rage to see Greece or travel the continent was "a symptom of a deeper unsoundness" (164). We don't need to copy, he assures us, because all we need is right at hand. Emerson urges America's questers to seek adventure on their own shores. Breaking into a long tradition of travel narratives, he sees America as a poem waiting to be written. For many, life on the road has been the poem and the road narrative has been the genre to best express the vision.

5

Journeys of Self-Discovery

In one way or another, every highway hero wants to get away from the distractions of everyday life and drive into a time and place where the inner self can emerge. Some drivers want to start over somewhere else and with new people where they can establish a new identity. Others follow the road to ethnic and racial awareness or to local and regional values that contribute to a national mythos. Some pursue individualism through satire, caricature, and inversion of accepted norms.

Over a century after Whitman's *Democratic Vistas* the balance between the "leveling average" and individual identity is as precarious as ever, and the road continues to be a place for a kind of self-discovery possible nowhere else.

The road is freedom from schedules, commitments, memberships, and credentials; the highway journey also suspends for a while definition according to one's origins, profession, and geography. Movement also leaves behind restricting ways of looking at oneself and brings at least temporarily a frozen time and ever-changing space where all is possible. Free from the constrictive contexts of the day-to day, life on the road brings what anthropologists have called a "liminal" process of "mid-transition in a rite of passage" (Turner and Turner 249) where people in motion are suspended not only in space and time but between what they think they know about the past and what they have reason to suspect will be inevitable when they get home. Highway travelers give up—or are released from—a social structure that impinges upon dreams and aspirations. The apparent powerlessness of the traveler living in a suspended state has its compensation in knowledge gained along the way. Road heroes refer often to the wisdom, power, and infusion of new energy they receive on the journey. As on the pilgrimage, the highway prescribes its own rituals and codes and creates its own community of fellow travelers. Among the benefits of liminality on the modern road is the opportunity to start over and discover one's inner resources and potential. The liminar as author or narrator expresses this potentiality in a prose narrative story, the reading of which becomes for readers a participation in a liminal experience of their own. Thus the telling, reading, and living of the story of life on the road bring texts, readers, and authors into a dialogue of self exploration.

One such traveler suspending time and space is William Least Heat Moon in *Blue Highways*. Separated from his wife and having just lost his job, he takes to the road where "a man who couldn't make things go right could at least go." He embraces the road as a place where he can "check routine" and "live the real jeopardy of circumstance" (3). His narrative is a journey of discovery, assembled as it goes along. Again, motion becomes therapeutic as he passes through the monotony of "No Place" back into his Native American heritage, where he experiences a death to self and rebirth into the new identity assembled from the unearthing of what is very old. Drawing attention to his search for form as he tells the story, Least Heat Moon invites readers to participate in the questioning and reshaping of his (and their) values and attitudes. While the result may not be the appearance of unity many formalist readers demand, *Blue Highways* is a prototypical vision of the liminality discovering potential. Moon thus underscores the evolution of genre conventions by making his own shifting narrative perspective a main emphasis of history. In Mikhail Bakhtin's terms, we catch an author in dialogue with himself as the discontinuities of an evolving state of consciousness unfold.

Least Heat Moon's initial plan is to start out on a "circular trip over the back roads of the United States" following the coming of spring in each region. He hopes to discover a purpose in his travels but is confident that, no matter what happens, the circle would "come around again." What begins out of necessity soon leads to " the addiction of the traveler" for "a sense of the unknown" (9), a journey "wherein passage through space and time becomes only a metaphor through the interior of being" (186). For Least Heat Moon, the road becomes "therapy through observation of the ordinary and obvious, a means whereby the outer eye opens an inner one" (17). He feels akin to Whitman's "profound lesson of reception" in his awareness that the self he seeks is not narrowly within his own consciousness but in the circle that extends outward to receive what the road will bring. It takes him a long time and a great deal of thinking about how he will construct his story in writing, but eventually with the help of Whitman, Black Elk, and the Hopi legends and symbols, Least Heat Moon discovers that he has "learned to travel, then traveled to learn" (84). He learns with Emerson that limitation is in the mind's eye, and that "boredom lies only with the traveler's limited perception and his failure to explore deeply enough" (273). He embraces a "skewed vision" of "a man looking at himself by looking at what he looks at" (219). In short, he opens himself up to changes that the road can bring. His initial search for self-discovery takes a turn he didn't expect and which he calls the great vision of the Grandfather: "To seek the high concord, a man looks not deeper within—he reaches farther out" (241).

Early in his narration, Least Heat Moon delivers a series of monologues on Whitman, though he doesn't seem to learn the lesson of "reception" until he is out on the highway a long while. The early narrator wants to be in control—perhaps to find the control he had lost back home—and so he carefully selects a pattern of back roads, oddly named places, and ordinary heroes he can analyze. His journey begins in the tradition of travel literature informed by Kuralt's video essays. Road genre conventions are firmly in place. The road is therapy (17), travel is a metaphor for inner quest (188), and the highway is an analog providing sacred space wherein inquiry is possible. Further, he finds that monotonous driving releases special perceptions (343) and that the fragments will somehow have to be pieced together in the telling of the story (206). This last worry about finding a narrative pattern—along with a deepening probing into his own Native American roots—causes him to question the very conventions he is using and to move in new directions. If his long book seems to get dull or less dramatic as it develops, the reason may be as much the change in pattern as the length. As the narrator draws attention to his own constructions of pattern, he lets go of the control he felt he needed at the outset. Finally, he learns his Whitman and Black Elk and feels and accepts the lessons of the Hopi labyrinth.

Least Heat Moon constantly looks for pattern in his journey, order in his experiences, and a narrative organization for his book. He makes tapes describing events as he goes along and then plays them back looking for "a core in what had been happening." He sorts through notes, and at one point even gives up using words and tries "diagrams in hopes an image might shake free an idea" (162) Three images redirect his quest. From Black Elk he learns the power of the circle (406). The Navajo wind chant praises the power of memory and cycles as "everything forgotten/returns in the circling winds" (412). The cycle of life is from birth to death to birth, the cycles of the seasons, and Least Heat Moon's own "wandering circle," now "a kind of map of the wandering soul" and "a reminder of cosmic patterns that all human beings move in" (185). In the Hopi evolution through four worlds, man becomes separated from his oneness with forces outside himself. Looking inward, man becomes selfish and materialistic: "A human being's grandest task is to keep from breaking with things outside himself" (186).

The quietly dramatic insights of *Blue Highways* emerge in a series of visits with people all over the country. Least Heat Moon's worries about how to present his experiences at first get in his way but then later cause him to listen more closely to what people are saying. He admires the Shakers and is intrigued by the young Hopi Indian who tells him that a journey is like the emergence symbol of the wandering soul. He comes to appreciate the silence of the monastics, the Rappite mazes in New Harmony, Indiana, and the point Alice Venable Middleton tells him about "olden day travelers" who kept an *Album Amicorum* of learned advice they received along their way. Least Heat Moon is looking for a core; he wants to "catch on to things" (192). The struggle moves him into a dialogue on revision and remaking that prompts readers to question the effects of the road on perception itself. The lesson he finally learns is the difference between *vacare* and *educare*. *Vacare*, he tells us early in the book, means "to empty out" and is linked to the vacuous. In his last ten pages the etymology looks back: "educate, from the Latin *educare*, to 'lead out'" (400). He discovers along his route, however, that a "leading out" requires also an emptying of self. Accordingly, in the course of telling his story, he revises some of his goals. Whereas he had been looking for insights and achieved only loneliness, he finds that "the only gift is a chance to inquire, to know nothing for certain. An inheritance of wonder and nothing more" (240). Remembering Tocqueville's observation that one result of democracy was "a concentration of each man's attention upon himself" (168), he becomes irritated by a man from Arizona who "never quit thinking of himself long enough to listen" (165). Increasingly in the living and writing of his narrative, Least Heat Moon opens himself up to others. Hunting for structure in his notes, he learns to be content with what looks like randomness, content at last to wait for the circles to come around. The danger always was that he'd miss those lessons and give in to a conditioned search for goals: "I couldn't break myself of the notion that whenever I hit good road it would hold to the end. I just couldn't remember the cycles, the circles" (209). The book offers few clear-cut answers. Instead, Least Heat Moon passes along Whitman's invitation to flow with the cycles. What had begun as a self-directed quest for order becomes an other-directed circling back to the self through "the power not of visions but of revision, the power to see again and revise" (399). Life on the road makes possible disentanglement, wonder, or skewed vision; moreover, the writing and reading of road literature emphasize an additional crucial insight:

A man cannot remake ego because it is able to grow only in size like a simple cell. A locked form unable even to change its structure, it is ever only what it is: Not so an angle of vision—as the old Jerseyman had called it—*that* a man could make over. To remake is his potential, his hope. (399)

Ultimately, Least Heat Moon remakes himself through his vision in the telling of his story, and he invites readers in on the process by drawing attention to the problems he faces in the construction of events. Without all the errors and blind alleys and misdirection, he says, the labyrinth lacks joy. "And worse," he adds, "Knowing the way made traveling it perfectly meaningless" (411). As he "loses the way," Least Heat Moon's frustration increases; but letting go and accepting the "moments of glimpsed clarity" (406), he finally learns his Whitman. Embracing Whitman's "life that does not exhibit itself" (83), he takes in rather than analyzes the "public road" (167), is cleansed by the immensity and vacancy of Whitman's space (189) and realizes that he cannot see God "better than this day" (261). Appropriately, he concludes his retelling of the story with the mystical Rappites of New Harmony, Indiana, whose 1820 circular privet-hedge labyrinth was symbolic of "the Harmonist concept of the devious and difficult approach to the state of true harmony" (411). Least Heat Moon the lecturer is back at the end but changed significantly by the journey. "Splendid gifts all," he notes about his experiences.

Journeys of self-discovery often express the residual cultural values of the American cowboy motif with its frontier spirit and adulation for the rugged individualist. James Leo Herlihy's *Midnight Cowboy*, for example, recombines elements of the Western genre to underscore initiation and personal growth on the road. Joe Buck leaves Houston to head East to seek his fortune. His travels take him through bus stations and cafeterias to the sleazy parts of Manhattan. Along the way, he feels "some kind of masterful participation in the world of time and space," like he is "moving forward into destiny" (75). He is the very essence of the quest romance as he exudes self-assurance and accomplishment at every juncture: "Sometimes his eyes were open, but even at such intervals he dreamed himself into whatever landscape he was passing through, still so confident of himself and his future that he gave them scarcely a passing thought" (75). The journey follows his schedule completely: "And there's a seat for you, two of them in fact, one for your butt and one for your feet, and you don't need a reservation, the whole world is reserved, and the minute you sling your horsehide suitcase on to the overhead rack, the driver shifts into gear and begins to back out on schedule. Maybe not on schedule from Greyhound's point of view, but from yours. Because you *are* the schedule, and that bus *moves*" (13).

Joe's inexhaustibility is soon shaken, however, by his experiences in Manhattan's underworld where he is introduced to the brutality behind all the glitter: "Having no sense at all of where he might be headed, Joe Buck simply meandered deeper and deeper into September" (112). Later he meets a swindler, Ratso Rizzo, and their escapades advance the book's theme of initiation into human suffering as a wiser and more sensitive Joe Buck tries to get the dying Ratso to the warmth of Florida. Looking out the window "at the dark landscape rushing by, Joe astonishes himself when he tells Ratso he'll take care of him. Along the way they laugh and experience feelings that "surprised him into wakefulness" (183). He even surprises himself by crying: "He wondered what these tears were all about on a day when he had been feeling so good" (185). When Joe confronts the "abandoned look" in Ratso, "head slumped to the side" ("the thing in charge had gone out of it"), he realizes that Ratso has arrived in Florida dead: "And wouldn't you know it would be a beautiful blue-sky day with palm trees swaying everywhere just exactly as pictured in Ratso's folders?" In a conclusion reminiscent of e.e. cummings' "man who fell among thieves," Joe "did something he'd always wanted to do from the very first night" he'd met Ratso: "He put his arm around him to hold him for a while, for these last few miles anyway. He knew this comforting wasn't doing Ratso any good. It was for himself. Because, of course, he was scared now, scared to death" (191). What had begun as a cocksure quest to make the world into his own image became for Joe Buck an initiation into terror and love.

Escape is also transformed into self-discovery in Jim Harrison's *A Good Day to Die.* Following the breakup of his marriage, the narrator is living in the Florida Keys with a woman in whom he has "no interest." In many ways, his life has the negative side of liminality's separation without the compensatory liberating power. The book's epigraph from Rilke introduces us to "disinherited children, to whom neither what's been, nor what's coming, belongs" (9). In search of purpose and direction, the narrator meets Vietnam veteran Tim and his girlfriend, Sylvia, and together they plan a holy quest across the country to blow up a dam and save the Grand Canyon from destruction. At first the road is a wearying and unproductive place, but as their journey takes on the trappings of a pilgrimage, the characters come more fully alive in the car's "awful silence." In his frequently omniscient tones the narrator summarizes: "Though the car was dark and the only sound was the rain and the metallic crackle of the engine cooling, our presences were so luridly real that we may well have been shouting" (159). Whizzing through the night, they are "in good spirits . . . cared less," and listened to "mournful" songs on "the tape deck up as loud as it would go" (153).

At least momentarily redeemed by participation in a sacred quest, Harrison's disinherited antiheroes find in their shared resolve a separation from their past and a triumph over the mundane. It doesn't really matter that their quest fails; it seems, in fact, that tenacity even in the face of further failure becomes the existentialist angst of their liminality. The narrator's one hope for a clear, heroic deed ends in Tim's death and the closing summation about his own inadequacy: "I knew it couldn't be me" (176). Only the hope suggested by the title remains. Even on a dead-end quest, there was always the memory of Chief Joseph's courage. On the spot where the Nez Percé fought in the face of slaughter, the narrator recalls then saying: "Take courage, this is a good day to die." Outrage at the brutality of the Cavalry brings courage of his own and this shocking comment on Chief Joseph's resolve: "Eerie to be able to say such a thing and mean it" (139). This bittersweet resolve of *A Good Day to Die* advances what began as frantic escape to the discovery of a new kind of tough optimism. Kerouac's bursts of joy have been drugged, and Whitman's reception has become hollow. Death-wish travesties and moon shots take over where the conventional Westward push had been abandoned or transcended. But the courageous inner journey toward acceptance returns. Harrison's spokesman for the disinherited also recalls what the Miniconjou Sioux had said on their last quest: "Take courage, the earth is all that lasts" (139). Perhaps also this narrator will survive because he can laugh while writing his own history: "I would climb one of the surrounding mountains, mistake a lightning bolt for a power vision, and die with my charcoaled body blasted into a crescent Big Smiley" (141).

While self-discovery is a prominent feature of every road narrative, some journeys are planned almost entirely for meditation. One such "inquiry into values" is Robert M. Pirsig's *Zen and the Art of Motorcycle Maintenance*, a motorcycle road book that achieved almost cult popularity in the 1970s. Pirsig's quest is not only a travel narrative but a compendium of the history of Western philosophy. On one level, the book searches the structure of philosophy to find the origins of our collective mental breakdown; on another level, we read the adventures of the technical writer-narrator traveling by motorcycle with his son Chris from Chicago to the West Coast and back into his own past. Their plans are "deliberately indefinite, more to travel than to arrive anywhere" (5). They take secondary roads for "relaxation and enjoyment." Alternating with the events of their vacation is a flashback to the life of Phaedrus, the narrator's alter ego, once a student of rhetoric at the University of Chicago and teacher of composition in Montana and at the University of Illinois in Chicago. Throughout the road journey the narrator travels back through his own past in an attempt to integrate areas of his personality long in conflict. At the same time, he explores the origins of various conflicts in Western culture including the dualism of mind and body, facts and values, rationality and feeling, art and technology, and the classical and romantic views of the world. The travel narrative and the philosophical quest complement each other just as the principles of Zen and the maintenance of a working machine come to be seen as one. The theme is stated early and then orchestrated with astonishing complexity: "The Buddha, the Godhead, resides quite as comfortably in the circuits of a digital computer or the gears of a cycle transmission as he does at the top of a mountain or in the petals of a flower. To think otherwise is to demean the Buddha—which is to demean oneself" (18).

The narrator and his son travel light. They ride their cycles on back roads, in close contact with nature where "tensions disappear." Riding in silence close to the road, enjoying each other's company over a campfire, the mood is meditative: "We keep passing unseen through little moments of other people's lives." No radio. Not much contact with other people and conversation only with each other and thoughts packaged later in philosophical monologues taking the form of traveling tent-show chautauquas that used to cross the country—"a series of popular talks intended to edify and entertain, improve the mind and bring culture and enlightenment to the ears and thoughts of the hearer" (7). In one of the many chautauquas, the narrator introduces us to Phaedrus—a person he had at first intended to mention only through his views rather than personally. But this journey of self discovery is particularly complicated because, as we learn, Phaedrus is the narrator in his life many years before: "To omit him now would be to run from something that should not be run from" (63). In sum, Phaedrus represents at once the narrator's own beliefs as well as what Western philosophy had been before the gradual triumph of Platonic dualism. The road journey brings the narrator to the realization that he can unite his present and past only by tearing apart and rebuilding the basic philosophical assumptions by which our culture lives. The pilgrimage to shrines from his past (the University of Chicago, the University of Montana) stir dim memories that become more vivid through the force of place.

The common link between past and present in this voyage is "quality." Phaedrus is attacked and ostracized because his thinking violates the usual adherence to oppositions between subject and object, the intuitive and the analytical, the artistic and the technological. Phaedrus had always been trying to bring these apparent oppositions together, and finally while on the road, he is able to fulfill that quest. The core of the problem is the supposed opposition between the subjective and the objective and the popular assumption that scientists observe fact objectively while artists intuit subjectively, or that any individual thinks objectively and feels subjectively, or that thinking is done with the mind and feeling through the body. The mistakes in these oppositions are the separation of a whole human being into conflicting entities and the attempt to take the art out of science or the science out of art. Though it appears to be easier to talk in such oppositions, the damage perpetrated on human sensibility is incalculable, though not fatal. With the help of Zen, the narrator becomes aware of the benefits of certain traps. "Stuckness," for example, is a necessary block that steers one to a new course, "the psychic predecessor of real understanding" (279). So, too, there is a need for "enthusiasm" (to "be filled with theos, or God") as well as gumption, or the ability to be "quiet long enough to see and hear and feel the real universe, not just one's own stale opinion about it" (297). Finally, Pirsig observes that the experience of quality depends on what Henri Poincáre calls the workings of a "subliminal self" wherein the scientist, thought to be "objective" and "factual," makes preintellectual, aesthetic selections every day. "Qualitative preselection of facts" depends not on objectivity but on caring enough to be able to "select the good facts from the bad ones based on quality" (Pirsig 275). Hence, value is "no longer an irrelevant offshoot of structure" but "the preintellectual awareness" that precedes and gives rise to structure (Pirsig 277).

This struggle to reclaim a total, integrated self and to "be one person again" (404) is one with the narrator's quest to know his son and to resolve the apparent dialectics of Western philosophy. Whether repairing his motorcycle, reconciling the apparent oppositions between classical and romantic, or refurbishing the history of rhetoric, the narrator learns that Zen provides an invaluable corrective to the excesses of the goal-oriented quest in American culture. When we head wildly in the wrong direction, Zen merely says "Mu" and "nothing" or "unask the question." Pirsig observes that "it's exactly this stuckness that Zen Buddhists go to so much trouble to induce; through Koans, deep breathing, sitting still, and the like" (279).

The narrator's ambitious pilgrimage of self-discovery revises many of the assumptions of the conventional road quest. Some differences between his trip and the more typical road quest are glossed in his discussion of classical and romantic sensibilities. Having been rebuffed by his friend for introducing the "boring" topic of motorcycle maintenance, the narrator analyzes the necessary conflict as well as the interaction between their two ways of thinking:

> That's the dimension he's in. The groovy dimension. I'm being awfully square talking about all this mechanical stuff all the time. It's all just parts and analyses and syntheses and figuring things out and it isn't really here . . . He's on the dimensional difference of the sixties, I think, and is still in the process of reshaping our whole national outlook on things. The "generation gap" has been a result of it. The names "beat" and "hip" grew out of it. Now it's become apparent that this dimension isn't a fad that's going to go away next year or the year after. (53)

The healing force of *Zen and the Art of Motorcycle Maintenance* is found in a realization of the continuity of art and technology, a meshing of classical and romantic perspectives. Though he struggles through the nightmares of his quest to find his identity in the contradictions of Western philosophy, ultimately the narrator reaches his wrenching philosophical examination with the calm of Zen. Kerouac's obsession with cars and speed give way to the quiet reading of an operation manual and a harmonious accord with the mechanism of a bike. Like any good highway quester, Pirsig's narrator still sees himself as a pioneer looking toward a promised land. He reroutes the journey, however, and takes pleasure in announcing that the only Zen you find on a mountain is what you bring with you.

Like many journeys of self-discovery, Pirsig's seems steady at the outset, almost brash in its monologic confidence about where this father and son pair are headed together. But in the reliving of Phaedrus' experience, they confront "stuckness" and eventually overcome "gumption traps" and discover quality. Physically, and philosophically in this case, keeping everything in motion creates the requisite liminality in which all the elements can be examined, carved into pieces, and resynthesized. A key mode of discovery for Pirsig's narrator is the chautauqua with its open-ended spirit of inquiry and sense of dialogue between narrator and audience. In a letter to actor-director Robert Redford, Pirsig noted that the purpose of the chautauqua was to remove the "*ex cathedra* effect, the talking down, the pontification which pure essays get into" (DiSanto and Steele 232-33). Putting the chautauqua in the mouth of someone fallible draws the reader into dialogue about philosophy with an emphasis the narrator is just trying to say something on the exploratory rather than the didactic. Using the old traveling tent-show format also has two other effects. Dialogue is intended to replace sermonic discourse and allow the narrator to converse with himself, his friends, Chris, and ultimately readers. Perhaps a less obvious use of the chautauqua is its function as the motorcycle equivalent of car talk. Not much conversation can be heard on a motorcycle, so the talk takes place over campfires and during other stops. By contrast in the closed-off space of a car, driver and passengers are prompted to talk freely in an environment particularly conducive to discourse that is risk-oriented, sometimes confessional, and almost always exploratory.

Sealed off in the high-speed meditative space of the large American automobile, drivers are given opportunities to experience the liminal. In pilgrimages throughout time, the vehicle of transience has traditionally afforded the pilgrim space "outside or between routine structures" where one can renounce home and move from town to town (Turner and Turner 250). Sitting together in the car, driver and passengers experience closeness and community. Not knowing whether they will ever see each other again, drivers and hitchhikers are free to develop relationships that are free of the restraints of everyday obligations. Even people who have known each other for years can go on the road and see each other in new ways. Old links can be disentangled, even old wounds healed in space that seems magical. In *Short Drive, Sweet Chariot*, William Saroyan marvels at the healing powers available on the road: "Americans have found the healing of God in a variety of things," he observes, "the most pleasant of which is probably automobile drives." At the age of 58 and already a famous author for three decades, Saroyan wrote in 1966 one of the most unusual and interesting of the American road narratives. In the early '60s he bought a 1941 Lincoln limousine in which to chauffeur around his family and pick up hoboes along the road and take them wherever they wanted to go. Viewing the limo as a kind of chariot and planning to treat his passengers to cigars, whiskey, and "crisp new money," Saroyan begins in London, Ontario, and winds down in South Dakota. Along the way, we are treated to detailed dialogue that philosophizes on every aspect of the American scene. One goal of the long drive is freedom. The ride is both symbol of that freedom and a precipitating factor in bringing it about, sustaining it, or renewing it from time to time. "I had known this freedom in myself," he continues, "most memorably, most unforgettably, getting into my car, going, and not stopping until I feel like it" (111). Just knowing the car is waiting is sometimes even enough. When one feels trapped, freedom is no farther away than the car keys: "Now, of course *anybody* in this country is free. If he's got a job he can't abide, he can quit. If he's captured by other things and he can't get out of them, he's got his car. And I've got *mine*" (120).

For Saroyan it's not just getting in the car but what happens to the mind during the journey that provides the healing he celebrates:

> Psychiatry of one sort or another is what happens on a long drive. It has *got* to happen, even if the driver is alone. Memory unburdens itself to that side of himself which is the great listener, and every man *has* that side—he's *got* to have it. Part of the machinery in man, in the mystery of him, is this listening personality, this willing listener to everything. (42)

Before Freud, he continues, "every man's built-in listener was the only psychiatrist." And this listener has been given several names later by Freud, Jung, and others. Nonexperts "have thought of the great listener as God, which is also the truth, for the listener is in fact so difficult to accurately identify that it is necessary to think of him, or of it, as God." This psychiatry along the road is perhaps best thought of as the "healing of God," Saroyan maintains, because the best healing is beyond comprehension.

Whether explicit or implied, the built-in listener is prominent in all American road narratives. Some listeners start out as companions; others may join the trip along the way or for even a short time as hitchhikers. One of the distinctive elements of *Travels with Charley* is the role of the dog as companion, confidant, and displaced conversationalist. Here Steinbeck modifies the companionship convention of the genre by enjoying the benefits of traveling alone as well as using the plot elements and manipulation of point of view made possible in the presence of "other." Charley is sounding board, excuse to start discussions with strangers, and symbol of Steinbeck's own aging. Whether getting to know someone close for perhaps the first time, confiding to a stranger, or talking to a dog, many hours over long miles in enclosed space will loosen the tongue for conversation and release powers of observation in drivers and passengers alike. Steinbeck speculates at length on why driving activates certain conscious and subconscious mechanisms in the human thought process. "If one has driven a car over many years," he begins, one's "driving technique is deeply buried in a machine-like unconscious. This being so, a large area of the conscious mind is left free for thinking." On short trips this time may be taken up with immediate plans and schedules. Long drives, however, seem to stimulate daydreaming and creative thought. Steinbeck recalls free-floating stretches of highway when he designed houses he never built, made gardens he would never plant, and allowed radio music to bring back long-forgotten memories. The dreaming, he reasons, works as a kind of compensatory device so that "the lonely man peoples his driving dreams with friends."

In the midst of speed and frenzy, even Kerouac's *On the Road* slows down once in awhile to celebrate the meditative self-awareness released by enclosed space: "All alone in the night I had my own thoughts and held the car to the white line on the holy road" (115). Movement inevitably frees the mind: "We were all delighted, we all realized we were leaving confusion and nonsense behind and performing our one and noble function of the time, *move*." Dean tells Sal "we gotta go and never stop going til we get there." When Sal questions their ultimate destination ("where we going, man?"), Dean replies, "I don't know, but we gotta go" (196). Biographer Ann Charters has established valuable connections between space and speed in these conversations between Dean and Sal along the road. Charters likens their moving with great speed through diminishing space to a "phonograph record speeded up faster and faster with less and less space to move in." Whereas the early explorers were able to "step forth into the wild space," road questers discover a different pattern:

> What you end up doing a hundred years later is driving back and forth in cars as fast as you can. Initially you were moving very slowly in a totally wild area. What you end up doing is going very fast in a densely populated area. Space becomes translated into speed. (*Kerouac: A Biography* 86)

Ultimately for Kerouac, there is an ambivalence about whether all the talk and listening along the road are healing or depressing. As their westward journey nears completion and the book winds down, Sal's speculations on "the ancient activities of human life" are as near as a drive through his own imagination. For Sal, getting behind the wheel is like entering the inner sanctuary: "I took the wheel and drove among reveries of my own. . . . The boys were sleeping, and I was alone at my eternity at the wheel, and the road ran straight as an arrow" (229).

Speeding through time and space in the enclosure of a car releases the flow of thinking and conversation in a wide variety of road narratives. With the conclusion of a conversation about to "come like a belch," Larry McMurtry's Cadillac Jack finds that driving is his Alka-Seltzer that fizzes him "back into a blank, relaxed state" (357). Only "the long roads and blue skies of America," it would seem, are able to restore Jack to "lucidity and a simple sense of purpose" (102). Floorboard

George finds that total strangers open up to him (*Not Fade Away* 106); Pirsig's philosophical chautauquas arise from the meditative silences moving along the road; Adele and Ann Armstrong fight throughout their journeys in Mona Simpson's *Anywhere But Here*; the protagonists of Jayne Anne Phillips's *Fast Lanes* confide in each other: "He talked. I talked. We told stories. We argued" (50).

Car talk is a prominent element of self-discovery in road narratives in at least four additional areas: dialogue with hitchhiking confidants, exchanges with people who want to go along, wisdom learned from minorities or other outsiders, and the omnipresent but vicarious presence of others through the car radio. In American road narratives, the champion hitchhikers are Sal Paradise and Sissy Hankshaw, though an entire body of vagabond and tramp literature lies beyond this study. Hitchhikers stand in as father-confessor figures, psychiatrists, philosophers, or other confidants in works by Saroyan, Least Heat Moon, Jim Dodge, and Anne Roiphe. In short, road narratives are populated by a memorable collection of mysterious strangers who enter and leave with swiftness and impact. Steinbeck, Duncan, and J.R. Humphreys encounter numerous people who wish they could go along on the journey. A gas station attendant wants to make the pilgrimage with Floorboard George. Sometimes people don't understand why the hero wants to take such a trip at all. Steinbeck recommends that it's easier to tell people you're going fishing than to dispel their incredulity and disapproval. Richard Reeves observes that a major difference between Tocqueville's and his insulated space was the radio's ability to bring the universe into his cabin: "I could freely change my perspectives and my environment, again and again, back and forth, by touching these buttons" (20). Finally, much car talk is conversation with representatives of America's forgotten minorities or outsiders whose objectivity and insight derive in part from their having lived as outcasts. From the wisdom of the ex-preacher in *The Grapes of Wrath* to Bob White's concluding monologue in *Seaview*, road narratives find special insights in the experiences of those living out of the mainstream. Least Heat Moon turns his quest around after talking with the young Hopi Indian in Utah. Kerouac, Holmes, and the Beats turn to non-Western philosophies. Pirsig finds the wisdom of Zen in the crankshaft. Sal Paradise seeks inspiration in black music. Captain America and Billy are drop outs in *Easy Rider*. New York City minority kids reassess the country in *Checking It Out*. Charles Kuralt showcases numerous heroes from minority cultures in his video magazines.

Not all American road authors are so sure, however, that being enclosed in an automobile creates a magical space of liminal possibility.

For many, there is a tension between the loosening of the tongue which the enclosure stimulates and the isolation from experiences unfolding outside. From the earliest days of automobile travel there has been considerable debate about whether the car is liberating transportation or an insulating and confining compartment. Exhilaration greeted the earliest horse-powered transformation of the landscape, but as early as 1937 Waldo Frank warned about the narcotic effect of self-motion that became "idealized into the delusion of 'progress.'" As Peter Marsh and Peter Collett have shown, the modern car provides not only "speed, excitement, and vitality" but also "a sense of cozy seclusion—a womb-like refuge" (25). The liberating enclosure and protective shell afforded by the automobile serve in the modern road quest much the same as what Joseph Campbell calls "the insulating horse" which for the ancients would "keep the hero out of immediate touch with the earth and yet permit him to promenade among the peoples of the world" (224). The automobile as insulating horse offers protection against threats of external elements as well as the potential loss of imaginative vision.

For centuries, vehicles have been more than transportation. The modern automobile is a badge of identity, an extension of our homes, clothes, jewelry, weapons, and fantasies (Marsh and Collett). In the literature of the American highway, the car has been a time machine in which drivers look for the past, a weapon of social protest, a psychiatrist's couch of therapeutic healing, a shrine of displaced theology. Movement while enclosed in protective space can be an expression of anxiety for Maria Wyeth in Joan Didion's *Play It As It Lays*, or a suicidal death-grip as in John Hawkes's *Travesty*. The truck is Sarah's protective shell for her grandfather in Janet Majerus's *Grandpa and Frank* or a "self-propelled box" in which Least Heat Moon could feel "clean and almost disentangled" (8). Her mother's Lincoln is a place of refuge for Ann Armstrong in *Anywhere But Here,* just as the Joads' truck provides the only shelter they can lay claim to in *The Grapes of Wrath*. More than protection against external threats, the automobile energizes the quest through the power released in compressed space. The speed and power of Kerouac's '49 Hudson are legendary, and the Merry Pranksters' psychedelic bus is a world unto itself. The Big Bopper's '59 White Eldorado looked 70 feet long to Floorboard George. In Anne Roiphe's *Long Division*, Emily Brimberg Johnson feels in orbit, "like a monkey in a capsule a billion miles above the earth" (29). In *Fast Lanes*, Jayne Anne Phillips describes driving as "love in a space capsule" (49). Larry McMurtry's Cadillac Jack drives a pearl-colored Cadillac with a peach velour interior, "the perfect vehicle in which to search the country for antiques" (12).

A "letting go"—a kind of free floating surrender—has always been a part of the American road narrative's healing power. The enclosed space seals off drivers from external distractions and helps them ward off pressures of the quest to "find" themselves. "The open road has always ministered to the American flight from self," Phil Patton observes:

> To drive without purpose—to "cruise"—is the central trope not only of Kerouac but of a hundred popular songs, in country music and rock and roll. Just driving without goal or purpose, surrendering the mind totally to the mechanical functions of steering wheel and gas pedal, figures in such songs as a solace. (250)

Patton notes that the car's private, enclosed space holds a particular attraction to Americans who resist mass transit. Thus, as numerous commentators have noted, Americans lose themselves in their cars as soon as they take to the highways in a quest for self-discovery. The paradox holds up in almost all American road narratives. Patton's link between thought and mechanical functions suggests that enclosed space, humming engines, and whirring tires provide a mantra for the driver's meditations: "The freeway driver, one half of his brain occupied by the immediate and mostly automatic decision making of driving, is, like the television viewer, in a peculiarly distracted and suggestible state of mind" (110). Pirsig, Least Heat Moon, Steinbeck, and others object to the mesmerizing, narcotic effect of the superhighway driving— preferring instead the motorcycle, the backroad, and the blue highways. Patton compares the open spaces of freeways to nature in Romantic literature and suggests that we come to treat the landscape cinematically. Just as Pirsig found no ultimate clash between "romantic" and "classical" in the maintenance of one's motorcycle, so also many road questers use the combination of enclosed space and the hypnotic mechanical functions of driving as a liberating experience. Patton suggests, for example, that the same people who cannot "stand to be on a bus or train full of strangers find managing their vehicle with the flow somehow refreshing, almost baptismal: a form of going down to the river" (111).

Commentators have long ago noted the central place of the pastoral in the American sense of quest. Automobile travel is a threat to virgin land and an intrusion into the paradise of the garden. In American road narratives, the automobile is at once an intruder in paradise and the creator of a new paradise within. While moving through—and at the same time becoming insulated from—the landscape, the American

highway hero rides into a new state of consciousness very like what
Karin Blair has identified in her analysis of the appeal of *Star Trek*. Blair
finds that the attraction audiences have for the *Enterprise* goes beyond
the extension of the frontier myths to the stars. In *Star Trek*, she finds,
the machine is not just accepted into the garden; the machine *becomes*
the garden. Blair sees the machine as "no longer the instrument of
opposition, war and destruction," but rather, a "vehicle which both
sustains and expresses the human psyche which created it." As the road
narrative tradition progresses, the garden or virgin land become
increasingly inaccessible or at least remote. Road questers thus recreate
paradise in the mythic patterns associated with the interior of the
automobile in motion. No longer are we limited to the machine moving
into the garden. Now the garden moves inside the machine.

In "Versions of Eden: The Automobile and the American Novel,"
David Laird has noted that characters in recent American fiction display
a fascination with machines that "promise power, mobility, freedom,
even a 'poetic' space that beckons from beyond the too familiar course
of things, from beyond the rush of time and time's sad waste" (qtd. in
Lewis and Goldstein 643). This promise of freedom and liberation into
Edenic space carry, however, their own "unforseen liabilities and
losses." Borrowing from Leo Marx, Laird contends that the automotive
machine "*is* the garden, opening the way to or itself becoming a
sheltering space, free from the conditioning, shaping influences which
beset the fallen world." Laird finds the automobile's provision of "a
space of one's own" an important stage in the development of "psychic
structures by which Americans, consciously or unconsciously, have
experienced and responded to the bewilderments and confusions of
modernity" (in Lewis and Goldstein 643). Whether one calls the process
an escape, a search for identity, or a mythic quest, Laird finds that the
cultivation of inner space has analogies in the Western literary tradition
at least as old as the Romantic Period. The yearning is not, then, for the
wild frontier only, and the lure of the road is not only for adventure and
expansive new experiences. The attraction is also for even the lonely,
isolated but redemptive enclosed space of modern novels. In Thomas
Pynchon's *The Crying of Lot 49*, Oedipa Maas "escapes the dull,
dispiriting uniformity of a planned community by fleeing to the
freeways" (qtd. by Laird in Lewis and Goldstein 642). In her rented car
she finds "deliverance from passivity and madness." In Walker Percy's
The Last Gentleman, Will Barrett seeks in the inside of his Trav-L-Aire
car a space that is "protected, self-contained, yet open to its
surroundings, mobile yet at home, compacted . . . in the world, yet not of
the world" (qtd. by Laird in Lewis and Goldstein 643). Laird sees in

these two novels and others a common "notion of an escape into a 'Poetic' space, a secret garden, a room of one's own, set off from the ordinariness of things by means of motion, memory, or encabined contemplation" (643).

While traditionally the insulating horse offers protection against threats to life and mythic vision, on the modern highway the compartmentalized vehicle has been seen also as a source of monotony and homogenization of experience. With so many hours on the road and so much space to cover, complacency is unavoidable. Because pioneers and explorers were actually clearing the brush and putting their names on new places, it is easy to see vehicles as protection in early quests. Baby-boom growth, however, soon cemented over the landscape, and expressways and larger cars placed drivers in increasingly enclosed space where the old external forms of adventure were closed off. This sealing off of the driver from the environment has become a central issue in road narratives of the past 30 years. Just how enclosed the modern highway quester has become can be seen as attacks against the automotive insulation become part of the road vision itself. Pirsig and Least Heat Moon put forth such objections.

Although for Pirsig boredom and "stuckness" can be liberating forces in moving travelers toward inner exploration, he believes that the automobile can lead to stagnation rather than adventure. Excessive speed, over-planned itineraries, and the trappings of superhighways insulate drivers and passengers alike from contact with the environs through which they move. Pirsig's road experience thus differs noticeably from the conventional patterns. Sal Paradise wants to follow "one great line across America," whereas Pirsig's "secondary road motorcycle buffs" learn how to find hills and traffic patterns on maps. With the right tools and a "lack of pressure to 'get somewhere'" it's possible to be on the road slowly and "have America all to ourselves." Here the contrasts between enclosure of the car and the expanse of a motorcycle reflect the differences in the two books:

> In a car you're always in a compartment, and because you're used to it you don't realize that through the car window everything you see it just more TV. You're a passive observer and it is all moving by you boringly in a frame. On a cycle the frame is gone. You're completely in contact with it all. You're in the scene not just watching it any more, and the sense of presence is overwhelming. (4)

Ultimately, for Least Heat Moon there is an ambivalence along the highway as the healing process of movement runs the risk of insulating the traveler through a kind of delusion. The author observes: "A car whipped past, the driver eating and a passenger clicking a camera. Moving without going anywhere, *taking* a trip instead of *making* one. I laughed at the photographs and then realized I, too, was rolling effortlessly along, turning the windshield into a movie screen in which I, the viewer, did the moving while the subject held still" (188). Chester Liebs has linked this windshield phenomenon to a transformation of modern sensibility intensified by a merging of car travel and the development of cinema: "The windshield of any car could be transformed into a proscenium arch framing one of the most fascinating movies of all—the landscape played at high speed." The same hypnotic lure is found in Jayne Anne Phillips's *Fast Lanes*: "There was the windshield and the continual movie past the glass. It was good driving into the movie, good the way the weather changed, the way night and day traded off" (49).

In *The Moving American* George W. Pierson has noted the effects of what he calls "the M. Factor" (Movement, Migration, Mobility) on American Society (223-25). He describes a habit of wandering in which a person can get addicted to the excitement, detachment, and even the loneliness of movement itself. Soon motion breeds optimism in the view that we can always change and that change is always for the better. Constant movement also creates activism and a love of novelty as well as what Pierson calls the "paradoxical conservatism" in which people in motion learn necessarily to live with less and to cling to the objects one moves for. Mobility also fosters narrower and more intense groups and appeals to cranks and fanatics. Finally, "the great mix master" of a mobile society promotes awakenings and is a leveler of status and values. The experience of being on the road contributes to and reflects these diverse strands of America's cultural values. Writing and reading about being in motion also open up a dialogue between authors, texts, and readers that itself contributes to changing values.

In the conventional quest romance there is often a place, a mantra, a formula, or a guru which comes to be seen as repositories of the wisdom sought. Returning to a special place or repeating a phrase become sources of enlightenment. But in a new twist on the old lessons of self-discovery, the hero sooner or later realizes that externals—teachers, creeds, even roads—must give way in favor of an ongoing, internal quest. As Sheldon B. Kopp has pointed out (*If You Meet the Buddha on the Road, Kill Him!*), "the Buddhahood of each of us has already been obtained. We need only recognize it" (188). Before the pilgrim can accept that Buddha within, however, the pilgrimage must first be other-directed. Opening oneself up to others is the essence of what Whitman called the lesson of "reception," the paradox of Goethe's "the self-seeker finds nothing," and the Christian view of the death of self as rebirth into new life. On the road, in *Midnight Cowboy,* Joe Buck finds himself only in Ratzo Rizzo, Sissy Hankshaw in *Even Cowgirls Get the Blues,* and Bob White in *Seaview* reach the ultimate movement in standing still. Least Heat Moon turns to others for the power of the circle that returns him to himself, and Pirsig's narrator reintegrates the pieces of a fragmented self through acceptance and the realization of what is wholly within.

In a variety of ways, the automobile in motion is the insulating vehicle which precipitates the modern journey of self discovery. Protected from external threats and enclosed in sacred space, road heroes find meditative silence, liminality, and heightened conversation. Interacting with passengers, hitchhikers, or the people they meet along the way, listening to the neglected wisdom of outsiders, or tuned in to the world through the radio, the hero behind the wheel finds the protective shell of the car to be both a shield and a source of renewable vision and energy. Journeys of self-discovery change over time, and the road genre evolves with those changes. New forms are not simply arbitrary combinations of elements but evolve because writers and readers discover in the writing and reading processes new ways to understand and express their views of the world. In journeys of self-discovery, narrators often begin with certain assumptions about their lives and the society in which they live. The journey, however, leads them to think and feel differently about the world they find and their place in it. Drawing attention to the search for order and meaning, the American road quest moves frequently from monologue to an increasingly dialogic narrative pattern. As narrators converse with the people they meet, as well as others along for the ride, readers are drawn into participation in the questioning and reshaping of values and attitudes. While the result may not be the structural unity formalist readers demand, this dialogical road of self-searching is particularly suited to capturing social and cultural changes in the making.

6

Escape, Experimentation, and Parody

After two decades of social protest, self-discovery, and the search for a national identity, the road for some turned sour. As the energy of Dean Moriarity's "Wild Yea Saying" diminished, the journey became discouraging. For others, by the late 1960s the road offered not hopeful renewal, but the frenzy of pure escapism. Disillusionment about what had been the hopeful 'open road' moved in three new directions. One group of narrators struggled with depression and anxiety as in works by John Updike and Joan Didion that emphasize survival motion in narratives of escape. The genre reshaped itself in the basic quest motif into experimental, spatiotemporal structures very like science fiction or the theater of the absurd. Road novels from Rudolph Wurlitzer to Roger Zelazny reflect the genre's brief venture into the metafictional. Still a third response created a series of quest parodies that ranged from the dystopic nightmares of Vladimir Nabokov's *Lolita* and Tom Engel-hardt's *Beyond Our Control* to the self-reflexive spoofing of Tom Robbins's *Even Cowgirls Get the Blues* and Toby Olson's *Seaview*, which turn road quest conventions inside out in a celebration of sitting still. The effect is not outright rejection of the road quest so much as what Bakhtin calls a parodic doubling, where a multiple perspective of self-mockery sets in motion a dialogical hybrid of corrective laughter at existing conventions (qtd. in Morson and Emerson 433-35). By means of deliberate undermining, the lure of the road, goal orientation, and the nature of the quest hero are opened for debate or revision within a range of predictable genre conventions. These three developments in narrative pattern—escape, experimental structure, and self-reflexive parody—result from recombinations of genre conventions and reflect changes in readers' tastes, demands, and values. In the later stages of the road genre's development, experimental form and self-reflexive parody arise from pressures to be original or the need to correct what goes wrong along the way.

John Updike's Rabbit Angstrom is one of the earliest examples of an ambivalent hero who drives to escape. *Rabbit Run* (1960) expresses an American dream that doesn't seem to be working. Attempting to soothe the disappointments of adulthood and relive earlier basketball heroics, Rabbit takes to reflex-action running and lengthy pointless driving. In an updated version of the story about the man who goes to the store for a gallon of milk and was never heard from again, he takes a short drive early in the novel that turns into a long search for escape. He drives too fast, ignores a stop sign, and decides he doesn't ever want to see his home town again. The road is speed, and his plan is simple: go south, "down, down the map into orange groves and smoking rivers and barefoot women," but the lure of escape is short-lived, and soon the road itself begins to take on features of the same trap. Rabbit's dreams of freedom are derived from what he has read and heard about the American quest. He remembers reading an article in the *Saturday Evening Post* about Highway 1 from Florida to Maine through lush scenery. To get to this dream road, however, he must endure long stretches of dullness; his disillusionment soon worsens when he hits the confused highway system of Baltimore. Trying to steer free, he uses maps to chart a course and avoid the traps of impulse. He imagines himself gliding right down into the middle of a warm and lush landscape, "into the broad soft belly of the land, surprising the dawn cottonfields with his northern plates." The old enthusiasm returns as his excitement about the quest builds: "Find the right road, zip on it, and you'll have a chute dumping you into sweet low cottonland in the morning. Yes. Once he gets on that, he can shake all thoughts of the mess behind him" (30).

Rabbit's anger and frustration, however, soon overwhelm his short-lived hopes for escape. The more he drives, the more surroundings bring back the same painful memories and associations. Conventional road rewards are bankrupt. What had been the lulling calm of motion becomes boring. Instead of winding gently, the road "unravels with infuriating slowness, its black wall wearilessly rising in front of his headlights no matter how they twist." Joy has turned to anger and frustration as he grinds his foot from accelerator to brake "as if to squash this snake of a road and nearly loses the car on a curve, as the two right wheels fall captive to the dirt shoulder" (32). Finally, in the extended snake metaphor, the road takes on a life of its own, "twisting wildly at first in its struggle to reach to the sky and then dropping down where, without warning, it sheds its skin of asphalt and worms on in dirt" (33). For Rabbit, the road becomes a hostile force and a barrier to his escape. He, therefore, becomes obsessed with maps, though he can't read them in the dark and can't remember where he's been. Struggling to make out the names of towns and rivers, he sees the map as a net of intersecting red and blue lines forming a maze in which he is trapped. What had been for Kerouac straight and fast stretches inviting power, speed, and energizing continent-crossing was now for Rabbit only another trap. In an astonishing moment of frustration he ritualistically destroys the map:

> He claws at it and tears it; with a gasp of exasperation he rips away a great triangular piece and tears the large remnant in half and, more calmly, lays these three pieces on top of each other and tears them in half, and then those six pieces and so on until he has a wad he can squeeze in his hand like a ball. He rolls down the window and throws the ball out, it explodes, and the bent scraps like disembodied wings flicker back over the top of the car. (34)

Rabbit tears apart the highway symbol of progress, only to have its remnants blow back in his face. Although the novel never returns directly to the road motif following this purge, Rabbit still drives and, ironically, he becomes a Toyota dealer. His urge to escape, however, slides over to the lighter and quieter metaphor of running (255).

While many road quests, like Rabbit's, sought the release of running away, others responding to the turbulence of the sixties found themselves mired in escapist nightmares and a fascination with wreckage. In *Play It As It Lays* (1970), Joan Didion stretches and modifies genre conventions to create a wrenching portrait of pain. Maria Wyeth drives the California freeways in a high-stakes crap game where there are seemingly no winners. Trapped by Hollywood drug culture, an unhappy marriage, an abortion, a hopelessly ill child, and incurable loneliness, Maria hopes motion itself will fill empty days and numb unbearable memories. Through stream-of-consciousness in monologue and flashbacks, Maria tells her own story. In 84 short chapters, the book is a personal epic quest for order and meaning in tones that are mock-heroic or biblical: "In the first hot month of the fall after the summer she left Carter . . . Maria drove the freeway." She didn't arrive anywhere in particular; in fact, she didn't even plan to get anywhere. Rather, she just drove to help organize her day—much in the way some people plan their time around TV or radio schedules: "It was essential (to pause was to throw herself into unspeakable peril) that she be on the freeway by ten o'clock. Not somewhere on Hollywood Boulevard, not on her way to the freeway, but actually on the freeway. If she was not, she lost the day's rhythm, its precariously imposed momentum" (15). Didion dislodges the road narrative's traditional goal orientation into psychological groping in a senseless existence. Back on schedule, the ritual is again carefully prescribed: "Once she was on the freeway and had maneuvered her way to a fast lane and turned on the radio at high volume and she drove. She drove to San Diego to the Harbor, the Harbor up to Hollywood, the Hollywood to the Gold State. . . . She drove it as a riverman runs a river, every day more attuned to its currents, its deceptions" (15-16). Maria dissects each crevice and groove to conquer the hostile forces that threaten passage and—most of all—to even briefly forget.

Challenged and totally absorbed by the road, Maria lies awake at night picturing road signs. She is haunted by the difficulties of one stretch of road that required a move crossing four lanes of traffic. The heroic road quester is back in full force: "On that afternoon she finally did it, without once breaking or once losing the beat on the radio, she was exhilarated, and that night she slept dreamlessly" (16). But the heroism is more like that of Prufrock than Odysseus. Though she is really going nowhere, Maria puts 7,000 miles on her Corvette in one summer and keeps a hard-boiled egg on the front seat so she won't have to stop to eat: "She could shell and eat a hard-boiled egg at seventy miles an hour (crack it on the steering wheel, never mind salt, salt bloats, no matter what happened she remembered her body) and she drank Coca-Cola in Union 76 stations, Standard stations, Flying A's" (18). Just as later at the supermarket she will buy large boxes of everything to ward off the pain of loneliness, these rituals of driving create at least the illusion of order and direction in a world that is falling apart. The depression intensifies, however, as everything reminds her of dead and maimed children and memories of her abortion. While he is making a movie out on the desert Maria's husband asks her to join the crew. She declines—choosing instead to stay behind at the motel office where she

> studied the deputy sheriff's framed photographs of highway accidents, imagined the moments of impact, tasted blood in her own dry mouth and searched the grain of the photographs with a magnifying glass for details not immediately apparent, the false teeth she knew must be on the pavement, the rattlesnake she suspected on the embankment. (197)

In these and other grotesque images, *Play It As It Lays* presents an anxious escapist road quest. The hero takes to the road in search of new direction and meaning, but the quest for peace of mind is lonely and ultimately unfullfilling. Didion's ritualized enactment of highway travel uses many elements of the road genre, but in this portrait the protagonist is trapped, pressures are unrelieved, and the movement becomes merely numbing—in the end a caricature of the conventional quest.

Not all escapist road narratives present Rabbit's anger or Maria's brooding. The same desire to flee on the American highway has also been treated with a humor typified by the lighthearted sophistication of William Faulkner. Set in 1905, *The Reivers* is the story of Lucius Priest's coming of age. His grandfather's car is a modern intrusion into their well-ordered lives and, at the same time, a symbol of freedom, escape, and excitement. Lucius, Boon, and Ned borrow the car for a frenzied trip from Jefferson, Mississippi, to Memphis on a journey of initiation that Olga Vickery has called a parody of chivalric romance. To the young Lucius, the car represents the freedom of that mesmerizing world behind the throttle: "We moved back and forth across that vacant sun-glared waste forward awhile, backward a while . . . out of time, beyond it, invulnerable to time until the courthouse clock striking noon a half-mile away restored us; hurled us back into the impending hard world of finagle and deception." With his appetite whetted for escape, Lucius becomes more enamored with the freedom of the road stretching before him on each subsequent short drive off on their machine-powered trek through the wilderness. These adventurers begin to feel they are part of a wagon train. Boon prophesies that the roads to Memphis would soon be "cluttered thick as fleas with automobiles" (70), and his expectations slowly come to pass when the land opens up, the farms get bigger, and they come to "a broad highway running string-straight into the distance and heavily marked with wheel prints." For the first time, Lucius anticipates what would become the country's heritage of highway questers. As he passes another car and they co-mingle their dust in a shared cloud, he begins to fear that mechanization will be the inescapable destiny of the nation (71). Their adventures are a foretaste of the road's bittersweet mix of exciting promise and dulling progress. The older Lucius as narrator later recalls his apprehension about not wanting "just to retrace but retract, obliterate" the journey they had undertaken. Mostly he wanted to take his grandfather's car back to Jefferson—driving in reverse if necessary, in the hopes of reversing the forces of "antilife" in their midst. Lucius knew already, of course, that this retraction of progress was not possible.

These worries about whether cars would bring improvements or dehumanizing experiences led some road authors to suffer from—even as they embraced—a kind of double jeopardy. Road heroes and antiheroes became annoyed with both progress and protest against progress. One way out, seen in road movies even more than books, is to revel in the power of motion itself. Anne Robinson Taylor has shown that restlessness and flight often dominate tales of adventure to the point that the quest itself can become boring and claustrophobic. Tracing the history of the road quest to its "hope of salvation," she finds that in road movies heroism has given way to speeding machines and the imprisonment of the violent and lonely rebellion. "At least Huck Finn was headed somewhere," she notes: "The modern river man is in trouble, and the modern river is merely a ribbon of concrete, colorless and banal" (143). Whether highway, river, or bicycle path, the road continues to be a hallowed space to get away, question, make new plans, talk with others, and write fascinating stories.

In addition to expressing escapist flight, road authors from the mid-'60s to the mid-'70s broke out of conventional patterns by experimenting with new time sequences and fictional forms. Metafictional road quests featured absurdist cross-country trips with Godot-type missing heroes and futuristic landscapes. For example, the American dream machine is satirized in Harry Crews's *Car,* an outrageous parody of the nation's worship of automobile culture. The story presents Easy Mack, proprietor of a towing service, automobile graveyard, and car-crushing service, and his son Herman whose efforts to enshrine the American car in its rightful place inspire him to create historical displays and liturgical ceremonies. Pushing society's craving for auto shows and museums to its extreme, Mack stages "Car Display: Your History on Parade" wherein people can relive the great moments of their lives through 50 years of cars. Eventually, Herman internalizes automobile culture by *eating* a car. A variation of this mockery is found in Walker Percy's *Love in the Ruins* in which cars no longer run, highways are overgrown, and motels sit empty in deserts and swamps. Humankind is sick, and only Dr. Thomas More tries for a cure with his modern "stethoscope of the spirit." Travel is found mostly in the flight of buzzards who circle a mile above the interchange. Shopping centers have been abandoned, and growth is found mostly on the flat roofs of abandoned stores alongside what used to be parking lots. Percy presents these road icons and literally empties them of life and motion.[1] A similar manipulation of conventional patterns is found in several novels by Joseph McElroy, where the quest motif pushes into fascinating experimentation with new spatiotemporal ordering. In his commentary on "total novels" of the 1970s, *American Fictions: 1940/1980,* Frederick R. Karl calls McElroy's technique a "defamiliarization of our normal expectations."[2] In *Ancient History,* for example, McElroy presents neither an escape nor a Kerouac-like high but what Karl finds reminiscent of Robbes-Grillet or Butor, wherein movement is not across the plains or even down the highway, but an inward tunneling. Conventional space and time are replaced by the mathematical plotting of a field theory.

In yet another example of metafictional experimentation, three novels by Rudolph Wurlitzer push life on the road further into absurdity, surrealism, and dystopia. *Nog* relates the tale of three characters on a bizarre journey where the character of the title never appears. The narrator buys a rubber octopus in Oregon and travels with Nog through the Midwest staging a sideshow. A year later in *Flats,* places become characters in a novel that Frederick Karl has described as a meditation on space in which Wurlitzer is trying to "limn a personal America," moving across a flat map, in flattened prose. Karl suggests that Kerouac's speedsters are transformed by speed itself, into aborted movement and constipated action. Conventional journeys are a distant memory as Wichita asks: "Is this a tailgate? Does this mark the end of the road?" (85). Finally in the third entry in Wurlitzer's trilogy *Quake,* the dystopia is total. Following an earthquake, travel is meaningless, there is no escape from the devastation and events are shaped as adaptations to chaos. Roads have been destroyed or rendered useless, fires rage throughout the city, and characters wander aimlessly down the center line on a road that has no more cars.

The road has become an escape hatch also in Gilbert Sorrentino's *The Sky Changes,* which depicts the entrapment and absurdity of modern life and offers the cross-country car trip as a desperate attempt to soothe the pain. The narrator, his wife, and their children start from Brooklyn wanting to escape to the light of Mexico, to the sunlight with "keen edges" (13). Discovering after seven years that he doesn't know his wife, he decides that on the journey he might learn to face her, to break out of the cocoon that he hid himself in. But the trip is ill-fated from the beginning, and the realization soon sinks in that this quest will be "a stupid groping for happiness," a confronting of life's absurdity on a journey that makes no sense. Along the way the futility grows, and the narrator comes to understand the real reason for their going: "That's why we made the trip. To separate, with manufactured reasons that would never have proved efficacious in the stability of living, together, in one place, the stability of residence. The trip was their exit, their opportunity" (85). Like most road narratives, *The Sky Changes* seeks self-discovery through a change of place and circumstance, but here the quest turns inside out and mocks the truths it seeks.

The Sky Changes is an absurdist road narrative with Beckett-like characters struggling to break through layers of anxiety and indecision. Many of the motivations of the conventional highway quester are openly mocked as this couple take their marriage on the road where they "were playing some sort of shabby drama out to the end, neither one of them with enough strength or honesty to terminate things" (103). Instead of the healing, expansive conversation of most highway journeys, *The Sky Changes* records terror and suspicion: "Outside the edge of the strained looks, and the quick banter which followed it, there was a lurking ominous silence, waiting to invade the car when the talk died" (161-62). Ultimately, the anxiety wins out even as the momentum of this journey is toward frustration, confusion, and massive repression. Sorrentino captures the experimental mode of the American road narrative at its painful best where heroes choose self-destruction, move only to forget, talk to block out silences, and rage at the absurdity of experience.

Just as *The Sky Changes* presents pointless and absurd obsessions, John Hawkes's *Travesty* is firmly mired in paranoia from the outset. This is an automobile trip to end them all, the ultimate quest for total self-destruction and revenge. In his 128-page monologue, the unnamed narrator travels with his daughter and her lover through the night at 149 kilometers per hour toward death. These reluctant fellow travelers never speak; there is no scenery, no sense of time passing, no feeling of movement at all. Distance, transformation, and progress cannot be measured by any known standard. Collage-like flashbacks piece together a fragmented story of modern dissonance where traditional linear extension directed outward has been violated.

Travesty mocks everything predictable in the road genre. The plot is all in the mind of the narrator who constructs the action piece by piece from his own fears and anxieties. He views himself as a hero and plans for the destruction of his passengers as a redemptive act. Fixated on speed, he pushes the car to its limits in a quest of his own: "Our speed is a maximum in a bed of maximums which happen to include: my driving skill, this empty road, the time of night, the capacity of the car's engine, the immensity of the four seasons lying beyond us between the trees or in the flat fields" (15). Preparing them for the end, he tells his passengers that he has often driven this alone and at the fastest speed possible. He sees his car as a bullet, moving the quest entirely inward, into his own search to regain lost control. It is only "the life of the mind," he coolly observes, "that holds the moving car to the road." Hawkes's sense of urgency is unremitting throughout this suicide trip. With his total sensibility tuned to the dashboard indicators, the narrator concludes that "the life of the car is running out, the end of the journey tonight is not as distant as one might think" (33-34). He plans, of course, to orchestrate that demise and to control its every phase. True to the genre conventions, *Travesty* has its say on the importance of maps in the planning and execution of the journey. "On a white road map," the narrator proclaims, movement along the road "looks exactly like the head of a dragon outlined by the point of a pen brutally sharpened and dipped in blood" (52). This image reminds him not to trust the road quester's illusions of progress or significance. The only answer is to survive long enough to be in command of one's own destruction. This driver's quest comes full circle—so that the goal is the annihilation of all goals and the triumphant recognition that in the end "there shall be no survivors. None" (128).

Ronald Sukenick's *Out* presents a similar journey of self-destruction,which obliterates not only people and landscapes, but the pages on which it is written. Sukenick's metafiction works imperceptibly at first toward the inevitable erasure of not only the road but also the words in which road stories are told. The loose plot of *Out* involves a group of dynamiters who cross the country to blow up buildings and roads. Alongside the explosions, the narrator's text diminishes as the margins of pages get larger and larger. One character hopes to erase all words until he finally reaches the unknown. The pattern thus runs the conventional acquisition model quest in reverse. The journey is still goal-oriented, but now the goal is an eventual whiteout in which the road, a sense of direction, space itself, and all the inner modes of the quest disappear.

In another rare but significant highway excursion into the metafictional, Roger Zelazny's *Roadmarks* runs the traditional American road metaphor in reverse. Red Dorakeen starts on the road as an old man and discovers that the purpose of traveling is to "grow young" and achieve maturity in the discovery of youth. Traveling through various countries and centuries in his Dodge pick-up, Red wants to bring weapons to the Greeks so they can defeat the Persians at Marathon. At the same time, Dorakeen's former partner in intrigue, Chadwick, is trying to kill him. The hired killers are waiting in the past and future along the road, and Red survives, finally, by counterattack on Chadwick. Zelazny portrays time as a superhighway with exits and entrances, main and secondary routes, where maps are ever changing and only a few people know how to find the access ramps (45). On a quiet section of road, Red passes futuristic vehicles, a coach and four, and a solitary horseman (4). Each branch of the road "traverses time—time past, time to come, time that could have been and time that might yet be. It goes on forever, so far as I know, and no one knows all of its turnings" (89). These inversions of chronology are skillfully crafted, and the intrigue of plot and experimental structure effectively modify conventional quest patterns.

The story in *Roadmarks* is in the tradition of Whitman and Kerouac. Two computerized characters make the journey—one named after Baudelaire's *Flowers of Evil*, the other after Whitman's *Leaves of Grass*. Dorakeen is a typical road hero who experiences the joy of motion, the restlessness of the quest and a profound joy in simply being (153). Finally, the road comes full circle as Red tells Flowers "we are born crooked and twisted and old and must discover youth, which is our maturity in this form" (157). *Roadmarks* blends successfully experimental structure and conventional patterns of the road experience.

Experimental narrative forms have brought to recent road literature contained and short-lived metafictional exploration. Purposeful motion gives way to pointless wandering in Percy's dystopic ruins. Conventional spatiotemporal categories are subsumed by McElroy's "field theory." Walking on the devastation of what used to be roads, Wurlitzer creates surrealistic and absurdist landscapes. Healing car talk is drowned out by the paralysis of making noise to forget in *The Sky Changes.* In *Travesty* self-destruction is pursued with zeal of the pilgrim's holy quest. Antinarrative narration in *Out* predicts the fading of books into a whiteout. *Roadmarks* runs chronology in reverse in a quest along the superhighway of time where old age must mature into youth. In all, experimental road narratives manipulate conventional patterns of motion, time, and space in order to explore further possibilities of the genre.

In addition to escapist flight and metafictional experimentation, the road narrative has expanded its range through parodic self-commentary—a way of critiquing itself from within that exposes the limitations of the road vision even as it celebrates the genre's strength and abiding popularity. Parodies of generic conventions can be found as early as *Lolita* (1955) in which Humbert Humbert kidnaps Lolita and travels the roads in a car which Mary F. Catanzaro has called a cell or "the vehicle that asserts human beings are trapped in a psychological and spiritual dilemma that offers no solution" (91). Humbert narrates their experiences in parodic catalogs of motels, bathrooms, gift shops, roadside restaurants, and other ubiquitous tourist attractions. Their movement is often frantic, sometimes perfunctory. Although Humbert provides detailed accounts of what they inspected on hundreds of scenic drives (158-59), he also confides that their hard, twisted, teleological itinerary was planned only to keep Lolita in good humor: "Every morning during our yearlong travels I had to devise some expectation, some special point in space and time for her to look forward to, for her to survive until bedtime" (153). Their movement is a parody of travel with Humbert hoping to set the geography of the United States in motion in order to give Lolita "the impression of going places; of rolling onto some definite destination." Satiric commentary develops as their actions reproduce typical travel itineraries of the American vacation which is going nowhere with deliberation.

Along the way, all the trappings of the road narrative come in for wry commentary and brutal parody. They "passed and re-passed through the whole gamut of American roadside restaurants," inspected rocks and log cabins and photo collections and frontier lore and hundreds of such items on display for their perusal. The repetition is at times suffocating: "Our twentieth Hell's Canyon. Our fiftieth Gateway to something or other *fide* that tour book, the cover of which had been lost by that time. . . . Our hundredth cavern, adults one dollar, Lolita fifty cents" (159-60). Humbert's parodies of the road quest culminate in an act of open defiance wherein movement along the highway becomes a metaphor for the act of writing itself: "The road now stretched across open country, and it occurred to me—not by way of protest, not as a symbol, or anything like that, but merely as a novel experience—that since I had disregarded all laws of humanity, I might as well disregard the laws of traffic." Deciding to drive on the left side of the road (in biblical tones he "checked the feeling and the feeling was good," he enjoys the abandon: "Cars coming toward me wobbled, swerved, and cried out in fear." He smashes the taboos: "Passing through a red light was like a sip of forbidden Burgundy when I was a child" (308). The tone of *Lolita* is whimsical as Humbert revels in mock epic mimickery of solemn road rituals.

A different kind of parodic double challenges readers with an angry, dystopic inversion of the quest romance. The laughter is dark in corrective parody which begins usually with the enthusiasm of a pilgrimage and then subverts many of the genre's conventions in response to the disillusionment encountered. Just as Henry Miller tried to imagine the pioneers' experience in *The Air-Conditioned Nightmare* and had to settle for traffic jams, Tom Engelhardt's *Beyond Our Control: America in the Mid-Seventies* starts out on "the classically American trip from coast to coast" (8) but runs up against "the vampirization of everyday life by corporate America" (109). Engelhardt takes to the road to break out of something and into something else. Together with his photographer-fellow-traveler, he is at first committed to "the virtues of movement" (33) only to conclude that "the 'On the Road' mystique had me fooled" (86). The problem is that Whitman's open road was now cluttered with mass-produced food, prepackaged camping, franchised experiences, freak shows, the worship of commodities, the "mechanical abomination" of recreation vehicles (37) and words in which everyone talks alike—as on a giant ocean-to-ocean TV screen. What had been the lure of discovery turns into "traveling in quicksand" (65), on roads "auctioned to corporate America" (149). The highway has become alien turf, "a controlled rut" (71), where "objects are imbued with all the power that was once placed in human beings" (72). People move along ready built roads that are "a strategic corridor jammed with all the profit-making hokum American industry can design" (150). Once upon a time, the road did symbolize freedom, opportunity, expanse, adventure; it was a place to find oneself, to go it alone, in what Engelhardt calls the best American tradition (186). While everybody looked the other way, however, that myth became a saleable commodity and the metaphors changed. The open road encouraging self-reliance turned into a consumerland of trendy conformity. Left with a realization that we have been uprooted with no sense of a future, the only adventure left involves ransacking the past. Hence, the myth still lives on—but as nostalgia rather than an ideal or a sense of achievement.

Engelhardt's parodic quest discovers underneath the road journey a betrayal wherein drivers, authors, and readers are lured to the persistent American habit of confusing movement with progress. Soon motion itself is a narcotic substitute for real freedom. The problem, as he sees it, is that we set out to change our location rather than ourselves. Drifting from one mediocrity to another through a succession of prefabricated experiences, we feel the illusion of progress as the car rolls along. The quest itself glosses over crises and avoids problems. When we are lost, confused, and alone, we can always still drive, and behind the wheel we always at least seem to be getting somewhere. Engelhardt's critique of our fascination with motion is reinforced by Wallace Stegner's recent regret that the American West has spawned a literature of motion rather than place. "In the midst of our perpetual motion," Stegner says we are homesick for a vanishing wilderness or nostalgic for the old folks at home. Rather than writing "loving place-oriented books," we have "made a tradition out of mourning the passing of things we never had time to know" and "made a culture out of the open road, out of movement without place" (*Bluebird* 203-04).

Nonetheless, whether or not *Beyond Our Control* is accurate about the closing up of the open road, Englehardt affirms through parody the enduring power of the highway mythos. The lure of motion, the need to escape, the mystique of the quest, and even the multiple intrusions of media and spectacle—all have been woven into the American experience through the symbolic power of roads and cars. In the midst of his diatribe about all that has been distorted, even Englehardt relents somewhat: "We bring shifting geography to bear on shifting emotions, and sometimes it does seem to slide over them easily enough, after all" (109).

The most recent friendly American road parody is Bill Bryson's *The Lost Continent: Travels in Small Town America*. Bryson comes from Des Moines, Iowa ("Someone had to," he quips); as soon as he was old enough, however, he moved to England so he could "be somewhere."

Years later he returned to his earlier haunts: first retracing his boyhood vacations, then in search of American popular culture myths, and finally on a quest for the perfect small town. Along the way, his sardonic wit takes aim at what he finds pretentious and empty in the American dream. By far the funniest of a usually serious genre, Bryson's satire is seething, but shows none of the bitterness of Engelhardt or Henry Miller or even the end-of-the road sadness of Kerouac and other gurus who come home with a mute vision. In the end, the Iowan finds staying away harder than he thought. "Friendly," "decent," "nice" wasn't what Bryson set out to find. He seems pleased, however, to settle for less. "I could live here" he thinks, and "for the first time in a long time" he feels "serene."

If imitation is said to be the greatest form of flattery, then parody may be the ultimate tribute to the power of the vision embodied in a genre. By using genre conventions to mock the form itself, authors celebrate the ability of the road to laugh at itself and to supply its own corrective. One of the most outrageous parodies is Tom Robbins's *Even Cowgirls Get the Blues* where Sissy Hankshaw redefines the freedom of the open road. Born and raised in South Richmond, Virginia, Sissy heads out West to Rubber Rose Ranch to follow her dream and become a cowgirl. Along the way she meets the Countess, an entrepreneur-tycoon; Julian, her esthete husband; Dr. Goldman and Dr. Robbins, who run the whole gamut in approaches to road psychiatry; and the guru Chink, who merges East and West. *Cowgirls* is an unabashed celebration of Sissy as Robbins parodies almost every convention of the road quest. Driving is replaced by hitchhiking; goal orientation is set aside for the transforming power of altered perception in the here and now; and the success-oriented mania of American life is called into question. Sissy was born with enormous thumbs. Though embarrassing to many, the offending digits became her glory and soon she made hitchhiking a way of life that has an "epiphanic impact" on everyone in the book. Sissy's mode of transport differs radically from the traditional road pattern. Whereas most heroes are drivers headed toward a destination, Sissy is a passenger to whom the going is far more important than the arriving: "Sissy never really dreamed of hitching *to* anywhere; it was the *act* of hitching that formed the substance of her vision" (27). Others might practice the art of perpetual motion, but Sissy champions the art of stillness. "I don't reside anywhere in particular," she announces, "I just keep moving" (85). When she is accused of being aimless, she responds in a totally undefensive way: "Not aimless. Not in the least. It's just that my aims are different from most." Her explanation further overturns the road narrative conventions. She assures us that the road is populated with enough aimless drifters out to find themselves, people who travel for kicks searching for America or looking for themselves. She prefers the process, the act of hitchhiking itself—something she defines as "the primacy of form over function . . . wherein an emotional and physical structure created by variations and intensifications of the act of hitching was of far more importance than the utilitarian goals commonly supposed to be the sole purpose of the act" (155). Sissy does more than move; she becomes movement itself:

> And when I am really moving stopping car after car after car, moving so freely, so clearly, so delicately that even the sex maniacs and the cops can only blink and let me pass, then I embody the rhythms of the universe, I feel what it is like to *be* the universe, I am in a state of grace. (54)

Foremost in Sissy's plan for liberating the human spirit (277) is her attack on the American mania for success. *Cowgirls* challenges the traditional American success myth as well as the euphoric triumphs often achieved by counterculture roadsters on the quest: "Success mustn't be considered the absolute. It is questionable, for that matter, whether success is an adequate response to life. Success can eliminate as many options as failure" (12). Sissy's parody of the road quest seeks options rather than the fulfillment of narrow goals, for "often it appears that in this life of experience and accommodation we pay just as dearly for our triumphs as we do for our defeats." Three of the cowgirls challenge each other and the readers to snap the blues by breaking out of traditional patterns and reinventing the quest. The straight-line, supercharged quest must be rounded and calmed, they warn, if there is to be any hope of avoiding past errors. They conclude that "the Power of the world always works in circles, and everything tries to be round" (348). Robbins has a plausible explanation for why American culture has ignored the power of the circle: "The male, in his rebellion against what is natural and feminine in the universe, has used logic as a weapon and shield." In contrast with man's straight-line grids, the cowgirls observe that nature creates and moves everywhere in circles: "Atoms and galaxies are circular, and most organic things in between. The Earth is round. The wind whirls. The womb is no shoebox." The damage, however, has been done: "The square is the product of logic and rationality. It was invented by civilized man. It's the work of masculine consciousness." The answer for Sissy is the redirection of that kind of quest. Like primitive tribes and ancient matriarchal cultures, she will pay homage to what is round. Debbie plans the new route for the quest in her summary pronouncement: "It's the duty of advanced women to teach men to love the circle again" (348).

By the 1980s, three decades of road narratives following the Beats had established a variety of genre conventions. In place were conventional highway patterns of heroic quest, the magic of movement, the lure of open spaces and new people, and a sense of the transforming power available through participation as either traveler or reader along for the journey. In 1982 Toby Olson reversed many of these conventional patterns in *Seaview*, a novel that turns road conventions upside down to celebrate the achievement of learning how to become fully present in one place at one still moment. Through manipulation of genre expectations about structure, heroic acts, and narrative perspective, Olson creates an antiroad narrative, reversing the frontier quest in an eastward movement from California to Cape Cod.[3] Olson's heroine, Melinda, is dying of cancer and wants to see one last time the seashore and home in which she was born. Her husband, Allen, golf-hustles their way across the country to finance the journey. Along the way, they pick up Pima Indian Bob White who wants to save tribal land on the Cape taken over by Seaview Links Golf Course. Two quests converge as Allen shares in Melinda's dying and Bob White instructs them about the art of recovering lost things. In a subplot Allen is stalked by unrequited drug dealers; in a mock-epic, anticlimactic ending that underscores Olson's inversion of the pilgrimage, all the protagonists come together on the golf course. The trio's drive across the country is vintage literary highway: motels, diners, road signs, small towns, back roads, hitchhikers, traveling dreams. The pace is slow, the mood quiet, the action everywhere understated. No one ever forgets that Melinda is dying, yet strangely she seems most alive, as she awakens into a clarity wherein her impending death "freed her to live in the elegance of the struggle" (12). From the outset, their journey is not an escape or a search for progress but a going home. The characters experience on the road what Bob White sees as a disentanglement, or a prolonged liminality that promises to break out of stifling routine. Through parody and inversion of conventional structures, readers are challenged to use road conventions to overcome them in a reexamination of the meaning of habits, relationships, and motion itself.

Each character in *Seaview* tells his or her own story moving back and forth across time and supplemented by an authorial reporter's distant and understanding voice. Characters present their own histories and relate events from different perspectives, drawing readers into a dialogue about plot, character, and theme. Working their way through the collage, readers are forced to reevaluate many conventional ways of seeing both the road and the questions raised along the way. In an especially interesting twist, Allen and Melinda speak through the impersonal pronoun, a style borrowed from late 19th-century stories by women writers. Like stage directions in readers' theater, the narrator enters Allen ("He no longer wondered . . .") and Melinda ("she had insight into . . .")—sometimes alternating the perspectives in quick succession to underscore their relationship in a pattern perfected by Katherine Anne Porter in "Rope."

Through multiple points of view, Olson brings together several distinct stories and perspectives. Melinda sees the trip as one of the few benefits accruing from her cancer: she gets to go home. Allen moves away from his involvement with drug dealers and into the sacred ritual of golf. On the journey their relationship grows in the intensity of their participation in Melinda's cancer and the eloquence of their struggle together. A pilgrimage of sorts, their journey is more a letting go than an acquisition: a silent and deepening resolve to let everything happen in its own time. What their relationship lacked before the disease is reflected in their "futile search for a body component" in mind work. Allen would reach for "something beyond and not in" Melinda—all the while ignoring what was there all along. Melinda, too, comes to have "the best time of her life." In her art, she has "no more interest in representation" at the expense of felt presence. Bob White brings to the book not only an additional goal—liberating his people's land from corporate embezzlement—but his home truth that through concentration and the achievement of noninterference people can reach the exclusionary form of stillness, silence, and the reintegration of body and mind.

In one of the two epigraphs to *Seaview*, Gabriel García Márquez proclaims that "the search for lost things is hindered by routine habits and that is why it is difficult to find them." Perhaps this is why pioneers, heroes of the quest romance, and sad Beats like Sal Paradise want to live on the road. In their traveling dreams Allen and Melinda experience a congruence of physical and spiritual journeys; together, they create a special harmony as they attempt to shake themselves free, undo the routine, and "live in the force of the habits clear through to the other side of them" (193). Typical of the road narrative patterns, in *Seaview* protagonists recover what had been lost as rituals take on the significance of holy ceremony. Allen anticipates Melinda's needs and identifies with her feelings, all with a deliberateness reflected in the narrator's understated style: "He did these things" (6). The description of the final stages of Melinda's cancer is crucial: "She knew that the result would be her death, but this, in its way, freed her to live in the elegance of the struggle" (12). Melinda and Allen break out of a pattern. In the simplest terms, they stop taking each other so much for granted .

Seaview offers an abundance of symbols for disentanglement. Cooking is for both Melinda and Allen an intensely sensuous, integrated process; their sex is "a mixture of passion and giving in to the faded effort of passion at the same time" (75). Juxtaposed with their sensuousness is the voyeurism and sadomasochism of Richard and Gerry. The book is dominated as well by rituals of golf with its meshing of body and mind, its pure motive, focus, and completeness. In golf there is silence, straight and clean lines, economy, concentration, the pleasure of the mechanistic, the achievement of "noninterference." Graceful in play, the golfers enact an interaction of mind and body that yields to necessity, defining nothing "in terms of any thing other than itself" (250). This liberating necessity and disentanglement often sought on the road are epitomized in Melinda's participation in dying. Freed from blame and responsibility and finished with rage, she settles in "the way one slips into a tub in a dark bathroom, into hot water, and soon the skin is no longer a barrier, an integrity and definition; one becomes part of the water, the cancer" (3). Bob White's farewell letter to Melinda and Allen speaks of the need to "shake ourselves free" from life and fancy talk. "Perhaps it is in the body only that we come to live. Closing in on death and other intensities is where we can best do it." The road is thus liberating not in the sense of heroic pilgrimage, frenetic picaro, or even promising *Bildung*, but in the resolution to let go. Bob White concludes, "Live in the force of the habits clear through to the other side of them" (193).

In keeping with the inversion of road convention patterns, the arrival at Seaview Links is presented as mock-epic chaos. Richard stalks Allen and the golf course itself becomes a battleground of violence, a tournament of destruction which liberates the land of Bob White's ancestors. The end of the road is thus anticlimactic, a triumphant use of metaphors of motion and quest to set aside restless yearnings in favor of an exquisite recovering of lost harmony. Melinda, Allen, and Bob White began the journey—each in his or her own way—struggling. Through Olson's reversal of conventions, their road quest calms the struggle and shapes a larger perspective. One overcomes, or at least sees through, trivial routine and recovers lost experiences by immersion in the right kind of rituals. For example, Bob White admires the movement of golf—powerfully concentrated, energies focused, with lines that are not so straight after all but when turned yield only to necessity. In *Seaview*, the road is a place to set oneself free from the entrapment of routine and to confront the self on its own terms.

American road narratives are popular with a wide range of readers because the genre expresses evolving road experiences and adapts to changing reading tastes. With narrative conventions flexible enough to encompass escapism, absurdist worldviews, parodies, and metafictional experimentation, these inverted parodies run parallel to the road journey and provide corrective commentary to a quest pattern that can otherwise lean toward single vision. Parody thus subverts conventions and opens the genre to greater potential. The effect is to draw readers into dialogue with authors, texts, and critics as cultural beliefs and values are reaffirmed, redefined, or otherwise renegotiated.

7

The American Highway and Cultural Diversity

Most American road narratives have been lived, written, and published by white males. This dominance is easy enough to understand, given the history of both American travel and American authorship. Native Americans, African Americans, women, and other minorities have moved around North America for centuries but not usually in the manner of the road quest conventions. We now have records of the tribal migrations of plains Indians, pioneer diaries by women, and stories of flight and migration in slave narratives and autobiographical prose by African American writers. For a variety of reasons, however, the automobile journey became the province of the white male—generally middle class, established, and free to embark on the kind of journeys around which road conventions would be shaped.

Not surprisingly, few road stories by women or minority writers were published before the 1970s. Whitman travels the "open road" alone, Willy Loman lives in the male world of the traveling salesman, and even Steinbeck travels only with Charley, his male French poodle. In several works by Jack Kerouac, as well as in John Clellon Holmes's *Go*, Clancy Sigal's *Going Away*, and Tom Wolfe's *Electric Kool-Aid Acid Test*, the women remain in the background, never portrayed as central to the important business the heroes pursue. In another well-known type of road story, women are absent as a result of separation or divorce. William Least Heat Moon begins *Blue Highways* in the hope of ordering the disarray of his life, the narrator of Jim Harrison's *A Good Day to Die* recounts his failure to sustain a relationship with his wife, and in *Zen and the Art of Motorcycle Maintenance*, the protagonist sets out with his son to put the pieces of his life back together.

Even in the most rebellious of countercultural road manifestoes, women faced a lockout. Discussing factors that blocked the emergence of feminism, Sheila Rowbotham numbers the counterculture of the 1950s among the obstacles. She recalls how Ginsberg's *Howl* and Kerouac's *On the Road* created in her postwar adolescent years a new rhythm that was "like a great release after all the super-consolation romantic ballads like 'Three Coins in the Fountain'" (14). Though Rowbotham found Kerouac's message exciting, she is quick to add: "The fact that the girls invariably get a rough ride in the beat movement never really dawned on me until later. I just thought it was somehow inevitable that girls were meant to be heroically tough and miraculously soft at the same time" (15). This rough ride was engineered, of course, by an "immensely mobile" light traveler who was a "mixture of James Dean and Marlon Brando" (15).

This same warping of experience is found as well in road-narrative depictions of minorities. The earliest automobile journeys ignored the presence of minority cultures in American life; later protest books beginning in the '50s glamorized the jazz life of Harlem cabarets or the Denver nightspots frequented by the Beats. This romantic idealization is described in Norman Mailer's *Advertisements for Myself* as "the white negro" who absorbs "the existentialist synapses of the Negro" but still manages to construct his inner life with nary a nonwhite or woman in sight.[1]

In spite of their curiosity about jazz and ghetto life, most American road narratives of the '50s and '60s presented a white male's world oriented toward success, fast movement, and little concern for women or multicultural experience.

Such distortions are not news in the history of American literature. As Annette Kolodny has outlined in two valuable studies, traditional American metaphors of travel and literary fantasies about the landscape have been shaped in male-dominated notions of conquest and erotic paradisal symbols. Kolodny shows how male frontiersmen traveled across virgin land with ambivalent, regressive, and exploitative consequences. As the pastoral impulse became confused with myths of progress, there developed a frustrating conflict between the passive and possessive, the nurturing and the conquesting. The American travel narrative came to repeat what Kolodny calls "a movement back into the realm of the Mother, in order to begin again, and then an attempted (and not always successful) movement out of that containment in order to experience the self as independent, assertive, sexually active" (*Lay of the Land* 153). In American road narratives the pattern is immersion in the landscape alternating with an endless search for new worlds to conquer. In a later study, Kolodny traces how 18th-century American women create a very different kind of landscape imagery that depicts the frontier not as virgin land to be exploited but as "sanctuary for an idealized domesticity." Women also moved across the plains, but their dreams never achieved the status of national myths, and their view of the garden as domestic space was not usually associated with the winning of the West. Kolodny demonstrates how women writers of the time produced no heroes considered legendary but instead challenged "the nation's infatuation with a wilderness Adam" (*The Land Before Her* xiii). Women's narrators created fantasies of their own to evade "male fantasy structures." Rejecting "privatized erotic mastery," they stressed home, settlement, relationships and community.

A closer look at early travel literature in America explains why there have been so few road narratives by women. Granted, there were fewer women behind the wheel; male-dominated canons of American literature also discouraged women who did travel from writing or even thinking their stories would interest anyone. Furthermore, what Kolodny observes about pioneer literature has continued to be true today: "Women's fantasies about the West took shape within a culture in which men's fantasies had already attained the status of cultural myth" (*The Land Before Her* 12). In the road tradition, Dean Moriarity crashing through the landscape took over where the frontier explorer's conquest of the virgin land left off. What women saved and restored in their own fantasies about the landscape was pushed into the background of America's developing mythos, while the male emphasis on the wilderness Adam pushing across the virginal landscape is repeated on the highway.

In "'Woman's Place' in American Car Culture," Charles L. Sanford has examined many of the attitudes, values, and institutions associated with automobiles. With an enormous economic base and numerous subcultures developing around it, car culture has fostered in America what Sanford calls "a neo-frontier spirit" with its own "rituals, taboos, folk songs, and legendary heroes" (in Lewis and Goldstein 533). Although each stage of life has its own car symbols signifying sexual prowess, status, or domestication, the foremost ritual is the important puberty rite when the adolescent male feels the power of acceleration and the freedom to shape his own destiny through movement. Not surprisingly, Sanford observes, the high priest of this high octane frontier quest is the modern version of the American Adam. "But," he asks, "Where is Eve?" While sociologists, historians, and urban planners debate whether car culture has liberated or further imprisoned the American woman, most early road narratives depict women as abstractions—when they appear at all.[2] In "Not From the Back Seat," Lydia Simmons recalls her experiences growing up with cars in America: "Like everything else in this country that involves speed, power and a lot of reckless insanity, the car has been associated with the male" (in Lewis and Goldstein 548). In this world of male automotive prerogatives, Simmons observes, women also have had definite opinions about, and have been influenced by, America's obsession with cars: "Just as there were women in covered wagons, there have also been women in cars. The car was not invented, hasn't existed, solely for the purpose of the American Adam" (548).

Just how preeminently life on the road has been a man's world can be seen in the criticism leveled against it by the women who do speak out. Women's presence on the road was felt at least a half century ago—first in *The Grapes of Wrath* where Ma calls a halt to the men's plans, and then in *Death of a Salesman* where Linda Loman quarrels with the world-running pretensions of Willy's brother Ben in a futile effort to save her husband from self-destruction. In *The Grapes of Wrath* the road is "the path of people in flight" and "the mother road," where men do the driving and make the plans, and women guide the inner journey and serve as correctives to isolation and fragmentation. Ma Joad understands the male psychology found in most road narratives. When Pa realizes that he "ain't no good any more," he objects nonetheless to a woman taking over the family. Ma isn't at all rattled. "Woman can change better'n a man," she notes. "Woman got all her life in her arms. Man got it all in his head" (467). When Pa thinks his life is over, Ma counters:

> It ain't, Pa. An' that's one more thing a woman knows. I noted that. Man, he lives in jerks—baby born an' a man dies, an' that's a jerk—gets a farm an' loses his farm, an that's a jerk. Woman, it's all one flow, like a stream, little eddies, like waterfalls, but the river, it goes right on. Woman looks at it like that. We ain't gonna die out. (467)

Over time, women on the road followed Ma Joad's lead and changed the metaphors from abrupt spurts to a smoother and more enduring flow.

At the end of the next decade, a classic of the American stage presented a similar critique of the male-dominated quest for success. Linda Loman in Arthur Miller's *Death of a Salesman* tries to diminish the false bravado of her husband Willy. Though she lives with three men, Linda's is not the world of the male-dominated chase to make it big. Never sympathetic to why Willy drives himself beyond what is reasonable, she doesn't appreciate his attempts to imbue their sons, Biff and Happy, with the same drive. She isn't even let in on the jokes the three make about the differences between being "liked" and "well-liked," and she is beyond crying at Willy's funeral because she doesn't quite understand it all. In her words, for the "first time in thirty-five years we were just about free and clear." Linda even tries to intervene in the talks between Willy and Ben. She isn't charmed to see Ben in the first place and even less enthralled with his proposition that Willy head for Alaska. With untypical common sense, she tries to caution Willy that he's got a "beautiful job" and is "doing well enough" already. The stage directions note that Linda is "frightened of Ben" as she retorts: "Don't say those things to him! Enough to be happy right here, right now." Then she turns to Willy and tries the ultimate softening of the quest mania: "Why must everybody conquer the world?" (85).

Fully delineated characters like Ma Joad and Linda Loman are rare but significant women's voices—at least as written from the male perspective—during the first few decades on the road. More recently, road narratives by women, African Americans, and Native Americans have significantly revised many of the traditionally male-dominated conventions and values of the genre. Women and minority authors have brought to the road a new range of heroes who rechart the course.

In Hilma Wolitzer's *Hearts*, a 26-year-old widow, Linda Reismann, and her stepdaughter, Robin, travel from New Jersey to California. Linda had been married only six weeks when her husband, Wright, died unexpectedly. As the book opens, she and Robin take to the road to deliver Wright's ashes to his family and to find a home for Robin. The novel chronicles as well the inner journey of these two women who experience the country together and, in the process, develop a remarkable relationship. What had begun as a collision of estranged driver and passenger develops into an internalized quest of growing together. Again, many conventions of the American highway create the narrative pattern. Just after Wright's death, Linda's sense of being alone is mirrored in the isolation of driving. On her trip to the hospital, the first she had made alone in heavy traffic, she drives very slowly, "braking every few hundred yards whether she had to or not, and honking warnings at cars and trucks that approached in the adjacent lanes." She wonders as other drivers honk back or make profane gestures in her direction whether she was supposed to respond according to "some unwritten code of the road" (4). With so little experience as a driver, Linda sees their cross-country trip as a challenge and a ritual. In a dramatic revision of male road symbols, she thinks of driving as a form of dancing and suspects there must be "a kind of music that everyone else heard and drove to." Linda envies the ability of these strangers to tune into what seemed to be an "inner song" with its own "flawless" rhythm (29).

Linda and Robin take many precautions. At first, they plan to follow Interstate 80 all the way through, because "if you don't get off, you can't get lost." Along that straight horizontal line they "would shoot across America like a guided missile, without seeing anything of beauty or interest." In the meantime, Linda reads on the map "wonderful names of cities she'd never visited: Sandusky, Toledo, Elkhart" and decides "they were going to see the country" after all (43). Their revised plan includes taking their time, traveling by daylight only, and stopping as soon as they tired. Shortly into the trip, Linda and Robin come to understand that they don't really know each other, and that their only mutual concern was the husband-father whose ashes they carried across the country. Mile after mile they struggle through an embattled relationship, peaking in a marathon of ignoring each other that is broken only when Linda gives in: "It was thrilling to speak again," she recalls, "like opening one's body willingly to love. Not really giving in at all" (204). Slowly they share more secrets from their past lives and they become receptive to each other's feelings as the plot moves forward to its culmination in California. Ultimately, the real journey of *Hearts* is the two women moving toward each other.

With many similarities to the journey of developing relationships in *Hearts*, Anne Roiphe's *Long Division* presents Emily Brimberg Johnson and her ten-year-old daughter, Sarah, who travel across the country to get a divorce. Sarah is a brooding, sullen TV addict who takes little interest in the landscape or the people and events they meet. With disarming candor, Emily describes their encounters with religious fanatics, seedy characters, and a bizarre group of seniors who hold them captive in Settlement Tomorrow. Little impresses Sarah—even when she nearly falls into a vat of chocolate in Hershey, Pennsylvania—until she is kidnapped by a band of gypsies who show her there is life after television. Elusive but unmistakable freedom hovers over this trip, for the two women come to understand that they are free to resettle anywhere they please. Emily recalls her immigrant grandparents for whom New York was the first stop and asks "why not move like the sediment in the bottle down to the bottom, or sideways, or crooked?" (13). She finds new courage behind the wheel: "By myself, I could forge across the country and, like my grandparents, I would learn to disconnect the past from the present, so the double albatross of loss and grief would fall from my neck when at last, like the ancient mariner, I had suffered enough" (118). In the West, Emily's metaphor for her quest is the Jews' wandering in the desert: "As we drove, a rage boiled inside of me—one Jewish girl from the Bronx divorced by an artist-fellow does not a diaspora make. And yet I seethed. I felt like Deborah, wise prophet, judge of sin, moral conscience of her time." She wonders at the same time, if she too is doomed to wander in a never ending exile.

The liberation at the end of *Long Division* is two-fold. Emily and Sarah don't climb mountains, slay dragons, or find the Promised Land. Repeatedly, however, they "learn something to make the trip worth-while" and, in the process, deepen and expand their understanding of each other. Encounters with fanatics and lechers teach Emily toughness.

At Madonna of the Trail they pay tribute to the women who settled the West and spread civilization. They avoid highways, deciding to drive instead on back roads where they can take their time and accumulate memories. The trip also makes it possible for mother and daughter to grieve together, and the ending breaks off with deliberately understated hope for the future of their new relationship.

Like *Hearts* and *Long Division*, Mona Simpson's *Anywhere But Here* is also about an embattled relationship between a mother and her daughter. Simpson presents their trip West as well as an inner journey that reshapes the quest in significant ways. Ann August and her mother, Adele, drive from Bay City, Wisconsin, to Hollywood in search of adventure and a better life. Ann tells most of the story with occasional shifts to the perspective of her aunt, Carol, or her grandmother, Lillian. Most of the book is about Ann's growing up in Wisconsin, her journey with her mother to California, and their life in and around Beverly Hills. The story is mostly reminiscence and observation; the developing relationship between mother and daughter is the central theme, and driving is everywhere the controlling metaphor and the operative myth.

Anywhere But Here is about movement itself and perpetually leaving in order to stay in motion. Longing to escape the suffocation of small-town life in the Midwest, Adele seeks the good life, fame, fortune, and recognition on the West Coast. Above all, she wants Ann to live with "the very best" (365) rather than risk becoming "a poor nothing girl in a factory town in the midwest" (530). Adele's compulsion keeps her behind the wheel of her white Continental where she is constantly searching, running away, leaving something or someone. Simpson takes her title from a famous passage by Emerson about the follies of travelers: "There are three wants which can never be satisfied: that of the rich wanting more, that of the sick wanting something different, and that of the traveler, who says 'Anywhere but here.'" (This is the same Emerson who called traveling "the fool's paradise" and who proclaimed with confidence "my giant goes with me wherever I am.") *Anywhere But Here* exploits the richness of America's metaphor of motion but warns also of its limitations and dangers. Movement for its own sake—with all its leavings and longings—is both celebrated and transcended. Adele embodies manic restlessness, whereas Ann is both a product of the myth and reroutes the quests in her own way.

When we first meet Adele and Ann, they are in motion, headed West. They plan their trip by reading magazines and using Ted's (Adele's soon-to-be-estranged husband's) credit card. They stay at Travel Lodges and eat long, elaborate meals, ritualizing the driving, the shopping trips, and their own ubiquitous quarrels. Adele is in a perpetual motion of driving, talking, planning; Ann seeks fresh air and is all expectation. Mostly they are in combat with the world and each other. When they aren't speaking to each other, Adele tells her daughter, "Get out, then," as she gently pushes her out of the car and drives away, leaving her alone to at first explore and later cry. Adele always comes back to pick her up, however, in a ritual reenactment of what would become their modus operandi and the book's central metaphors of leaving and longing. Repeatedly, Adele and Ann are separated and reunited in the rhythm of their combat: "It did something for my mother, every time she let me off on the highway and then came back . . . she'd be nodding, grateful-looking, as if we had another chance, as if something had been washed out of her" (19).

Everywhere in the book, driving is a metaphor for the constant motion of their lives. The long drive to California is the dominant quest of the story, and Adele's white Continental is their home on the highway, a sanctuary in times of uncertainty or confrontation. Many of Ann's earliest memories recall drives in and around Bay City or of the times her mother drove her to the orphanage and told her "this is where you'll end up if I can't make you mind" (320). Driving not only mirrors Adele's restless urges but also provides the times when she and Ann are most alive. In their motel rituals, looking for a house together, or always spending more than they can afford, mother and daughter create a new relationship. When they call grandma and she asks what they're doing, Ann responds, "I don't know. Nothing much. Driving" (22). Their relationship develops further in a succession of shorter trips, like the jaunts to dozens of Red Owl food stores trying to get a bag with a lucky letter for a contest. Ann daydreams about a fantasy trip to Disneyland with her mother and father, "in our old brown car, with rounded feathers, floating down an old canal" (225). Adele spends so much time behind the wheel that Ann begins to equate her mother's esteem with her driving style: "Sometimes I really liked my mother. She drove easily, with one hand, as she pumped the gas with the toe of her high-heeled shoe. We looped on the freeway ramps smoothly."

Adele has the manic qualities of Dean Moriarity, Ann the patient rebelliousness of Huck Finn. Although they are in perpetual motion, the emphasis is on their relationship far more than on goals they seek. Even Adele's desire to hit it big for Ann in Hollywood is overshadowed by what Kolodny calls a woman's desire for relationships and stability. Adele's is the single-minded pursuit of class, recognition, and whatever they can't afford. She chases recognition, seeks escape, and threatens suicide when it won't work. Ann is in a love-hate relationship with her mother and these same myths. She admires her mother's savvy and is lured to some of the same goals. Somehow, though Ann transcends it all and survives, she benefits from all her mother wants for her and yet manages not to get devoured by it. With Ann it's as if all the leavings and the chasings and the cravings can be set aside. During one of Ann's visits from college, when they discuss growing up, and aging, the whole process is so painful that for once they can't get in the car, hit the accelerator and laugh it off. Instead, their exchanges sharpen. "I feel like you're always leaving," Adele says—to which Ann responds, "That's what kids do, they leave." Finally, Ann the narrator adds the telling comment that her mother might not even understand: "I only left home once and that was years ago" (502). Home for Ann was always back in Wisconsin in the house on Lime Kiln Road. It was the house Adele always wanted to leave but which for Ann was "the particular place we were meant to be" (315). In spite of, or perhaps because of, her mother's wanderlust, a part of Ann did stay there forever, and like the nineteenth-century women pioneers—she learned to carry that home with her wherever she went.

These three pairs of mother-daughter heroines draw from and contribute to American road genre memory. Linda and Robin, Emily and Sarah, Adele and Ann find kindred spirits in the numerous neglected narratives by American women of the past two hundred years who show less need to keep moving, or to conquer the unknown than their male counterparts. As Kolodny demonstrates, the women searched for not more and ever new territories to conquer, but a place "in which to continue and even hollow the past" (*The Land Before Her* 11). The women, therefore, "transferred many more of the tokens of prior homes and earlier gardens than male migration patterns allowed." Without leisure time for exploration or even to enjoy her own garden, the pioneer woman mastered "defiant survival" and learned to carry her own roots with her wherever she was forced to move (35). Ann Armstrong's concern with home in *Anywhere But Here* is prefigured repeatedly in what Kolodny calls "metaphors of intimacy" that permeate narratives of the 19th century. This is not to say that women's and men's metaphors on the road were always dramatically opposed, but rather that the fantasies of women were adjustments to the male-oriented patterns that had come to be associated with speed, power, and goal orientation.

American road narratives by women slow the pace, rechart the itineraries, and reassess the goals within the conventions of the typical road quest. Just as the domestic novel of western relocation presented images of the city to "evade" certain consequences of urbanization (Kolodny, *The Land Before Her* 173), so also women on the road hoped to evade some of the less appealing dimensions of the highway hero's single-minded, self-centered and exploitative frenzy. Women bring a calming influence to the American road. With not as many highs to seek and maintain, the accompanying lows are modulated. The quest is not so manic, the goals are more realistic, and the state of mind is more even. In travel narratives from the 19th century to present American road narratives, women have attempted to correct what they felt was going wrong with the quest. Their imagery was meant to counter what they felt was misguided in the male fantasies. Kolodny shows that women often rejected further moves west not because they feared the perils of the wilderness, but because "irrevocable separation from friends and family wasn't worth it" (*The Land Before Her* 93). In American road narratives by and about women there is generally also less pervasive sadness. There isn't as much of Sal Paradise's depression, Least Heat Moon's melancholy, Pirsig's protagonist's struggles, or the anguished self-pity expressed in *A Good Day To Die*.

When women go on the road or write road novels, the recorded experiences and the literary conventions change significantly. The same is true in road experiences where many African-Americans, Native Americans, and other minorities have different road stories to tell, and they thus modify the conventions of the road quest to reflect very different perspectives. Because many conventional road heroes are outsiders politically or socially, the genre has developed against the grain of dominant cultural norms. This critique of the status quo, however, is even more apparent when members of minority cultures invite readers to redefine personal and national goals. As people previously excluded or ignored enter the community of fellow travelers, it is easier to observe why certain genre conventions developed and how those patterns can be modified to different ends.

African Americans have seldom felt safe traveling long distances on American highways. Problems with everything from accommodations and restaurants to law officers and mechanics have been acute. John A. Williams's *This is My Country Too* outlines some of these dangers and illustrates as well several ways in which the African American road quester alters sharply the shape of the journey. Williams traveled the country for four months over 15,000 miles in 40 states. He drove through New England first and then flew to Detroit where he purchased a new car for the journey into the South, out West, and then back home. He was on assignment for *Holiday* magazine, investigating the political and racial climate in 1963. The book followed the magazine articles by almost a year and records his search for America, particularly what he "had learned of America as a Black American."

An accomplished writer and storyteller, Williams is also a keen historian and a tough political observer. He chooses the road experience and the road quest genre for predictable reasons: the journey gets him out where people live, where he can hear and feel their opinions and values. He also feels "the freedom to go" born within him: "I never feel as good as when I am pointing myself away from where I've *been*" (12). His road journey begins in Syracuse, where he is first attracted to speed, the power behind the wheel, and what he calls "the ground-level height of Everyman's automated existence" (86). He accepts the assignment, apprehensive about road travel as an African American, but intrigued by the writing challenge and the "wild, joyous feeling" awaiting him with all that horsepower in "the land of big sky" (92). Here the book's use of predictable road genre conventions ends, however, as Williams alters the patterns and emphasis for his own needs.

For the African American on the highway, the road is not always open and dangers cannot be for long overlooked. "I do not believe white travelers have any idea of how much nerve and courage it requires for a Negro to drive coast to coast in America," Williams notes. "Nerve, courage, and great deal of luck" (22). African Americans do travel and do write about traveling, but not usually for the same reasons and with none of the reckless abandon of the white male on a quest for self-discovery. Williams takes with him a list of places in America where African Americans can stay without being "embarrassed, insulted, or worse." He speaks of the need in the South to always "remember where you are," recalling that Northern Negroes traveling in the South would wear a chauffeur's cap or at least have one on the seat. They would often pretend they were delivering their car for white folks and never feel safe until with friends in a Negro neighborhood. An African American isn't supposed to own anything, Williams notes, and, if he does, he's seen as a thief. Everywhere he has to watch for traffic police and subtle Jim Crow rules of movement in and around public places, and he endures the "insults of clerks, bellboys, attendants, cops, and strangers in passing cars" (138). The "unforgivable sin," he learns, would be at any given time to relax and forget to keep his mind on danger (64). Not only does he encounter overt threats and racial slurs, but even where he is accepted, there are clear expectations about the limits beyond which his observations cannot range and prescribed sets of topics he is supposed to be concerned about. Even well-intentioned people force him into a box, assuming he is interested only in civil rights. Along the way he has to pick his spots, people, and situations carefully; he regularly "expects to be rebuffed" and worries about traveling alone. "People have a way of disappearing on the road" he is told (6). Finding a meal can be a struggle, car trouble is an occasion for harassment, and everywhere people stare.

This constant presence of danger alters the road subjects Williams discusses and reshapes the nature of his quest. In discussions that are more history lessons and cultural analysis than personal narrative, he analyzes the accomplishments of his ancestors at Tuskeegee, Martin Luther King's March on Washington, and the militaristic mania for football in the South. In addition to carrying out his professional assignment as historian and commentator on life in America in the year John F. Kenndy was assassinated, Williams also notices the people and events that go unmentioned in the usual road journey. He talks for example, to old black men and women along the road and listens in ways even Whitman's "lesson of reception" would miss. The caution he must remember to feel everywhere prohibits the freedom of movement available to the conventional road quester, but the same restrictions also enhance his acute sense of freedom, his view of the automobile as both protection and danger, and his dedication to life on the edge. The car is protection for African Americans traveling through real or trumped-up legal problems that bring down the law. Everywhere he faces the threat of lynching or beatings from the night riders. Rather than retreat, however, Williams drives into the danger. Advised to take a less dangerous route, he nonetheless wants to "drive the cliff edge" in order "to live with myself and in order to overcome the shame I suddenly felt to confess my tiredness, my tension," to the white man (80). Danger thus restricts and reshapes Williams's experiences and leads him to modify road genre conventions.

This Is My Country Too changes the way of telling road stories by using dream sequences and internalizing the physical journey. After every reported lynching, Williams pictures himself in a custom-built car with friends heading south. The car is bulletproof, equipped with machine guns and a supercharged engine and they feel "nothing on the road could catch us" (57). At another point he feels the power of each horse under the hood and imagines that with enough speed he can touch the sun. He awakens from every dream, however, and returns from every imagined road to get back in step everyday events once more. Reminded of the need to come back from the dream, Williams recalls "how lonely and even ugly is the craft of writing" (154) and sets out to interpret and communicate his experiences in ways his readers can understand. Eventually, all the road trappings come together—his quest, the driving, the people he met, the dangers avoided and confronted, the political commentary, his dreams—in an assessment that turns the journey inward. Concluding that there is a "great emptiness" as well as a growing alienation about who we are as a nation and where we are going, on returning home he emphasizes the good will as well as the anger he saw in people. After much hostile mail following the publication of his *Holiday* articles, however, Williams feels that many Americans are "evil in the primitive, possessive, and destructive sense," a violent people who "defied natural laws of territory and possession" to all but eliminate the American Indian. His resolution is deliberately ambiguous as his disgust about bigotry, fundamentalist righteousness, and hypocrisy is accompanied by the hope that the search will go on. The point of the quest, he decides, is not to observe ancient temples or monuments but to bring American ideals to realization. Though too few people pursue this search, he warns, the road continues to symbolize the movement and energy of "living up to the ideals we have set for ourselves" (162). For Williams, the dangers of the road and the isolation of the writing process paradoxically immerse him in community not only with the people and places he meets but with his African American ancestors who tried long ago to help America "sing its greatest songs." *This Is My Country Too* modifies many of the genre's conventions in the direction of the journeys toward freedom found in the spirituals, slave narratives, and the poetry of the oral tradition. In the process of stretching the genre, Williams renegotiates cultural values of the 1960s and speaks to us about problems we still face thirty years later.

For reasons Williams suggests, the automobile journey has not figured prominently in African American literature. Classic works by Ralph Ellison, Richard Wright, and Toni Cade Bambara feature travel, but the vehicles are usually public transportation. Many road authors from Steinbeck to Least Heat Moon discuss civil rights issues and the lives of blacks in America, and visitors from other countries have noted the wide gap between reality and promise in America's treatment of cultural diversity. Only one additional full-length road narrative, however, features African American automobile travelers, and that is one of the rare large-group trips in the genre. In *Checking It Out: Some Lower East Side Kids Discover the Rest of America*, Michelle Cole and Stuart Black take 50 kids in several vans on a six-week cross-country trip to see America. Cole and Black are teachers who want to share their view of the country with the kids, while the kids lend their perspective in a "reciprocal education pact." They leave New York in mid-summer for California via Chicago and points in between. The journey begins in the Lower Eastside Action Project (LEAP): "In a cold storefront with no recreational facilities and no Monopoly games and no money for trips or baseball leagues or camp or sometimes even coffee, we came together with thirty-five kids to share our sense of optimism with their astounding and almost miraculous ability to survive" (x). The idea is to show the kids the country they couldn't otherwise see; in reality, the kids opened up much the authors would never find.

From the start, the kids see through veneer culture; they aren't impressed by college campuses, for example, where they see middle-class blacks trying to act like street people as well as SEEK and Upward Bound students who had "nothing but complaints about being segregated off from the rest of the students, about being treated 'specially,' about campus roles and uncaring professors and irrelevant classes" (212). They visit so many off-limit places, the authors consider writing "a Mobil Ghetto Guide for families like ours driving across the country" (45). *Checking It Out* is unconventional as well because the travelers become the objects of attention as the folks along the way gawk. Tired of congestion and false attention, the kids discover at last in North Dakota "a darkness New York never sees, a quiet it never hears, a loneliness it would love" (103). It's as if the New York experience took many miles to wear off, because this road journey never really goes into full swing until they hit the Northern Plains: "The trip has just opened up for us. 'America' started in Fargo. We feel open, land and space for all, the kids now more consistently into the trip. The need to get high is just about dead. The trip is getting us all high" (108). Dazzled by the country's size, the "thick, happy trees," and the overwhelming Oregon coast, the kids observe changes in themselves and begin to drop what Cole and Black call their "lifetime of defenses." The spontaneity of their travel makes *Life* magazine's plans to photograph the trip an imposition: "We didn't have every day charted out. That bothered them" (187). Above all, these road questers don't want to be overprogrammed. "'Just' traveling had its own message," they conclude (187).

Checking It Out includes a wide variety of experiences, consider-able dialogue, and captivating *cinema verite* photos and reads like an insider's travel diary of a journey that very few Americans could ever take. Cole summarizes how the trip affected her: "Living in the 'social problem' in New York had made my lifestyle much like the kids'. I lived from day to day, crisis to crisis. But the cross-country trip returned me to my former state of 'overall consciousness.' The kids had nothing to 'return to': They were still living day to day." Traveling underscores Cole's analysis of the differences between her own socio-economic position and that of her students: "They live in New York, and from that base they are visitors to San Francisco. I live in the United States and reside in New York. That's a big difference" (208). Because it is a multicultural experience compressed into six short weeks, *Checking It Out* communicates an urgency about the group's reentry into the problems they left behind. Through the kids' eyes, Cole and Black invite readers to reconsider America's commitment to diversity, fairness, and equal rights.

The journey motif has also been a part of Native American storytelling for centuries. Most tribes moved in circles, however, rather than in the linear quest pattern of later road narratives; for native Americans, travel was more a collective ritual than an individualist quest. Standing Bear observed that the white man moves not as a sacred ritual of interaction with space but because he is not connected with true American roots. Movement for European Americans was born of separation; the native American, on the other hand, was caretaker of the earth, not so restless, and not so intent on conquering space, speed, and progress. Without romanticizing, it is fair to expect few if any Native American writers to be attracted to the road narrative genre unless it is to undermine or parody many of its conventions.

David Seals's *The Powwow Highway* exploits road narrative conventions to reconnect contemporary Native American characters with their own heritage while demythologizing romantic stereotypes and debunking narrow audience expectations with mock epic zest. Seals wraps his story in elaborate road icons. Chapter numbers are illustrated with highway signs. The major characters embark on a pilgrimage, orchestrate high-speed chase scenes, and soak up elaborate Western scenery. The narrator describes his tale as "the story of a machine and of the people who made a story of its movements" (vii). In a mock-epic tone, the events of the journey are outlandish and everything is open to parody: sociological analysis, radical chic cocktail-party conversation, and even stereotypical Indian wisdom. At the same time, the narrator challenges his readers: "Oh, Whitman, get yer cryptic shit together and cut out this reason hogwash! It gums up the story" (159). In *The Nation,* Seals has objected to critical focus on what he calls the new Custerism or the stereotypical reduction of the complexity of native American life to a packageable Hollywood image. In *The Powwow Highway*, he attacks that commercialized sentimentality by setting in place recognizable road motifs and then providing correctives to the pattern through irony and mock-epic commentary.

Seals's plot is vintage road quest. Philbert Bono and Buddy Red Bird set out to free Buddy's sister from prison. At the same time, Philbert immerses himself in an ancient warrior's journey to rediscover his heritage. Their vehicle is an old "shit-brown" Buick, Philbert's warrior pony which he names "Protector." During their picaresque adventures, they free Bonnie Red Bird and Philbert rides Protector into a past of legends, myths, and "sweet medicine." In the process, Philbert overcomes both Buddy's skepticism and the narrator's mock-optimism to emerge as an unlikely hero who is healed and reunited with his inner being. Seals places his story along Interstate 25 from Montana toward New Mexico, where movement is on two plains: through the contemporary scene of former AIM activists and government-manipulated reservation life and through the past of Philbert's visions of ancient warriors and sacred rituals. Pointed descriptions of the underbelly of the contemporary scene serve to at once de-romanticize the treatment of Native American life and provide a narrative frame within which Philbert's visions and fantasies can flourish. Along "the endless wanderings of the Powwow Highway," Philbert unites with his ancestors to become "a trickle on an ancient river" (vii). In this quest, community rather than individual heroism is the goal: "Like all the refugees of the Powwow Highway, they had friends in just about every reservation in the country" in a network of "such haphazard and chaotic symmetry that the FBI spent millions of dollars a year worrying about it" (139).

The mythic dimensions of *The Powwow Highway* flourish in Philbert's dreams and in his response to the landscape. Trying to be a warrior with his mind on myths, Philbert doesn't fully understand what he has missed. He learns his Indian name over the CB radio, takes a new interest in powwows and the history of the badlands, wades with Buddy into the water to chant, and looks deeper into national monuments where he sees himself in a "sweat hut of the old days." Irreverently, the narrator pokes fun at Philbert's desire to ride with the hum of his pony and the flow of the land into "these many absolute moments of purity that only occasionally visit other lesser men" (5).

Seals's mock epic tone explodes myths about "noble savages," the desire for unity among tribes, America's pilgrim quest, and the goals of American business. Episodes accumulate into a series of battles, fairy tale quests, and what Philbert calls "stories that tell of problems and of how the old ones handled the problems" (203).

In a book dominated by wry commentary and ironic overtones, Philbert triumphs through determination and because "he was too stupid to know what was futile" (180). These two unlikely heroes travel through contemporary America "above it all, apart from it all," and only Philbert's sense of history saves them: "Secretly desperate to be a part of it all, and yet openly incapable of being anything but above it, they sank with scorn to be below it all. They did not belong, they could not accept it, they could not understand it." Like many drop outs and counter-cultural road questers, they survive by making fun of what they rejected: "It was the way of all disenfranchised folk who were only tributaries to the great mainstream" (59). Philbert thrives by rediscovering the ancient native-American sense of memory which sees past events as present realities. Whereas the white man hated history which he saw as past, Philbert feels the sorrows of Little Wolf in a clump of dirt, hears the great buffalo herd still on the plains, and becomes one with the ancient spirits who are now "the stuff of the soil and stones" (180). Like Williams in *This Is My Country Too* and the women who have moved into the driver's seat, Seals uses road narrative conventions to call into question many American myths and cultural values.

Throughout its history, the American road narrative has been sensitive to the nation's multicultural heritage. Henry Miller reminds us that our true national history is in the ancient Southwest, while Jim Harrison celebrates Chief Joseph and the Nez Percé. Exploration of the national myths about minorities is also a major part of Dayton Duncan's demythologizing or William Least Heat Moon's discovery of his heritage in *Blue Highways*. American minorities do not generally share, however, the middle-class white male's fascination with the open road and hence have come to the genre later and often with different purposes. The road may still have a lure, but it isn't always "open," the nature of heroism changes, and the people and experiences related along the way take on new dimensions. Authors modify narrative perspective as well as the history remembered, and different kinds of relationships develop with people missing in earlier road stories. Finally, the power and speed of the car itself doesn't hold the same attraction it had for white males still exploring the residual frontier.

In spite of a few notable exceptions, America's minority authors still are not taking to the road in big numbers. The reasons are no doubt obvious, as we have lived through decades of progress and backlash against the civil rights Williams and others sought. On the other hand, three books of the late 1980s reflect ways in which women continue to reshape the road genre. Michelle Carter's *In Other Days When Going Home* (1987) expresses 18-year-old Annie's desire to leave home and join the male outside world "where people lived by moving, not standing still" (65). Her explorations take her from San Francisco to Cape Cod with highway songs and naive hopes ringing in her ear. Not surprisingly, however, Annie asks all the wrong questions and discovers in the end there is "no highway song for me" (257). "It's not there for us," a friend finally tells her: "The streets are all about power, Annie, and the closest we can get is the back of a motorcycle and what they offer us in exchange for spreading our legs" (205). Annie's journey celebrates, in her words, "what I knew different now." In "a world full of men," she doesn't turn out to be "the kind of strong" she wanted to be. Modifying the conventions of the road quest, she does have the last word on what counts: "Those things I saw while waiting were more important than what it was like to leave. What mattered most was my having been there, and then, even more, my having gone" (257).

The next year Mary Morris's *Nothing to Declare: Memoirs of a Woman Traveling Alone* confronts the road's gender barriers head on. With what she calls "a terrible feeling of isolation and a growing belief that America had become a foreign land" (4), Morris travels from Chicago to Mexico to search for connections and to "make sense" again. Conventionally she eschews maps and the company of others, preferring to travel alone and trust her own instincts. Seeing herself as "an adventurer, a pioneer, a woman hero" (76), Morris structures the narrative as a loosely chronological collage of essays juxtaposing reportorial distance, essay commentary, and dream sequences. "Women who travel as I travel," she notes, "are dreamers" who live lives of "endless possibility." Nostalgia has no place in such forward motion that reaches "a kind of high, a somewhat altered state of consciousness" (164) wherein the outward journey sets in motion "another journey inside my head." *Nothing to Declare* uses escapist road conventions to explore how a woman can unlearn the lessons of false dependence on a man and other limiting roles society offers. Morris finds many restrictions not impinging on her male road counterparts, but she also enjoys discovering "how easy it was to be with myself" (243). In her dreams she is a "warrior," an explorer, "an interpreter of magical signs." For Morris, the journey and the telling of the story merge: "While the journey is on buses and across land, I begin another journey inside my head, a journey of memory and sensation, of past merging with present, of time growing insignificant" (164).

In a 1989 road novel, *The Widows' Adventures* Charles Dickinson turns the highway quest narrative frame to seriocomic and bittersweet commentary on aging in America. Two sisters travel from Chicago to California to see relatives. Conventional patterns give way early in this story of Helene who is blind and drives the car with the front-seat guidance of her sister Ira who can't drive at all. They are in motion only between midnight and 4:00 a.m. at low speeds and on back roads. "Fear of the unexpected" is what Ira both "desired and feared most from this trip," where it's "you and me bickering across America" (150). Their adventures are enormously funny as the two women travel with 120 cans of beer and $12,000 in twenty-dollar bills. Dickinson uses multiple perspective as Helene and Ira alternately tell their stories undaunted by road restrictions. In the trappings of a Westward quest, a highway vacation, and a visit to relatives, these widows from the outset are after something bigger. While Ira tells everyone including Helene that it's just a brief trip to get away, from the start she doesn't ever want to go back home. These are unswerving women on the road: "We're further west than anybody else we know," they proclaim at the end. As their journey has shown, however, it might not matter at any time where they are: "We have skipped away before; we could do it again" (375). Dickinson convinces us they could and would.

Road narratives by and about women and non-white males dramatize what is alluring about the genre on the whole: getting away, staying away, and searching have the effect of questioning the status quo. From Whitman to the present, the road has invited travelers and readers alike to challenge norms and values, to ask new questions and to make an impact upon reentry. Women, African Americans, and Native Americans have traveled the literary highways for over five decades. Culturally diverse road protagonists in the future are likely to continue modifying crucial elements of the road genre. With Ma Joad, they know that straight lines get "jerky" finding their way back into "the flow." They are not likely to be caught up in Sal Paradise's speed or Willy Loman's bravado. They may ride Philbert Bono's sacred pony looking for his "sweet medicine." They will probably identify with John A. Williams's internalized journey toward making the promises come true. Though some may be candidates for Maria Wyeth's frustrating search, many will ride with Linda Reismann, Emily Brimberg Johnson, and Ann Armstrong who revise as much as they relive the past. However much the American road narrative is likely to remain dominated by the white male experience, women and minority authors are planning different kinds of itineraries. Alongside such otherwise different models as Black Elk and Sissy Hankshaw, they are following the circles to what is within, and in the process, putting new kinds of lines on the map.

8

Reentry and the Road Mythos

In *The Hero with a Thousand Faces* Joseph Campbell describes the necessity of the hero's return in the completed cycle of the monomyth:

> When the hero-quest has been accomplished, the adventurer still must return with his life-transmitting trophy. The full-round, the norm of the monomyth, requires that the hero shall now begin the labor of bringing the runes of wisdom . . . back into the kingdom of humanity, where the boon may rebound to the renewing of the community, the nation, the planet, or the ten thousand worlds. (193)

The road journey requires coming home as well, though the inevitable return voyage and experience of reentry are often fraught with problems. The hero's reluctance to return is increased by the lure of continued adventure, visionary insight, or the modern automotive equivalent of what Campbell calls the bliss of the deep abode. To restore equilibrium and keep the mythic cycle going, to satisfy the curiosity and jealousy felt back home about those who leave, and to complete the journey in the telling of the story, the hero must return—even if at times "the world may have to come and get him" (207).

Most of the motivation for a road journey is spent on the going forth, the search for new experiences, people, and places. The freshness, excitement, and challenge of pursuing a goal are lost or diminished on the trip back: sometimes faster, sometimes duller, mostly less adventuresome, often anticlimactic, and always problematic. Behind the wheel of a car, finding the way home no longer means relocating the ancient trail in the forest. More than likely, modern roads and detailed maps increase the boredom of the return trip, now missing the fresh wonder of the initial quest. Some avoid possible monotony by choosing an alternate path home, plotting out a circular journey, or avoiding preplanning or maps of all sorts. No matter the itinerary, there comes a time when the traveler senses that the going forth is over and the heading back home must begin. Dayton Duncan likens this realization to the closing of the frontier when the traveler had to turn back and face that our myths of success and progress could not be expressed forever in images of moving on. Just as crucial a part of the quest motif, the turning back is what Duncan calls "a new and different national experience." In one sense, heading home means that the trip is over and the innocence of exploration on the outbound road is lost. At the same time, however, being homeward bound brings new and indispensable insights that were unavailable earlier. On the way home, the hero is more experienced and wiser, and what had been boundless enthusiasm gives way to a measured and more mature judgment.

In their research on the pilgrimage as a liminoid phenomenon, Victor Turner and Edith Turner describe the route of the religious journey as a series of "overlapping, interpenetrating ellipses" with the shrine at the center of the overlap (22). The route to the shrine traditionally includes numerous devotional stops and places designated for penance and preparation for reaching the goal. On the way back, however, the pilgrim wants to relax, reap the benefits taken away from the shrine, and get home as fast as possible. Therefore, even if those returning choose the same physical route home, psychologically the way home differs significantly from the path of the quest. The ellipse rather than the straight line captures this real or psychological difference between going out and coming back. Life on the road is not always a pilgrimage, of course, but the pilgrimage system provides a helpful gloss on the rituals of routing and the narrative patterns used in telling the story.

The dilemma of turning back provides a focal point of theme, character development and narrative structure in the literature of the highway. In *On The Road*, a return route is never at issue since neither Dean nor Sal after him express any desire to return anywhere. Instead of heading home with the wisdom of the journey, Sal is what Joseph Allen Boone calls the prototypical "social outcast whose true self can only exist *outside* the parameters of his culture, in a 'wild zone' analogous to . . . the moors in *Wuthering Heights*" (229). Boone compares these wild zones to moments of rebirth that reject the road home to the status quo. In the exceptions that prove the rule, in four other types of narrative patterns. In *Zen and the Art of Motorcycle Maintenance*, the entire trip is a moving outward toward discovery; once the narrator's synthesis of opposites is reached, the arrival home is instantaneous. Whitman's invitation to "come along with me" is, indeed, intended to last beyond the text. In *The Widows' Adventures*, Helene and Ira remain in California. Several narratives end with explosions that allow no choice: mass destruction at *Seaview,* a suicidal crash in *Travesty*, and the killing of the protagonists in *Easy Rider*. A more typical pattern approximating the pilgrimage ellipse is repeated in Least Heat Moon's circular route following the coming of spring in *Blue Highways.*

The choices of where, when, and why to turn back are crucial factors shaping the quest. Some head home following a clear plan, others by necessity and still others try to keep going. With a sense of mission completed, many road heroes are eager to get home. Floorboard George has completed his pilgrimage to honor the Big Bopper (*Not Fade Away*). Pirsig's narrator has reconceptualized Western philosophy and reemerged as a whole person. Others long to return to a lost place: Ann Armstrong recalls a particular house in Wisconsin, Henry Miller praises the ancient Southwest, and Dayton Duncan regrets the loss of a rich Native American heritage that has been corrupted by conquest. In most road narratives, the realization hits early, nonetheless, that for a variety of reasons going back home will be a painful necessity. In the pattern of English Romantic odes, some drivers seek to make their visionary insights permanent only to realize that they can't live in a car or stay forever in motion. Just as the characters on John Keats's Grecian urn are not living or breathing, so also the hitch-hikers picked up and soon dropped off along the road continue to live only in memory. Robert Frost's birches bend back to earth, Dorothy longs for Kansas in *The Wizard of Oz.* Adam and Eve accept God's prevenient grace and Michael's instruction and go their "solitary way" back into the garden to toil and sweat and to grow in regenerate experience in Milton's *Paradise Lost.* Many road narratives stop before the return trip is completed and the difficulties of reentry begin; others make the arrival home a central ingredient of the plot. Most frustrating for protagonists is coming home to find out that no one really wants to hear about the trip.

The most dispiriting problem of reentry is the realization that others don't care about, understand, or appreciate hearing or reading about one's travels. In *Checking It Out,* Cole and Black call this challenge the coming home problem and carry the burden for the kids in their charge who arrive home pumped up about their trip and eager to tell others about their experiences. The question "How was your trip," they warn, is "synonymous with the casual 'how are you?' Neither of these questions wants an answer" (309). On the way back, they consider how experiences on the road would disrupt the equilibrium they had with family and friends who might actually try to return them to a "pre-trip state." Equally frustrating is the feeling after only two days home that they had never been away at all. The downside of reentry brings, however, positive effects as well. Having no one back home who will listen to stories about the trip increases the motivation for writing a narrative that will create its own audience. A failed quest may even prompt a writer to make it all come out right in the narrative reconstruction. Conversely, a successful trip eagerly awaited by folks back home brings its own rewards and diminishes the motivation or urgency directed to the writing process.

Anticipation of reentry is part of an audience's expectations for road narratives. Even in the action of holding a book physically, readers have a sense of when they are going to run out of pages. Moreover, genre conventions develop predictable patterns of reentry, depending on whether the narrative is fiction or nonfiction. In road novels, a narrator-participant generally has the last word in an epilogue or short concluding chapter. In *Anywhere But Here*, Adele Armstrong makes judgments about her daughter in a concluding monologue. The protagonist-narrator of *A Good Day to Die* interprets the futility of the failed climax. Huck Finn resolves to "light out again." Humbert speculates on the immortality of his book in *Lolita*. Omniscient nonparticipant narrators generally provide a final assessment of their protagonists' educative experiences as in *Midnight Cowboy, Hearts*, and *Long Division*. In *Not Fade Away*, Floorboard George's story is framed in an opening and conclusion told by an auditor who listens to, and speculates about, the curious storyteller. Most of *Seaview* is told by an omniscient non-participant, but the concluding chapter is an epilogue spoken by Bob White about the home-truth of being present in everything one does. In nonfiction road journeys, reentry often includes the narrator's interpretation of the trip's significance. Henry Miller corroborates his intuition about the native land he left. Least Heat Moon, Duncan, Steinbeck, Pirsig, and Whitman, or their protagonists, look back on their travels, discover the pattern, resolve to keep the journey going, and in various ways challenge readers to set out for themselves.

Reentry often brings self-knowledge for narrators. In Jim Harrison's *A Good Day to Die*, the narrator is haunted by Tim's death and the futility of their failed quest: "An act that I had conceived of as heroic would probably go unnoticed except by a rancher who might wonder why his dam had never washed away before, or why his Doberman was dead, or why he was missing two of his cattle" (175). They plan to escape and wonder what to tell Tim's parents. Wanting to comfort Sylvia, the narrator finds his "brain had become wordless" and he wonders "who would miss Tim besides Sylvia?"—to which he adds: "And perhaps myself" (175). He considers for a moment blowing up more dams to honor Tim, but doubts he could pull it off. He adds valium to his whiskey, tries unsuccessfully to snap himself out of it with fantasies of fishing ("I caught an endless succession of tarpen"), but nothing relieves the despair. Curiously, he feels "oddly alive" in this closing scene—wet with Sylvia's tears, his arm asleep from her pressing against it. As the first light of dawn eases through the window, he realizes that "someone should take care of her, but if I had any qualities of kindness and mercy left, any perceptions of what I was on earth, however, dim and stupid, I knew it couldn't be me" (Harrison 176).

Accepting his limitations, the narrator rises above self-pity and regains his ability to care about someone else. Educative experience in the road journey is often represented during reentry in symbols of death and rebirth wherein knowledge is born through death of the self—a conventional paradox of losing one's life to gain it. In Campbell's terms, "the road of trials" in the classic hero journey involves a cleansing and humbling of the senses which leads to "self-purification." Foremost among the perils of the road quest is the confrontation with death. Dying into life is a crucial part of the journey at every stage of Melinda's cancer in *Seaview*, a book dominated by death and the transforming power of water. Through the intensity of Melinda's cancer, Allen learns a certain kind of integrity. To Allen, Melinda "seemed the healthy one." When he saw her sitting or occasionally standing beside some structure, holding it for support, "he'd feel himself slide into a kind of awakening, a clarity that rendered most of the rest dreamlike" (Olson 11). Melinda's dying is the central fact of the book, but her life on the edge intensifies every sensation and causes her to reexamine people, events, and daily rituals often overlooked. Knowing the end was near "freed her to live in the elegance of the struggle" (12). In *Not Fade Away*, Floorboard George undergoes a mythic dismemberment or crucifixion during reentry after his pilgrimage. He redirects the goal and purpose of his journey from what had started as a trip to the Big Bopper's grave side to a celebration of the Holy Ghost in the rhythms and spirit of music. His "Doo-Wop" to the Bopper's grave is interrupted by the Pilgrim Ghost who, with Goethe, tells him that "the self-seeker finds nothing" (Dodge 201). Nailed to the accelerator, George is released into the power of music. With his own ghost assaulting his ego along the way and haunted by the memories of eight-year-old Eddie killed on the way home from school, George arrives at the scene of the Big Bopper's death where he tap dances on the hood of the Cadillac and proclaims: "If you want to live you must throw yourself to death like a handful of pennies into a wishing well" (283). What begins with the Big Bopper's plane crash on "the day the music stopped" ends with Kacy's death and George's total immersion in the power of suffering: "I held her a moment real in my arms before she disappeared" (285). As in many road reentries, the narrator of *Not Fade Away* has the final say in an epilogue which points back to the book itself as the message brought back from the quest.

Death also haunts American road literature as an ever-present reminder of the dangers of speed and the limits of the journey itself. No matter how expansive and exciting the lines of the open road become, danger is never far away. Easy Mack explores the horrors of crashes in Harry Crews's *Car*. Maria Wyeth broods over photos of highway death scenes in Joan Didion's *Play It As It Lays*. John Hawkes's *Travesty* is an uninterrupted monologue of a suicidal death march. Still other pilgrimages are motivated by death as in Linda Reismann's journey to return her dead husband's ashes to his home town in Hilma Wolitzer's *Hearts,* or Emily Brimberg Johnson's coming fully alive only in the fears that her daughter has been killed in Ann Roiphe's *Long Division*. Death to self brings wholeness as in Pirsig's narrator's madness, hospitalization, and rebirth into one person again. The road hero's dismemberment, crucifixion, and resurrection bring what Joseph Campbell calls "atonement or at-one-ment," which is Whitman's urging that "we stick by each other" on the open road. Whitman's famous conclusion to "Song of Myself" repeats the cycle of death into life on the road: "If you want me again, look for me under your boot soles . . . I stop somewhere waiting for you." In the shadow of accidents and the threat of death, highway adventures create a community of heroes united by motives and shared stories.

Though many road heroes drive alone, reentry involves the repair or growth of relationships when two people travel together. One typical reentry pattern involves the working out of new understandings between mothers and daughters. Wolitzer's *Hearts* presents stepmother and stepdaughter in their westward journey to return the cremated ashes of their husband-father to his home town. Approaching Los Angeles (on the "last night of your old life"), Linda talks and Robin eats to avoid the unspeakable. They identify with the pioneers on this last leg of their quest. In the end, these two questers realize that they are bound to each other, that they become a family by not only accident but will, and that they have a duty to console each other. Reentry concentrates on the growth of the mother-daughter relationship also in Roiphe's *Long Division* where Emily Brimberg Johnson and her daughter, Sarah, experience many tests and trials in their cross-country drive. When Sarah is kidnapped by a group of gypsies, her mother is tempted to let her go, "cut the cords," "be without her, sparse, clean like a bone," and above all not having to watch her make the same mistakes, not having "to live it again through her" (185). Such freedom is lonely, however, and Emily's reentry is her realization of her embattled closeness with Sarah: "I feel an anguish open in me, hers and mine commingled—a terrible black pot of love and need and caring, an iron maiden into which we were both forced" (185). Their reunion brings not only relief, but a new vitality: "and she hugged me again, my daughter, my soul, my own love" (188). Similarly, in Simpson's *Anywhere But Here*, mother and daughter are combative throughout their journey from Wisconsin to California. Adele's concluding monologue is ironic in its analysis of how other mothers "never took the time to give the real total love" (530) or how Ann, her daughter, hasn't yet learned to let go of her fears. In Adele's reentry, Ann has gone off to college and by this time in the story they are together only for brief visits. Nonetheless, the same conflicts that sent them in motion together pull them apart, yet keep them together forever. No matter how much they fought, Adele feels confident that Ann would "find her own grace" if only she would learn "to just Be" (534). The healing force of their journey brings, upon reentry, the love of their connectedness.

Many questing heroes adjust to the difficulites of reentry by expressing the hope that even though the trip is over, the journey will continue. In *Travels with Charley,* Steinbeck concludes that people don't take trips, "trips take people." With home in sight, he feels that the quest will continue long after the actual travels have ended. This indefinitely postponed reentry is in the tradition of what Campbell describes as the hero's refusal to return to the mundane (218). The trick is to keep moving even at the point of reentry, as Dean Moriarity manages to do in *On the Road,* or to coax readers out onto the road—as Whitman does repeatedly—or at least to vow to go again soon as Huck Finn resolves. Continued movement at the point of reentry is found also in Least Heat Moon's circles, Wolitzer's image of driving as dancing in *Hearts*, and Floorboard George's "Wop-bop-a-loop-bop-a-wham-bam-boom" to the Holy Ghost of music in *Not Fade Away*. If the quest hero is what Campbell calls "the champion of things becoming, not of things become" (243), the reentry is not so much an arrival someplace as it is Sissy Hankshaw's realization of the totality of all being and movement in the stillness of a present moment.

Most returning heroes of the American road quest come home with messages of self-knowledge, death to ego and rebirth of the self, and improved relationships. Even with these successes, however, neither the reentry nor the imparting of the message is easy or without a significant price. As Campbell has pointed out, the hero's most difficult tasks are to be understood and to make intelligible pronouncements to people trapped in the mundane and the banal. After a soul-satisfying vision of fulfillment the hero must be able to accept the existential anguish and tedium of the ordinary. "Why reenter such a world?" Campbell asks and quickly answers: "The easy thing is to commit the whole community to the devil and retire again into the heavenly rock-dwelling, close the door, and make it fast" (218). That temptation on the highway is the hypnotic romance of the road itself, the desire to stop only for gas and follow the white line to power, speed, and perpetual motion. American road heroes transcend or evade much of the anguish of reentry through the force of optimism and exuberance. Even that enthusiasm, however, can be yet another reentry trap. Campbell warns that "as dreams . . . momentous by night may seem silly in the light of day, so the poet and the prophet can discover themselves playing the idiot before a jury of sober eyes."

Coming off the road to rejoin the community back home is especially painful when friends and family can't understand what the road hero wants to tell them. Much of Kerouac's sadness, for example, is triggered when his narrators are unable to reach the people back home. Journey's end in Kerouac's *Desolation Angels* captures the always beat Jack Duluoz when he is at first eager to bring his message to friends and then—disappointed at their reactions—he becomes "sick of the whole subject." After the trip to the mountain top and the reentry into daily life, he finds himself "disgusted with any new experience of any kind" (330). At a time when he should be exhilarated, he feels instead "empty voidness," "horror and unhappiness" (359). Ultimately, Jack's friends teach him that his vision is not easily understood by those who haven't been there, that insight is often brittle, that the wise returning hero must be rejected by his friends so that they can go on traveling themselves rather than merely following him: "Besides, the vision of the freedom of eternity which I saw and which all wilderness hermitage saints have seen, is of little use in cities and warring societies such as we have" (66). As the last stages of *Desolation Angels* turn sour, Duluoz finds himself changing from a youthful adventure to "nausea concerning experience in the world at large, a *revulsion* in all the six senses" (300). Facing his limitations and his friends' unwillingness to accept his mountaintop vision, he is resigned: "A peaceful sorrow at home is the best I'll ever be able to offer the world, in the end, and so I told my Desolation Angels goodbye. A new life for me" (366). Unable to sustain his own vision or communicate it to others, Duluoz feels the anguish of what Campbell calls trying to "communicate to people who insist on the exclusive evidence of their senses the message of the all-generating void" (218).

Beyond the difficulties of communicating the message, re-entry is damaged irreparably by the tarnishing or collapse of the vision during the journey. In *Beyond Our Control*, for example, Tom Englehardt set out to rediscover America only to learn that the road had been closed off by corporate "vampires." He abruptly ends his journey when he discovers that he had become part of the problem he was critiquing.

Henry Miller came back for one last look at the country only to discover that he could have "put in thirty pages . . . everything worth saying about the American way of life." Miller's hero-journey concludes that the utilitarian and the mercenary have locked out the dreamer-poet in America. The temptation to retreat or otherwise withdraw is felt in the failed quest of *A Good Day to Die*, in the self-parody of *Lolita*, where the highway is called "a container for self-centeredness" (198), and in Floorboard George's rejection of white-line fever. In spite of the difficulties and challenges faced, the majority of highway heroes are enthusiastic about coming home and eager to share their stories. Most narrators return with sermonic single-mindedness. Duncan reinterprets the mythic dimension of Westward migration, Reeves reaffirms and updates Tocqueville's speculations, Least Heat Moon takes new resolve in Hopi emergence, Steinbeck and Moyers are homiletic about what they learn listening to America, and even the camera in *Easy Rider* innocently and unabashedly celebrates the lush countryside and the power of motion. Such confident observation and analysis upon reentry are in the American tradition of optimism stretching back to Whitman's "*Allons*, the road is before us.*" Similarly positive but painful resolutions are reached in the existential anguish of Harrison or Didion, the therapeutic healing of *Long Division, Seaview,* or *Hearts,* and the parodic irony of *Huckleberry Finn, Lolita,* and *Even Cowgirls Get the Blues.* At times the hero's eagerness to tell the story takes on the religious zeal of Whitman's "holy road," Dean Moriarity's search for It, or Pirsig's narrator's discovery of Zen in a crankshaft. This displaced theodicy of the highway is summarized in Duncan's Road Rule 10: "The theology of the road forms its own religion, combining bits and pieces of other beliefs. It relies on technology (a vehicle) yet respects the forces of nature. Its deity is the Road Spirits; its principal practice is the pilgrimage" (140).

At once the most triumphant and the most burdensome act of reentry is proclaiming the word in the actual writing of the road narrative. Whether travelers record events in notes along the way, follow William Wordsworth's emotion recollected in tranquility, or study successive revisions, they compose meaning into the road experience most fully in the writing process itself. Research on the composing process has shown writing to be a mode of discovery, a way of learning, a development of insight as it takes shape on the page. Reentry also involves a self-consciousness about how narrative patterns take shape. Least Heat Moon, Steinbeck, Pirsig, and others search for order in their notes and conclude that the search itself is the order they were seeking. Duncan observes that the order found in the journey depends ultimately on who is taking the notes. In road novels especially, the use of limited perspective often draws attention to the constitutive nature of the composing process—as in the dramatic monologue frame of *Not Fade Away* or the multiple perspective of *Anywhere But Here,* where readers are reminded that a story's events are observed, described, and structured from several different points of view. Reentry for readers requires sorting out which versions of events they accept.

While a narrator's individual perspective is often masked as objective reporting as a story unfolds, journey's end is a special place to highlight the structuring mechanism of the story teller's subjective responses. The genre thus involves readers in this self-reflexive process by exposing the narrative machinery and taking a look at how plots take shape. Prose narratives are generally more self-reflexive on reentry than other media. While highway songs and road films celebrate adventure stories and action-packed experiences, prose discourse is more reflective in analyzing the construction of the journey as it takes shape. The prose narrator fills in detailed descriptions that "travelin' songs" and road movies don't develop. Behind the wheel, writers take "pictures" of the landscape and explore states of mind—stretching over the car, the highway and countryside what Henry James has called "the immense spider web of sensibility." Phil Patton notes that just as a photographer or filmmaker frames and composes the elements of a snapshot or movie, so also behind the windshield America's road story tellers compose an order into the roadside (225). Like the photographer who freezes the flux, the prose narrator stops the car for moments of introspection and analysis. Whether this windshield view of the world has been liberating or restrictive becomes another recurring problem to be sorted out during reentry.

Coming home means writing the story—a process that takes place not in isolation, but under the influence of journeys already made and books already written: each new road quester heads down well-worn highways. Whitman is, of course, the great American inspiration, his voice heard everywhere from Kerouac and Least Heat Moon to Duncan and Zelazny. Similarly, *Travels with Charley* becomes a model of cautious adventure, and Duncan shows adulation for Lewis and Clark. Writing his story partakes as well in theirs and begins a dialogue with readers that becomes an ongoing revision of the "tradition." Taking one's place alongside others, however, runs the risk of living in the shadow of their accomplishments. Road questers seek their own space by setting off in new directions launching direct attacks on those who have gone before, or swerving from the pattern through parody. Indeed, satire is an effective way of being heard on reentry. Direct attack can be found, for example, in Sissy Hankshaw's jibes about Kerouac, Engelhardt's critiques of the delusive power of motion, or the self-destructive parody of *Travesty*.

During reentry in both nonfiction and fiction, storytellers often draw attention to their participation in the journey as well as to their construction of the narrative. In fiction this self-consciousness is particularly prominent. We know, for example, that a narrator constructs the details of a story from a particular perspective, and often readers receive information from a variety of sources and must participate in the assembly of the pieces. Some narrators will distance themselves from their experiences in a mock frame that reminds readers that they are reading fiction. Dr. Robbins mocks author Tom Robbins's storytelling in *Even Cowgirls Get the Blues* when he cautions readers against being taken in by the illusion of the story. His authorial intrusions alienate readers from the comfortable verisimilitude that postpones or smooths over reentry. A similar distancing effect is achieved as fictional narrators refer to earlier road quests, emphasizing self-consciousness about how this new story will take its place in the tradition. Though an adventure tale of smuggling and intrigue, John Keeble's *Yellowfish* quotes generously from the journals of Simon Fraser and other pioneers of the Northwest. The effect is to make storytelling itself a major concern of the story. Road fiction also uses dream sequences and stories within stories as in the narrator's fictional dream in *Not Fade Away*. Multiple perspective also places storytelling in the middle of the story—and often in the moving car—as in Simpson's *Anywhere But Here*, Dickinson's *The Widows' Adventures* and Olson's *Seaview*, where events are related by different characters in ways that require readers to participate in the construction of sequence, causality, and motivation. Less obvious is the case of the singular, unnamed, fallible, participant narrator who is confident, but limited in a presentation of information that invites readers to wonder. Jim Harrison's narrator in *A Good Day to Die*, for example, is a strong personality who struggles to make sense out of his story as he pieces it together.

Perhaps because the "real" events of nonfiction road narratives are assumed to be truer than the "fiction" in novels, participant-narrators in nonfiction refer less often to how the story is being constructed and reconstructed. For some, the writing is often masked as merely a recording of what happened or a sorting and organizing of notes or taped interviews. Thus Henry Miller, Clancy Sigal, and even John Steinbeck give only brief glimpses of how they kept records or put together materials. Kuralt takes viewers behind the scenes in the CBS truck from time to time, recognizing technical crews for their roles in the making of "on the road" experiences. Even these nonfiction road authors make narrative machinery more transparent to enhance aesthetic distance. Henry Miller and Mary Morris create extended dream sequences; Michelle Cole and Stuart Black dialogue with "the kids" for multiple perspective in *Checking It Out*; Duncan presents himself talking to himself about Lewis and Clark in *Out West*. Letting readers in to see the writing process in action breaks the illusion of objectivity and underscores the artistry at the center of the road experience.

Nonfiction road narratives often direct attention to how stories are written—perhaps to dispel the suggestion that authors merely record without reconstructing events. Sometimes the attention given to the gathering and arranging of details is a way of bringing readers along on the trip. Just as Whitman wrote poems that urge readers to transcend poetry, nonfiction road narratives at times draw readers into a self-reflexive examination of the hows and whys of composing the road experience into literary form. After observing that the way back doesn't repeat the journey out but is a journey all its own, Duncan devotes considerable attention to how writing about life on the road is itself a part of the myth-making power of the quest. Whether reentry brings self-knowledge, rebirth, a heightened experience of everyday life, or the tentativeness of lapsing vision, the hero discovers the meaning of the quest only in the proclaiming of the word. Writing a story is a way of finding order in experience. Each new story preserves and destroys something of the old stories as it passes on and revises the road mythos.

Drawing attention to the construction of a story further involves readers in dialogue about who and what shapes personal identity and the national mythos. "Keep a journal of your travels," Duncan advises, "as a reminder of where you have been." But more than just memory, the recording is an act of creation wherein the details observed and described make the history and the mythology by which we live. An important corollary to Road Rule 25 explains what Duncan feels he is accomplishing: "If travelling with other people, always volunteer to be the journal writer. That way, yours will be the version of history that is recorded" (407). As he reads Lewis and Clark and writes his own journal, he comes to understand the way authors use existing conventions to discover and construct their own truths. While the initial goals may set the quest or pilgrimage in motion and keep it going, new discoveries along the way are reconstructed in the telling of the story back home or while composing it on paper. "The final value of any expedition is not what you failed to discover but what you found in its place," he concludes. Ultimately the experience and the record of that experience—though distinct—can move closer together. Duncan draws readers into this self-reflexive pattern by creating a dialogue between author, reader, and text (and earlier texts such as Lewis's journals) on how the recorder of the history becomes the myth-maker. In *Out West* and in many other road narratives that draw attention to the writing of the story, readers are invited to understand how the processes of the author's writing and their own reading can again and again create a new life on the road.

Of course there are other ways to study how road narratives are written—beyond what narrators and texts draw attention to. Kerouac's newspaper end rolls of *On the Road* are a matter of record, as are his long nonstop "automatic" writing sessions where he wove the mythology in 12-foot-long unbroken paragraphs of jazz improvisation. With the help of *Steinbeck: A Life in Letters*, it is possible to compare side-by-side passages of *Travels with Charley* and letters he wrote to his wife at the same time. A massive *Guidebook to Zen and the Art of Motorcycle Maintenance* makes available maps, chronological charts, detailed footnotes and indexes, and passages deleted from Pirsig's original manuscript (DiSanto and Steele). Research on textual origins and authorial intention are part of the routine scholarship on how manuscripts get started and progress through revisions until a text appears. Beyond the standard scholarship, however, road books make how they were written a part of the journey itself. Writing or reading about the road is never quite the same as life on the road itself, but that deficiency is also one strength of the artistic vision that endures. Road heroes may not bring home the elixir as in quests of lore, but they do come home to write stories that keep the journey going.

Epilogue

In one way or another, reentry is a crucial stage of every road quest: whether from pilgrimage or picaresque, road heroes return home, and the dynamics of that reintegration become an interpretation of the journey itself. In reentry, *Bildung* heroes emerge, protestors shape an alternative vision, and those searching for a national or personal identity propose definitions. Even nomads wander through a return stage of their encircling—measured by contrast with a more conventional homeward settling. Writing about road narratives also requires that I too reenter after a long journey of reading and analyzing what began as a few dozen and turned into well over a hundred novels and nonfiction prose accounts. Taking stock, I come to each new road narrative with some recurring questions: Who are these road heroes? When and why do they set out, and where are they going? How do they decide the best ways to tell their stories? Who reads these books? What is the enduring appeal of the stories, and why are they significant?

The answers to those questions reflect the many perspectives expressed in the genre.

Road narratives feature ordinary people trying to learn something about themselves and their country, to seek new experiences, to find more and better space, and to meet new people and explore alternative values. On the road and in their books, we meet everyone from established people getting away from confinement to counterculture dropouts protesting the hypocrisy of the establishment. They enter the sacred space along the highways where they discover adventures and endure trials that are educative, healing, and expansive. Narrators share stories of down-and-out characters hoping to recover from misfortune, fallen creatures looking for healing, the anxious or angry hoping for at least the temporary relief of escape. Heroes of the highway are a diverse group including the academic and the popular, students of American culture who retrace previous heroic journeys to rediscover what is very old; retired persons who forsake a permanent address in favor of actually living on the road (perhaps in a recreational vehicle); and the lost or disinherited groping for answers in the fast lane and in movement itself.

In the telling of so many kinds of stories, American road narratives display rich variety. Heroes and rogues alike come back home to sort out what they encountered and to share the insights they reached while gone. Audiences listen and read because the stories are good and because the narrators use familiar genre conventions modified for innovation. Books written on reentry are as complex as the experiences, cultural symbols, and genre conventions allow, and invite readers into a dialogue on evolving cultural values. In the communities where reading, discussion, and critiquing take place, new works remake the literary tradition they enter and suggest new ways of looking at personal and national goals. The same community of people who take the trips and shape the visions also write, read, and evaluate the books; that ongoing dialogue also decides what counts artistically. For almost 50 years, this dialogue with the road has provided reassurance about our cultural identity as well as a way to question social developments and national goals. Swapping road stories is also a chance to explore and define the American individual in the context of the larger community.

Drawing from a long history of travel-writing, the road narrative is nomadic and restless with patterns resembling rhizomatic multiplicity more than the apparent stability of roots. Whatever the itinerary, however, the open road offers freedom, escape, speed, and the liminal state experienced while in motion. Because reentry means giving up that liminality, getting off the road is painful in several ways. Returning home means exchanging timelessness for measured limits, the intensity of heightened experience for the boredom of routine. Having been free of obligations for at least a while, the traveler comes back to prescribed roles and duties; with the sanction or excuse for wandering used up or elapsed, pragmatism reasserts its dominance. The daring of speed and power vanish into dullness. What had been sacred space is now zoned commercial; what had been clear and simple is soon muddled and cluttered. In short, the romance is gone and, in its place, the pain of loss.

In spite of all that is relinquished on reentry, however, coming home also brings its recompense. In some road narratives, the heroes either reach their goals or trade them in for something better along the way. Most hear or see what they set out to find or rediscover what was lost. Just as road pilgrims generally reach their destination, so also protestors proclaim emergent values in opposition to the dominant culture. While many commentators think or hope they have found the soul of the nation along the road, others want to keep looking—sure only about numbing the sadness of loss with the exhilaration of speed. More than a few redirect their courses or trade goal orientations for the satisfaction of being richly and fully present anywhere. If, for some, the journey gives way to mystical brooding, coming home offers a much-needed opening up to others once again. Reentry can then prevent time on the road from becoming a salvation trap rather than a discovery of self through others. Experimental forms—especially parody—provide a check on white line fever and other road traps that postpone the painful growth of reentry.

No matter how abrupt or anticlimactic coming home might be, the temporary paradise of life on the road must eventually come to an end in yet another type of loss. What remains, however, is the telling of the story wherein salvation is found not in an escape from daily experiences but rather in a reintegration into what had been left behind. The road hero's rewards include both the extended release from life back home as well as a return that brings fuller participation in the community of story tellers and readers. Road questers are compelled to wander. Whether they keep goals in clear view or their paths seem to go nowhere, the journey at least for a while becomes all—and then they go back home. The community they return to, however, is not exactly the one they left—the crucial difference being the addition of the published record of their journey: the road narrative which is read and interpreted and becomes part of the ongoing conversation about where we have been and what we might yet become.

Notes

1. Introduction: Road as Genre

1. *Problems of Dostoevsky's Poetics*—as quoted in Gary Saul Morson and Caryl Emerson, *Mikhail Bakhtin: Creation of a Prosaics*, 295. I am indebted to Morson's and Emerson's selections and commentary throughout my discussion of Bakhtin and genre.

2. These and other approaches are summarized in John A. Jakle, *The Tourist: Travel in Twentieth-Century North America.*

3. For more on these topics, see Peter Marsh and Peter Collett, *Driving Passion: The Psychology of the Car.*

4. I am indebted to my colleague Bruce Roscoe for the term "reluctant companion," suggested in class discussion and in further helpful conversation over time.

5. For more on the reader response views of Iser (and Culler, Riffaterre, Bleich, Fish, and Holland who follow in this section), see Jane M. Tompkins, ed., *Reader-Response Criticism* and *The Reader in the Text*, Susan R. Suleiman and Inge Crosman, eds.

2. Backgrounds: A Chronology of Genre Memory

1. Henry Nash Smith, *Virgin Land: The American West as Symbol and Myth* is still a valuable commentary on literature and the frontier. For a more recent contribution of the "New Western" historians, see William Cronan, George Miles, and Jay Gitlin, *Under an Open Sky: Rethinking America's Western Past.* See also Annette Kolodny, *The Lay of the Land: Metaphors of Experience and History in American Life and Letters* and *The Land Before Her: Fantasy and the Experience of the American Frontiers, 1830-1860* for a very different reading of the frontier. (See also chapter 7 on how road narratives by women draw from and modify road genre memory.) On the term "myth," Patrick Brantlinger has suggested that "ideology" is a more appropriate term because the national identity is made rather than found. In Crusoe's *Footprints: Cultural Studies in Britain and America*, he suggests that Henry Nash Smith, Leo Marx, and others have come around to this view, 32.

2. Quoted in Julian Pettifer and Nigel Turner, *Automania: Man and the Motorcar*, 59.

3. For further discussion of the role of the automobile in American fiction, see the special isssue of *Kansas Quarterly* 21.4 (Fall 1989)—especially the articles on Sinclair Lewis, Dos Passos, Fitzgerald, Bellow, Nabokov, and Flannery O'Connor.

4. For further discussion of Kerouac's drafts, see Tim Hunt, *Kerouac's Crooked Road: Development of a Fiction.*

3. Disharmony and Protest

1. For an overview of road films that extends beyond this study, see Mark Williams, *Road Movies: The Complete Guide to Cinema on Wheels.*

2. For a guide to commentary on Kerouac, see Robert J. Milewski et al., *Jack Kerouac: An Annotated Bibliography of Secondary Sources 1944-1979 .*

3. Portions of the following on Kerouac and the open plains have appeared in different form in "The Endless Poem: Jack Kerouac's Midwest," *Great Lakes Review* 3 (1976): 73-86.

4. For a more recent contribution to the Pranksters' voyages, see Ken Kesey, *The Further Inquiry.*

5. See Jan Kerouac's *Trainsong* for further road adventures and the observation that her father bequeathed to her his "restless blood," 100.

4. Search for a National Identity

1. "Television News and the Television Documentary," in *Television Myth and the American Mind.* See also Charles Kuralt, *My Life on the Road.*

6. Escape, Parody, and Experimental Form

1. For a valuable discussion of "ambiguity in the dreams of freedom and success" as well as the "nightmares of constraint and failure in America's love hate relationship with the automobile," see Cynthia Golomb Dettelbach, *In the Driver's Seat: The Auto in American Literature and Popular Culture.* Dettelbach discusses works by, among others, Fitzgerald, Faulkner, Dos Passos, Agee, and Nabokov.

2. In what follows I am indebted to Karl's fascinating commentaries on American metafiction on the road.

3. I am indebted to my colleague Barry Alford for the suggestion that *Seaview* is an antiroad narrative—and for continuing invaluable discussions over time.

7. The American Highway and Cultural Diversity

1. See also Andrew Ross, *No Respect: Intellectuals and Popular Culture.* "Hip is the first on the block to know what's going on, but it wouldn't be seen dead at the block party," 101.

2. For a study of the history and social implications of women and "the coming of the motor age," see Virginia Scharff, *Taking the Wheel.*

Works Cited

Abrams, M.H. *Natural Supernaturalism: Tradition and Revolution in Romantic Literature.* New York: Norton, 1971.

Agee, James. "The Great American Roadside." *Fortune* 10 (Sept. 1934): 53+.

Allisop, Kenneth. *Hard Travellin': The Hobo and His History.* New York: New American Library, 1967.

Amory, Cleveland. *The Last Resorts.* New York: Harper, 1952.

Anderson, David D. *Route 2, Titus, Ohio.* Deerfield, IL: Lake Shore, 1993.

Anderson, Nels. *The Hobo.* Chicago: U of Chicago P, 1923.

Anderson, Rudolph E. *The Story of the American Automobile: Highlights and Sidelights.* Washington, DC: Public Affairs Press, 1950.

Anderson, Warren H. *Vanishing Roadside America.* Tucson: U of Arizona P, 1981.

Anderson, William C. *The Two-Ton Albatross.* New York: Crown, 1969.

Appleton, Victor, Jr. *Tom Swift and His Electric Runabout or the Speediest Car on the Road.* New York: Grosset, 1910.

Asch, Nathan. *The Road in Search of America.* New York: Norton, 1937.

Atkinson, Alex, and Ronald Searle. *By Rocking Chair Across America.* New York: Funk and Wagnalls, 1959.

Baeder, John. *Diners.* New York: Abrams, 1979.

——. *Gas, Food and Lodging.* New York: Abbeville, 1982.

Bainbridge, Beryl. *English Journey.* London: Duckworth/BBC, 1984.

Bakhtin, Mikhail. *Speech Genres and Other Late Essays.* Ed. Caryl Emerson and Michael Holquist. Trans. Vern W. McGee. Austin: U of Texas P, 1986.

Barthes, Roland. *Image, Music, Text.* New York: Hill and Wang, 1977.

——. *Mythologies.* New York: Hill and Wang, 1972.

Bartlett, Lee, ed. *The Beats: Essays in Criticism.* Jefferson, NC: McFarland, 1981.

Bate, Walter Jackson. *The Burden of the Past and the English Poet.* Cambridge: Belknap P, of Harvard UP, 1970.

Baudrillard, Jean. *America.* London: Verso, 1989.

Bauer, Fred. *How Many Hills to Hillsboro?* Old Tappan, NJ: Hewitt, 1969.

Becker, Robert H. *Thomas Christy's Road Across the Plains.* Denver: Old West, 1969.

Bedell, Mary C. *Modern Gypsies: A 12,000-Mile Motor Camping Trip Encircling the United States.* New York: Brentano's, 1924.

Belasco, Warren James. *Americans on the Road: From Autocamp to Motel.* Cambridge, MA: MIT P, 1979.

Beagle, Peter S. *I See By My Outfit: Cross Country by Scooter.* New York: Viking, 1964.

Bel Geddes, Norman. *Horizons.* New York: Random, 1932.

——. *Magic Motorways.* New York: Random, 1940.

Bennett, E.D., ed. *American Journeys: An Anthology of Travel in the United States.* Convent Station, NJ: Travel Vision, 1975.

Benson, Adolph, ed. *Peter Kalin's Travels in North America.* New York: Dover, 1937.

Bercovici, Konrad. *The Story of the Gypsies.* New York: Cosmopolitan, 1928.

Berger, Michael C. *The Devil Wagon in God's Country: The Automobile and Social Change in Rural America, 1893-1929.* Hamden, CT: Archon, 1979.

Berger, Thomas. *Little Big Man.* New York: Dial, 1964.

Bissell, Richard. *How Many Miles to Galena?* Boston: Little, Brown, 1968.

Blair, Karin. "The Garden in the Machine: The Why of *Star Trek.*" *Journal of Popular Culture* 13 (Fall 1979): 310-20.

Bleich, David. *Subjective Criticism.* Baltimore: Johns Hopkins UP, 1978.

Bliss, Carey S. *Autos Across America.* 2nd ed. Austin and New Haven: Jenkins and Reese, 1982.

Bloom, Harold. *A Map of Misreading.* New York: Oxford, 1975.

——. *Ringers in the Tower: Studies in Romantic Traditions.* Chicago: U of Chicago P, 1971.

Bluefarb, Sam. *The Escape Motif in the American Novel: Mark Twain to Richard Wright.* Columbus: Ohio State UP, 1972.

Boone, Joseph Allen. *Tradition Counter Tradition: Love and the Form of Fiction.* Chicago: U of Chicago P, 1987.

Boorstin, Daniel J. *The Americans: The National Experience.* New York: Random House, 1965.

Borth, Christy. *Mankind on the Move.* Washington: Automotive Safety Foundation, 1969.

Botkin, B.A. "Icon on Wheels: Supericon of Popular Culture." Fishwick and Browne. 47-62.

Brantlinger, Patrick. *Crusoe's Footprints: Cultural Studies in Britain and America.* New York and London: Routledge, 1990.

Brautigan, Richard. *Trout Fishing in America.* San Francisco: Four Seasons, 1967.

Brevda, William. *Harry Kemp: The Last Bohemian.* Lewisburg: Bucknell UP, 1986.

Brinkley, Douglas. *The Majic Bus: An American Odyssey.* New York: Doubleday-Anchor, 1994.

Brooks, John. *The Landscape of Roads.* London: Architectural Press, 1960.

Brown, Lester R., Christopher Flavin, Colin Norman. *Running on Empty: The Future of the Automobile in an Oilshort World*. New York: Norton, 1979.

Bruce-Briggs, B. *The War Against the Automobile*. New York: Dutton, 1977.

Bryson, Bill. *The Lost Continent: Travels in Small Town America*. New York: Harper, 1989.

Buel, Ronald A. *Dead End: The Automobile in Mass Transportation*. Englewood Cliffs, NJ: Prentice-Hall, 1972.

Burman, Ben Lucien. *It's a Big Country: America Off the Highways*. New York: Reynal, 1956.

Burns, Olive Ann. *Cold Sassy Tree*. Ticknor and Fields, 1984.

Buryn, Ed. *Vagabonding in the USA*. Berkeley, CA: And/or Press, 1980.

Caldwell, Erskine. *Around About America*. Garden City, NY: Doubleday, 1964.

——. *Tobacco Road*. New York: Grosset, 1932.

Campbell, Joseph. *The Hero with a Thousand Faces*. Princeton, NJ: Princeton UP, 1949.

Carter, Michelle. *On Other Days While Going Home*. New York: Morrow, 1987.

Cassady, Carolyn. *Heart Beat: My Life with Jack and Neal*. Berkeley, CA: Creative Arts, 1976.

Cassady, Neal. *The First Third*. San Francisco: City Lights, 1971.

Catanzaro, Mary F. "The Car As a Cell in *Lolita*." *Kansas Quarterly* 21 (Fall 1989): 91-96.

Charters, Ann. *A Bibliography of Works by Jack Kerouac*. New York: Phoenix, 1967.

——. *Kerouac: A Biography*. San Francisco: Straight Arrow, 1973.

——, ed. *The Portable Beat Reader*. New York: Viking, 1992.

Chase, Harold, B. *Auto-Biography: Reflections of a Pioneer Motorist, 1896-1911*. New York: Pageant, 1955.

Cobb, Irvin S. *Roughing It Deluxe*. New York: Doron, 1914.

Cobley, Evelyn. "Mikhail Bakhtin's Place in Genre Theory." *Genre* 21 (Fall 1988): 321-38.

Codrescu, Andrei. *Road Scholar: Coast to Coast Late in the Century*. New York: Hyperion, 1993.

Cohen, Erik. "A Phenomenology of Tourist Experiences." *Sociology* 13 (May 1979): 179-201.

Cole, Michelle, and Stuart Black. *Checking It Out: Some Lower East Side Kids Discover the Rest of America*. New York: Dial, 1971.

Collett, Peter, and Peter Marsh. *Driving Passion: The Psychology of the Car*. Winchester, MA: Faber and Faber, 1987.

Cook, Bruce. *The Beat Generation*. New York: Scribner, 1971.

Cooper, James Fenimore. *The Pioneers*. New York: Townsend, 1859.

Copeland, Estella M. *Overland by Auto in 1913: Diary of a Family Tour From California to Indiana.* Indianapolis: Indiana Historical Society, 1981.

Cowley, Malcolm. *Exile's Return.* New York: Viking, 1951.

Craik, Kenneth. "Human Responsiveness to Landscape: An Environmental Psychological Perspective." *Response to Environment.* Raleigh: North Carolina State U, Student Publications of the School of Design 18 (1969): 170-93.

Crews, Harry. *Car.* New York: Morrow, 1972.

Crompton, John L. "Motivations for Pleasure Vocation." *Annals of Tourism Research* 5 (Oct.-Dec. 1979): 408-24.

Cronon, William, George Miles, Jay Gitlin, eds. *Under an Open Sky: Rethinking America's Western Past.* New York: Norton, 1992.

Culler, Jonathan. *Structuralist Poetics: Structuralism; Linguistics, and the Study of Literature.* Ithaca: Cornell UP, 1975.

Darby, William. *A Tour From the City of New York to Detroit.* 1819. Chicago: Quadrangle, 1962.

Darling, J.N. *The Cruise of the Bouncing Betsy: A Trailer Travelogue.* New York: Stakes, 1937.

Davidson, Robyn. *Tracks.* New York: Pantheon, 1980.

Davis, H.L. *Beulah Land.* New York: Morrow, 1949.

Deleuze, Giles, and Felix Guattari. *A Thousand Plateaus: Capitalism and Schizophrenia.* Trans. Brian Massumi. Minneapolis: U of Minnesota P, 1987.

Dettlebach, Cynthia Golomb. *In the Driver's Seat: The Auto in American Literature and Popular Culture.* Westport, CT: Greenwood Press, 1976.

De Voto, Bernard, ed. *The Journals of Lewis and Clark.* Boston: Houghton Mifflin, 1953.

Dickinson, Charles. *The Widows' Adventures.* New York: Avon, 1989.

Didion, Joan. *Play It As It Lays.* New York: Farrar, 1970.

Dimond, Bill, and Kathy Dimond. *Across the U.S.A.—by Boat.* New York: John Day, 1970.

DiSanto, Ronald L., and Thomas J. Steele. *Guidebook to Zen and the Art of Motorcycle Maintenance.* New York: Morrow, 1990.

Dodge, Jim. *Not Fade Away.* New York: Atlantic Monthly, 1987.

Donovan, Frank. *Wheels for a Nation.* New York: Crowell, 1965.

Doolittle, James Rood. *The Romance of the Automobile Industry.* New York: Klebold, 1916.

Dos Passos, John. *The Big Money: Third in the Trilogy USA 1933.* 1946. New York: Signet, 1969.

——. *1919.* New York: Harcourt, 1932.

Doty, Carolyn. *A Day Late.* New York: Viking, 1980.

Dreiser, Theodore. *A Hoosier Holiday.* New York: Lane, 1916.

Driskell, Leon. *Passing Through: A Fiction*. Chapel Hill, NC: Algonquin, 1983.

Duncan, David James. *The River Why*. New York: Bantam, 1983.

Duncan, Dayton. *Out West: An American Journey*. New York: Viking, 1987.

Dunn, Katherine. *Truck*. New York: Harper, 1971.

Earle, Alice Morse. *Stagecoach and Tavern Days*. New York and London: Benjamin Bloom, 1900.

Eastlake, William. *Portrait of an Artist with Twenty-six Horses*. New York: Simon and Schuster, 1963.

Eckert, Allan W. *The Wilderness Empire: A Narrative*. Boston: Little, Brown, 1969.

Eliot, T.S. *Selected Essays, 1917-1922*. New York: Harcourt, 1950.

Emerson, Ralph Waldo. *Selections from Ralph Waldo Emerson*. Ed. Stephen E. Whicher. Boston: Houghton Mifflin, 1957.

Engelhardt, Tom. *Beyond Our Control: America in the Mid Seventies*. Berkeley, CA: Riverrun, 1976.

Evans, Walker. *American Photographs*. New York: Museum of Modern Art, 1938.

Faris, John T. *Roaming American Highways*. New York: Farrar, 1931.

Farrell, James T. *Studs Lonigan*. New York: Random House, 1938.

Faulkner, William. *The Reivers: A Reminiscence*. New York: Random House, 1962.

Felsen, Henry Gregor. *Hot Rod*. New York: Dutton, 1950.

Finch, Phillip. *Haulin'*. Garden City, NY: Doubleday, 1975.

Fish, Stanley. *Is There a Text in This Class? The Authority of Interpretive Communities*. Cambridge, MA: Harvard UP, 1980.

Fisher, Harriet White. *A Woman's World Tour in a Motor Car*. Philadelphia: Lippincott, 1911.

Fishwick, Marshall, and Ray B. Browne, eds. *Icons of Popular Culture*. Bowling Green, OH: Bowling Green State University Popular Press, 1970.

Fiske, John, and John Hartley. *Reading Television*. London: Methuen, 1978.

Flagg, James Montgomery. *Boulevards All the Way*. New York: Doran, 1925.

Fletcher, Colin. *The Man Who Walked Through Time*. New York: Knopf, 1972.

Flink, James J. *America Adopts the Automobile, 1895-1910*. Cambridge, MA: MIT P, 1970.

——. *The Car Culture*. Cambridge, MA: MIT P, 1975.

Flower, R., and M. Wynn-James. *100 Years on the Road: A Social History of the Motor Car*. New York: McGraw-Hill, 1981.

Fonda, Peter, Dennis Hopper, and Terry Southerne et al. *Easy Rider*. New York: New American Library, 1969.

Foster, Edith Caroline. *Yesterday's Highways*. Ed. Joe L. Norris. Detroit: Wayne State UP, 1951.

Foster, Mark. *From Streetcar to Superhighway*. Philadelphia: Temple UP, 1981.

Frank, Robert. *The Americans.* New York: Grove, 1959.

Frazier, Ian. *Great Plains.* New York: Farrar, 1989.

French, Warren. *A Companion to The Grapes of Wrath.* Clifton, NJ: A.M. Kelly, 1972.

Fussell, Edwin. *Frontier: American Literature and the American West.* Princeton, NJ: Princeton UP, 1965.

Fussell, Paul, ed. *The Norton Book of Travel.* Norton: New York, 1987.

Garland, Hamlin. *Main-Travelled Roads.* New York: Harper, 1899.

Garvey, Timothy J. *Popular Monuments of the Midwest: Roadside Colossi as Regional Expression.* Bloomington, IL: Wesleyan UP, 1982.

Gass, Patrick. *A Journey of the Voyages and Travels of a Corps of Discovery.* Minneapolis, MN: Ross and Haines, 1958.

Gastil, Raymond D. *Cultural Regions of the United States.* Seattle: U of Washington P, 1975.

Gifford, Barry, and Lawrence Lee. *Jack's Book: An Oral Biography of Jack Kerouac.* New York: St. Martin's, 1978.

Ginsberg, Allen. *Collected Poems: 1947-1980.* New York: Harper, 1984.

——. *The Fall of America.* San Francisco: City Lights, 1972.

——. *The Visions of the Great Rememberer.* Amherst, MA: Mulch P, 1974.

Gladding, Effie Prince. *Across the Continent by the Lincoln Highway.* New York: Brentano's, 1915.

Goffie, Luc. *Jack Kerouac: The New Picaroon.* New York: Postillon P, 1977.

Goodman, Paul. *Growing Up Absurd.* New York: Vintage, 1962.

Gordon, Jan, and Cora J. Gordon. *On Wandering Wheels: Through Roadside Camps from Maine to Georgia in an Old Sedan Car.* New York: Dodd, 1928.

Gordon, John. *Overlanding: How to Explore the World on Four Wheels.* New York: Harper, 1975.

Gray, Elizabeth Janet. *Adam of the Road.* New York: Scholastic, 1942.

Grayson, David. *The Friendly Road: New Adventures in Contentment.* New York: Grosset, 1913.

Guthrie, A.B., Jr. *The Way West.* New York: Sloane, 1949.

Gutman, John. *The Restless Decade.* New York: Abrams, 1984.

Gutman, Richard, and Elliot Kaufman with David Slovic. *American Diner.* New York: Harper, 1979.

Hailey, Arthur. *Wheels.* Garden City, NY: Bantam, 1973.

Hardwick, Elizabeth. *Sleepless Nights.* New York: Vintage, 1980.

Harrison, Jim. *A Good Day to Die.* New York: Delta, 1973.

Hassan, Ihab. *Radical Innocence: Studies in the Contemporary American Novel.* Princeton, NJ: Princeton UP, 1961.

Hassrick, Peter. *The Way West: Art of Frontier America.* New York: Abrams, 1977.

Hawkes, John. *The Blood Oranges*. New York: New Directions, 1971.

——. *Second Skin*. New York: New Directions, 1964.

——. *Travesty*. New York: New Directions, 1976.

Hayes, Joseph. *Like Any Other Fugitive*. New York: Dial, 1971.

Heinmann, Jim, and Rip Georges. *California Crazy: Roadside Vernacular Architecture*. San Francisco: Chronicle, 1980.

Hellmann, John. *Fables of Fact: The New Journalism as Fiction*. Urbana: U of Illinois P, 1981.

Henfrey, Colin. *Manscapes: An American Journey*. Boston: Gambit, 1973.

Herlihy, James Leo. *Midnight Cowboy*. New York: Dell, 1969.

Hernadi, Paul. *Beyond Genre: New Directions in Literary Classification*. Ithaca: Cornell UP, 1972.

Hillaby, John. *A Walk Through Britain*. Boston: Houghton Mifflin, 1969.

Himmelstein, Hal. "Television News and the Television Documentary." *Television Myth and the American Mind*. New York: Praeger, 1984. 197-231.

Hipkiss, Robert A. *Jack Kerouac: Prophet of the New Romanticism*. Lawrence: Regents P of Kansas, 1976.

Hoffman, Daniel. *Paul Bunyan: Last of the Frontier Demigods*. New York: Columbia UP, 1966.

Hogan, William. *The Quartzsite Trip*. New York: Atheneum, 1980.

Holdt, Jacob. *American Pictures: A Personal Journey Through the American Underclass*. Copenhagen: American Pictures, 1985.

Holland, Norman O. *Poems in Persons: An Introduction to the Psychoanalysis of Literature*. New York: Norton, 1973.

Holmes, John Clellon. *Go*. 1952. Mamaroneck, NY: Appel, 1977.

Holwerk, David. "Left Nut: The 1957 Chevrolet." Fishwick and Browne. 131-36.

Howells, W.D. *Their Wedding Journey*. Boston: Osgood, 1872.

Hulbert, Archer Butler, ed. *Historic Highways of America*. 16 vols. Cleveland: Clark, 1902-1905.

Hulme, Katherine Cavarly. *How's the Road?* San Francisco: Colophon, 1928.

Humphreys, John R. *The Lost Towns and Roads of America*. Garden City, NY: Doubleday, 1961.

Hunt, Tim. *Kerouac's Crooked Road: Development of a Fiction*. Hamden, CT: Shoe String, 1981.

Iser, Wolfgang. *The Implied Reader: Patterns of Communication in Prose Fiction from Bunyan to Beckett*. Baltimore: Johns Hopkins UP, 1974.

Jackson, Carlton. *Hounds of the Road: A History of the Greyhound Bus*. Bowling Green, OH: Bowling Green State University Popular Press, 1984.

Jackson, William Turrentine. *Wagon Roads West*. New Haven: Yale UP, 1984.

Jakle, John A. *The Tourist: Travel in Twentieth-Century North America.* Lincoln: U of Nebraska P, 1985.

James, Henry. "The Art of Fiction." *The Art of the Novel: Critical Prefaces.* New York: Scribner, 1934.

Janeway, Elizabeth. *The Early Days of Automobiles.* New York: Random House, 1956.

Jencks, Charles. *The Language of Post Modern Architecture.* New York: Rizzoli, 1977.

Jenkins, Peter. *A Walk Across America.* New York: Fawcett, 1979.

——, and Barbara Jenkins. *The Walk West.* New York: Fawcett, 1981.

Jerome, John. *The Death of the Automobile: The Fatal Effect of the Golden Era, 1955-1970.* New York: Norton, 1972.

——. *Truck: On Rebuilding a Worn-Out Pick Up and Other Post-Technological Adventures.* Boston: Houghton Mifflin, 1977.

Judson, Phoebe Goodell. *A Pioneer's Search for an Ideal Home.* Lincoln: U of Nebraska P, 1984.

Kaplan, Max. *Leisure in America: A Social Inquiry.* New York: Wiley, 1960

Karl, Frederick R. *American Fictions: 1940/1980.* New York: Harper, 1983.

Karolides, Nicholas J., ed. *Reader Response in the Classroom.* New York and London: Longman, 1992.

Keats, John. *The Insolent Chariots.* Philadelphia: Lippincott, 1958.

Keeble, John. *Yellowfish.* New York: Harper, 1980.

Kellner, Douglas. "TV, Ideology and Emancipatory Popular Culture." Newcomb 471-503.

Kemp, Harry. *Tramping on Life: An Autobiographical Narrative.* New York: Boni and Liveright, 1922.

Kennedy, Douglas. *In God's Country: Travels in the Bible Belt, USA.* London: Unwin Hyman, 1989.

Kerouac, Jack. *Desolation Angels.* New York: Coward-McCann, 1960.

——. *The Dharma Bums.* New York: Viking, 1958.

——. *Jack Kerouac: Selected Letters, 1940-1956.* Ed. Ann Charters. New York: Viking, 1995.

——· *Lonesome Traveler.* New York: Grove, 1960.

——. *Mexico City Blues.* New York: Grove, 1959.

——. *On the Road.* New York: Viking, 1957.

——. *The Portable Jack Kerouac.* Ed. Ann Charters. New York: Viking, 1995.

——. *The Subterraneans.* New York: Grove, 1958.

——. *Visions of Cody.* New York: McGraw-Hill, 1972.

Kerouac, Jan. *Baby Driver.* New York: St. Martin's, 1981.

——. *Trainsong.* New York: Holt, 1988.

Kesey, Ken. *The Further Inquiry.* New York. Viking-Penguin, 1990.

——. *One Flew Over the Cuckoo's Nest.* New York: Signet, 1963.

——. *Sometimes a Great Notion.* New York: Viking, 1971.

Keyton, Clara. *Tourist Camp Pioneering Experiences.* Chicago: Adams Press, 1960.

Knight, Arthur, and Kit Knight, eds. *The Beat Diary.* California, PA: Tuvoti, 1977.

——, eds. *The Beat Journey.* California, PA: Tuvoti, 1978.

Knowles, John. *Double Vision.* New York: Macmillan, 1964.

Kolodny, Annette. *The Land Before Her: Fantasy and the Experience of the American Frontiers, 1630-1860.* Chapel Hill and London: U of North Carolina P, 1984.

——. *The Lay of the Land: Metaphors of Experience and History in American Life and Letters.* Chapel Hill: U of North Carolina P, 1975.

Kopp, Sheldon B. *If You Meet The Buddha on the Road, Kill Him!* New York: Bantam, 1976.

Kouwehoven, John A. *The Beer Can By the Highway.* Garden City, NY: Doubleday, 1960.

Kramer, Jane. *Allen Ginsberg in America.* New York: Random House, 1969.

Kreuge, Robert. *Gypsy on 18 Wheels: A Trucker's Tale.* Ed. Sam Yanes. New York: Praeger, 1975.

Krim, Seymour. *Shake It for the World, Smartass.* New York: Dial, 1970.

Kuralt, Charles. *My Life on the Road.* New York: Ivy, 1990.

——. *On the Road With Charles Kuralt.* New York: Fawcett, 1985.

Lawrence, D.H. "Whitman." *Studies in Classic American Literature.* New York: Thomas Seltzer, 1923. 241-64.

Least Heat Moon, William. *Blue Highways.* Boston: Little, Brown, 1982.

Lee, Raymond. *Fit for the Chase: Cars and the Movies.* South Brunswick, NJ: Barnes, 1969.

Leeflang, Gerald. *American Travels of a Dutch Hobo.* Ames: Iowa State UP, 1984.

Levin, David, ed. *Emerson: Prophecy, Metamorphosis, and Influence.* New York: Columbia UP, 1975.

Lewis, David L., and Laurence Goldstein, eds. *The Automobile and American Culture.* Ann Arbor: U of Michigan P, 1980.

Lewis, Eugene W. *Motor Memories: A Saga of Whirling Gears.* Detroit: Alved, 1947.

Lewis, R.W.B. *The American Adam: Innocence, Tragedy, and Tradition in the Nineteenth Century.* Chicago: U of Chicago P, 1955.

Lewis, Sinclair. *The Man Who Knew Coolidge.* New York: Harcourt, Brace, 1941.

Liebs, Chester. *Roadside Architecture: From Main Street to Miracle Mile.* New York: Graphic, 1986.

Lincoln Highway Association. *The Lincoln Highway: The Story of a Crusade That Made Transportation History.* New York: Dodd, 1935.

Lipton, Lawrence. *The Holy Barbarians*. New York: Messner, 1959.

Lively, Penelope. *The Road to Lichfield*. London: Penguin, 1977.

Llewellyn, Sam. *The Worst Journey in the Midlands*. London: Heinemann, 1983.

Low, Ann Marie. *Dust Bowl Diary*. Lincoln: U of Nebraska P, 1984.

Luxemberg, Stan. *Roadside Empires: How the Chains Franchised America*. New York: Viking, 1985.

Lynn, Kenneth S. *Mark Twain and Southwestern Humor*. Boston: Little, Brown, 1960.

___. "Roughing It." Smith, *Mark Twain* 40-46.

MacCannell, Dean. *The Tourist: A New Theory of the Leisure Class*. New York: Schocken, 1976.

MacDowell, Syl. *We Live in a Trailer*. New York: Messner, 1938.

Madden, Virginia Mudd. *Across America on the Yellow Brick Road*. Alamo, CA: Crow Canyon, 1980.

Mailer, Norman. *Advertisements for Myself*. New York: Putnam, 1959.

Mailloux, Steven. *Interpretive Conventions: The Reader in the Study of American Fiction*. Ithaca and London: Cornell UP, 1982.

Majerus, Janet. *Grandpa and Frank*. Philadelphia: Lippincott, 1976.

Mandel, George. *Flee the Angry Strangers*. New York: Charter, 1962.

Mandel, Leon. *Driven: The American Four-Wheel Love Affair*. New York: Stein and Day, 1977.

Manfred, Frederick. *Wanderlust*. Denver: Alan Swallow, 1962.

Marc, David. *Demographic Vistas*. Philadelphia: U of Penn P, 1984.

Margolies, John. *The End of the Road: Vanishing Highway Architecture in America*. New York: Penguin, 1981.

Marling, Karol Ann. *The Colossus of Roads: Myth and Symbol Along the American Highway*. Minneapolis: U of Minnesota P, 1984.

Marsh, Peter, and Peter Collett. *Driving Passion: The Psychology of the Car*. Boston and London: Faber and Faber, 1987.

Marshall, James Vance. *Walkabout*. Littleton, MA: Sundance, 1984.

Marx, Leo. *The Machine in the Garden: Technology and the Pastoral Ideal*. New York: Oxford UP, 1964.

Massey, Beatrice Larned. *It Might Have Been Worse: A Motor Trip From Coast to Coast*. San Francisco: Harr Wagner, 1920.

Maughan, Somerset. *Razor's Edge*. Philadelphia: Blakeston, 1945.

McCarthy, Eugene. *America Revisited: 150 Years After Tocqueville*. Garden City, NY: Doubleday, 1978.

McCullers, Carson. *The Heart Is a Lonely Hunter*. Boston: Houghton Mifflin, 1940.

McElroy, Joseph. *Lookout Cartridge*. New York: Knopf, 1974.

——. *Plus*. New York: Knopf, 1977.

McEvoy, Bernard. *From the Great Lakes to the Wild West.* Toronto: Briggs, 1902.

McGill, Vernon. *Diary of a Motor Journey From Chicago to Los Angeles.* Los Angeles: Grafton, 1922.

McLaughlin, Russell J. *Roaming Holidays: A Preface to Post-War Travel.* Detroit: Arnold-Powers, 1943.

McLuhan, Marshall. *The Mechanical Bride: Folklore of Industrial Man.* Boston: Beacon, 1951.

——. *Understanding Media: The Extensions of Man.* New York: Signet, 1964.

McMurtry, Larry. *Cadillac Jack.* New York: Simon and Schuster, 1987.

McNally, Dennis. *Desolate Angel: Jack Kerouac, the Beat Generation, and America.* New York: Random House, 1979.

Medoff, Mark. *When You Comin' Back, Red Ryder?* Clifton, NJ: White, 1973.

Meegan, George. *The Longest Walk.* New York: Dodd, 1988.

Mikhailov, Nikolai. *Those Americans: A Travelogue.* Chicago: Regency, 1962.

Milewski, Robert J. et al. *Jack Kerouac: An Annotated Bibliography of Secondary Sources: 1944-1979.* Metuchen, NJ: Scarecrow, 1981.

Miller, Arthur. *Death of a Salesman.* 1949. New York: Viking-Penguin, 1976.

Miller, Henry. *The Air-Conditioned Nightmare.* New York: New Directions, 1945.

Millstein, Gilbert. "Books of the Times." *New York Times* 5 Sept. 1957: 27.

Milton, John R., ed. *Conversations with Frederick Manfred.* Salt Lake City: U of Utah P, 1974.

——. *The Novel of the American West.* Lincoln: U of Nebraska P, 1980.

Mitchell, Don. *Thumb Tripping.* 1970. New York: Bantam, 1971.

Moberg, Vilhelm. *A Time on Earth.* Trans. Naomi Walford. New York: Simon and Schuster, 1965.

——. *Unto a Good Land.* Trans. Gustof Lamerstock. New York: Simon and Schuster, 1954.

Monahan, Valerie. *An American Postcard Collector's Guide.* Poole, Dorset: Blanford, 1981.

Morris, Jan. *Destinations.* New York: Oxford/Rolling Stone, 1980.

——. *Journeys.* New York: Oxford, 1984.

Morris, Mary. *Nothing to Declare: Memoirs of a Woman Traveling Alone.* New York: Penguin, 1988.

Morson, Gary Saul, and Caryl Emerson. *Mikhail Bakhtin: Creation of a Prosaics.* Stanford, CA: Stanford UP, 1990.

Moyers, Bill. *Listening to America: A Traveler Rediscovers His Country.* New York: Harper, 1971.

Mumford, Lewis. *The Highway and the City.* New York: Harcourt, 1956.

Nabokov, Vladimir. *Lolita.* 1955. New York: Putnam, 1958.

Nader, Ralph. *Unsafe at Any Speed: The Designed-in Dangers of the American Automobile.* New York: Grossman, 1965.

Nairn, Ian. *The American Landscape*. New York: Random House, 1965.

Nash, Roderick. *Wilderness and the American Mind*. New Haven: Yale UP, 1979.

Neihardt, John. *Black Elk Speaks*. New York: Washington Square P, 1932.

Newcomb, Horace, ed. *Television: The Critical View*. 4th ed. New York: Oxford UP, 1985.

Nicosia, Gerald. *Memory Babe: A Critical Biography of Jack Kerouac*. New York: Grove, 1983.

Norris, Frank. *The Octopus*. Garden City, NY: Doubleday, 1947.

O'Connor, Flannery. *The Complete Stories*. New York: Sunburst, 1972.

Olson, Toby. *Seaview*. New York: New Directions, 1982.

Ong, Walter J. "The Writer's Audience Is Always a Fiction." *PMLA* 90 (Jan. 1975): 9-21.

Parkinson, Thomas, ed. *Casebook on the Beats*. New York: Crowell, 1961.

Parkman, Francis. *The Oregon Trail*. 1849. New York: Penguin, 1982.

Parry, Albert. *Garrets and Pretenders: A History of Bohemianism in America*. New York: Dover, 1960.

Partridge, Bellamy. *Fill 'er Up: The Story of Fifty Years of Motoring*. New York: McGraw-Hill, 1952.

Patton, Phil. *Open Road: A Celebration of the American Highway*. New York: Simon and Schuster, 1986.

Pearson, Carol S. *The Hero Within: Six Archetypes We Live By*. San Francisco: Harper, 1989.

Pearson, Carol, and Katherine Pope. *The Female Hero in American and British Literature*. New York: Bowken, 1981.

Peck, Anne M., and Enrid Johnson. *Roundabout America*. New York: Harper, 1933.

Pellec, Yves Le, ed. *Beat Generation*. Rodez, France: Entretiens, 1975.

Percy, Walker. *Love in the Ruins*. New York: Farrar, 1971.

Perelman, Sidney. *Eastward, Ha*. New York: Simon and Schuster, 1977.

Perkins, Pamel Gruninger. *Autoscape: The Automobile in the American Landscape*. New York: Whitney Museum of Art, 1984.

Perry, Paul, and Ken Babbs. *On the Bus: The Complete Guide to the Legendary Trip of Ken Kesey and the Merry Pranksters and the Birth of the Counterculture*. New York: Thunders Mouth, 1991.

Pettifer, Julian, and Nigel Turner. *Automania: Man and the Motorcar*. Boston: Little, Brown, 1984.

Phillips, Jayne Anne. *Fast Lanes*. New York: Dutton, 1987.

——. *Machine Dreams*. New York: Dutton, 1984.

Pierson, George. *The Moving American*. New York: Knopf, 1973.

Pirsig, Robert M. *Zen and the Art of Motorcycle Maintenance*. 1974. New York: Bantam, 1975.

Pomerey, Earl. *In Search of the Golden West: The Tourist in Western America.* New York: Knopf, 1957.

Porter, M. Gilbert. *The Art of Grit: Ken Kesey's Fiction.* Columbia, U of Missouri P, 1982.

Post, Emily. *By Motor to the Golden Gate.* New York: Appleton, 1916.

Powell, Tom. *The Restless American: A Middle-aged Man on a Middle-aged Horse.* Boston: Little, Brown, 1968.

Priestley, J.B. *English Journey.* London: Heinemann, 1934.

Primeau, Ronald. "The Endless Poem: Jack Kerouac's Midwest." *Great Lakes Review* 3 (1976): 73-86.

——, ed. *Influx: Essays on Literary Influence.* Port Washington, NY: Kennikat, 1977.

Pynchon, Thomas. *The Crying of Lot 49.* Philadelphia: Lippincott, 1966.

——. *V.* New York: Bantam, 1964.

Raban, Jonathan. *Old Glory: An American Voyage.* New York: Simon and Schuster, 1981.

Rae, John B. *The American Automobile: A Brief History.* Chicago: U of Chicago P, 1965.

——. *The Road and the Car in American Life.* Cambridge, MA: MIT P, 1971.

Rae, William. *Western by Rail.* New York: Arno Press, 1973.

Rapson, Richard L. *Britons View America: Travel Commentary.* Seattle: U of Washington P, 1971.

Reck, Franklin M. *A Car Traveling People: How the Automobile Has Changed the Life of Americans—A Study of Social Effects.* Detroit: Automobile Manufacturers Association, 1945.

Reeves, Richard. *American Journey: Traveling with Tocqueville in Search of Democracy in America.* New York: Simon and Schuster, 1982.

Reigelman, Milton M. *The Midland: A Venture in Literary Regionalism.* Iowa City: U of Iowa P, 1975.

Riffaterre, Michael. *Semiotics of Poetry.* Bloomington: Indiana UP, 1978.

Rittenberg, Caroline. *Motor West.* New York: Vinal, 1926.

Rittenhouse, Jack. *Guide to Highway 66.* Los Angeles: Self-published, 1946.

Robbins, Tom. *Another Roadside Attraction.* New York: Ballantine, 1972.

——. *Even Cowgirls Get the Blues.* 1976. New York: Bantam, 1977.

Robinson, John. *Highways and Our Environment.* New York: McGraw-Hill, 1971.

Robinson, Rose. *Eagle in the Air.* New York: Crown, 1969.

Roiphe, Anne. *Long Division.* New York: Simon and Schuster, 1972.

Rosen, Gerald. *The Carmen Miranda Memorial Flagpole.* San Rafael, CA: Presidio Press, 1977.

Rosenbaum, Jean. *Is Your Volkswagen a Sex Symbol?* 1972. New York: Bantam, 1973.

Ross, Andrew. *No Respect: Intellectuals and Popular Culture*. New York: Routledge, 1989.

Roszak, Theodore. *The Making of a Counter Culture*. 1969. Garden City, NY: Anchor, 1969.

Rothschild, Emma. *Paradise Lost: The Decline of the Auto-Industrial Age*. New York: Random House, 1973.

Roueche, Berton. *Sea to Shining Sea*. New York: Avon, 1985.

Routledge, Janette. *How to Tour the United States for Thirty-One Days for One Hundred Dollars*. New York: Harian, 1938.

Rowbotham, Sheila. *Woman's Consciousness, Man's World*. New York: Pelican, 1973.

Rowsome, Frank, Jr. *The Verse by the Side of the Road: The Story of the Burma Shave Signs and Jingles*. Brattleboro, VT: Greene Press, 1965.

Ruthven, Malise. *The Divine Supermarket: Travels in Search of the Soul of America*. London: Chatto and Windus, 1989.

Saroyan, William. *Short Drive, Sweet Chariot*. New York: Phaedra, 1966.

Scarritt, Winthrop. *Three Men in a Car*. New York: Dutton, 1906.

Scharff, Virginia. *Taking the Wheel: Women and the Corner of the Motor Age*. New York: Free Press, 1991.

Schmitt, Peter. *Back to Nature: Arcadian Myth in America*. New York: Oxford UP, 1969.

Schneider, Kenneth R. *Autokind vs Mankind*. New York: Norton, 1971.

Scott, Quinta, and Susan Croce Kelly. *Route 66: The Highway and Its People*. Norman: U of Oklahoma P, 1988.

Seals, David. "The New Custerism." *The Nation* 13 May 1991: 634-39.

——. *The Powwow Highway*. 1979. New York: Penguin-New American Library, 1990.

Sears, Stephen. *The Automobile in America*. New York: American Heritage, 1977.

Sharp, Dallas L. *The Better Country*. Boston: Houghton Mifflin, 1928.

Shepard, C.K. *Across America by Motor Cycle*. London: Logmans Green, 1922.

Sigal, Clancy. *Going Away*. Boston: Houghton Mifflin, 1962.

Simons, Herbert W., and Aram A. Aghazarian. *Form, Genre, and the Study of Political Discourse*. Columbia: U of South Carolina P, 1986.

Simpson, Louis. *The End of the Open Road*. Middleton, CT: Wesleyan UP, 1960.

——. *A Revolution in Taste*. New York: Macmillan, 1968.

Simpson, Mona. *Anywhere But Here*. New York: Vintage, 1987.

Slotkin, Richard. *Regeneration Through Violence: The Mythology of the American Frontier 1600-1860*. Middletown, CT: Wesleyan UP, 1973.

Smith, Henry Nash, ed. *Mark Twain: A Collection of Critical Essays*. Englewood Cliffs, NJ: Prentice-Hall, 1963.

——. *Virgin Land: The American West as Symbol and Myth.* Cambridge: Harvard UP, 1950.

Snow, W. Brewster, ed. *The Highway and the Landscape.* New Brunswick: Rutgers UP, 1959.

Snyder, Tom. *A Route 66 Traveler's Guide: A Roadside Companion.* New York: St. Martin's, 1990.

Sorrentino, Gilbert. *The Sky Changes.* New York: Hill and Wang, 1966.

Spengeman, William C. *The Adventurous Muse.* New Haven: Yale UP, 1977.

Staten, Vince. *Unauthorized America: A Travel Guide to the Places the Chamber of Commerce Won't Tell You About.* New York: Harper, 1990.

Stegner, Wallace. *The Big Rock Candy Mountain.* New York: Duel, Sloan, and Pearce, 1943.

——. *Where the Bluebird Sings to the Lemonade Springs.* New York: Random House, 1992.

Steinbeck, Elaine, and Robert Wallsten. *Steinbeck: A Life in Letters.* New York: Viking, 1975.

Steinbeck, John. *The Grapes of Wrath.* New York: Bantam, 1946.

——. *Travels with Charley.* New York: Penguin, 1962.

——. *The Wayward Bus.* New York: Viking, 1947.

Stern, Jane, and Michael Stern. *Trucker.* New York: McGraw-Hill, 1975.

Sterne, Lawrence. *Tristram Shandy: An Authoritative Text.* New York: Norton, 1980.

Stewart, George R. *U.S. 40: Cross Section of the United States of America.* Boston: Houghton Mifflin, 1953.

Stockett, Maria Letitia. *America: First, Fast, and Furious.* Baltimore: Norman-Remington, 1930.

Sturmey, Henry. *In an Autocar through the Length and Breadth of the Land.* London: Iliffe Sons and Sturmey, 1897.

Sukenick, Ronald. *The Death of the Novel and Other Stories.* New York: Dial, 1969.

——. *98.6 A Novel.* New York: Fiction Collective, 1975.

——. *Out.* Chicago: Swallow, 1973.

——. *Up: A Novel.* New York: Dial, 1968.

Suleiman, Susan R., and Inge Crosman, eds. *The Reader in the Text.* Princeton, NJ: Princeton UP, 1980.

Sutton, Horace. *Travelers: The American Tourist from Stagecoach to Space Shuttle.* New York: Morrow, 1980.

Swope, Mary, and Walter H. Kerr, eds. *American Classic: Car Poems for Collectors.* College Park, MD: SCOP, 1985.

Szarkowski, John. *Walker Evans.* New York: Museum of Modern Art, 1971.

Taylor, Anne Robinson. "Prisoners of the Road: Flight and Isolation in American Films." *Southwest Review* Spring 1981: 141-56.

De Teran, Lisa St. Aubin, ed. *Indiscreet Journeys: Stories of Women on the Road*. London: Virago, 1989.

Terkel, Studs. *Division Street: America*. New York: Pantheon, 1968.

Theroux, Paul. *The Great Railway Bazaar*. New York: Ballantine, 1976.

——. *Kingdom by the Sea: A Journey Around Great Britain*. Boston: Houghton-Mifflin, 1983.

Thompson, Hunter S. *The Great Shark Hunt: Strange Tales From a Strange Time*. New York: Fawcett, 1979.

Thoreau, Henry David. "Walking." *Walden and Other Writings*. Ed. Brooks Atkinson. New York: Modern Library, 1950. 597-632.

Tocqueville, Alexis de. *Democracy in America*. 1835. Trans. Henry Reeve, New York: Knopf, 1945.

Toffler, Alvin. *The Third Wave*. New York: Morrow, 1980.

Tompkins, Jane, ed. *Reader-Response Criticism*. Baltimore: Johns Hopkins UP, 1980.

Townroe, P.M. *Social and Political Consequences of the Motor Car*. London: David and Charles, 1974.

Tubbs, D.B. *Art and the Automobile*. London: Lutterworth Press, 1978.

Turner, Frederick Jackson. *The Significance of the Frontier in American History*. Ann Arbor: University Microfilms, 1966.

Turner, Victor. *The Ritual Process*. Ithaca: Cornell UP, 1969.

——, and Edith Turner. *Image and Pilgrimage in Christian Culture*. New York: Columbia UP, 1978.

Twain, Mark. *Adventures of Huckleberry Finn*. Ed. Henry Nash Smith. Boston: Houghton Mifflin, 1958.

——. *Mississippi Writings*. New York: Library of America, 1982.

——. *Roughing It*. 1872. New York: Harper, 1904.

Tytell, John. *Naked Angels: The Lives and Literature of the Beat Generation*. New York: McGraw-Hill, 1976.

Updike, John. *Rabbit, Run*. 1960. New York: Fawcett, 1974.

——. *Rabbit Is Rich*. 1960. New York: Fawcett, 1974.

Van de Water, Frederic F. *The Family Flivvers to Frisco*. New York: Appleton, 1927.

Van Goethen, Larry. *The Fifth Horseman Is Riding*. New York: Macmillan, 1974.

Van Schaick, John, Jr. *Cruising Cross Country*. Boston: Universalist, 1926.

Vernon, Paul E. *Coast to Coast by Motor*. London: Black, 1930.

Vickery, Olga. *The Novels of William Faulkner: A Critical Interpretation*. Baton Rouge: Louisiana State UP, 1964.

Vieyra, Daniel L. *"Fill'er Up": An Architectural History of America's Gas Stations*. New York: Collier, 1979.

Wachenbarth, Horst, and Kevin Clark. *The Red Couch.* New York: Vander-Mark, 1984.

Wallis, Michael. *Route 66: The Mother Road.* New York: St. Martin, 1990.

Webb, Walter Prescott. *The Great Frontier.* Boston, 1952.

Weedar, Jeannie Lippitt. *Rhode Island to California by Motor.* Santa Barbara, CA: Pacific Coast, 1917.

Weesner, Theodore. *The Car Thief.* New York: Random, 1967.

Weinreich, Regina. *The Spontaneous Prose of Jack Kerouac: A Study of the Fiction.* Carbondale: Southern Illinois UP, 1987.

Welty, Eudora. *Thirteen Stories.* New York: Harcourt, 1965.

West, Ray B., ed. *A Country in the Mind.* Sausalito, CA: Angel Island, 1962.

Westbrook, Margaret. *Highway Travelers: 68 Days on Southern Highways.* Los Angeles: Suttonhouse, 1939.

White, G. Edward. *The Eastern Establishment and the Western Experience: The West of Frederick Remington, Theodore Roosevelt and Owen Wister.* New Haven: Yale UP, 1968.

White, Lawrence J. *The Automobile Industry Since 1945.* Cambridge, MA: Harvard UP, 1973.

Whitman, Walt. *Leaves of Grass.* Ed. Sculley Bradley and Harold W. Blodgett. New York: Norton, 1973.

Whyte, William. *The Last Landscape.* New York: Doubleday, 1968.

Williams, John A. *This Is My Country Too.* New York: New American Library, 1965.

Williams, Mark. *Road Movies: The Complete Guide to Cinema on Wheels.* New York: Proteus, 1982.

Williams, Raymond. *Marxism and Literature.* Oxford: Oxford UP, 1977.

Wolfe, Tom. *Electric Kool-Aid Acid Test.* New York: Farrar, 1968.

——. *The Kandy Kolored Tangerine-Flake Streamline Baby.* New York: Pocket, 1966.

——. *The Pump House Gang.* New York: Farrar, 1968.

——. *The Purple Decades: A Reader.* New York: Farrar, 1982

——. *The Right Stuff.* New York: Bantam, 1980.

Wolfe, Tom, and E.W. Johnson, eds. *The New Journalism.* New York: Harper and Row, 1973.

Wolitzer, Hilma. *Hearts.* New York: Farrar, Straus and Giroux, 1980.

Woods, Phyllis Anderson. *I Think This Is Where We Came In.* Philadelphia: Westminster, 1976.

Woolf, Virginia. *The Voyage Out.* London: Hogarth, 1915.

Wurlitzer, Rudolph. *Flats.* New York: Dutton, 1970.

——. *Quake.* New York: Dutton, 1972.

Zelazny, Roger. *Roadmarks.* New York: Ballantine, 1979.

Zelinski, Wilbur. *The Cultural Geography of the U.S.* Englewood Cliffs, NJ: Prentice-Hall, 1973.

Zinsser, William, ed. *They Went: The Art and Crafts of Travel Writing.* Boston: Houghton Mifflin, 1991.

Zube, Ervin H., and Margaret J. Zube, eds. *Changing Rural Landscapes.* Amherst: U of Massachusetts P, 1977.

Index

CPSIA information can be obtained
at www.ICGtesting.com
Printed in the USA
FFOW04n1412081116
29082FF